Political Parties in the Middle East

This comprehensive collection addresses the important question of political parties in the Middle East and North Africa (MENA). Written by historians, political scientists, and sociologists of the region, the book provides a pertinent analytical framework to understand the often complex and turbulent histories of these political parties, their role within the region, and their prospects in the wake of the post-2011 Arab Uprisings. The authors explore a rich and varied range of case studies including Iran, Turkey, Palestine, Egypt, Lebanon, and Morocco.

This book examines where political parties and organizations have been crucial to shaping contemporary historical events and political contestation, but also highlights their shortcomings and failures to deliver on the ambitions and hopes they had often evoked amongst their supporters. Furthermore, it looks at how political parties and their activities have intersected with important issues and themes such as gender, human rights, international solidarity, revolution and social transformation, and sectarian identity.

This book will be of great interest to students and researchers of political science, particularly within the MENA region. It was originally published as a special issue of the *British Journal of Middle Eastern Studies*.

Siavush Randjbar-Daemi is a Lecturer in Modern Middle Eastern History in the Faculty of History at the University of St Andrews, UK. His research interests lie in the evolution of the state in modern and contemporary Iran, and the contribution to the public sphere—particularly in periods of relative pluralism, such as the early 1950s or 1979–1981—of a variety of actors, from crowds formed by subaltern parts of society to socio-political elites.

Eskandar Sadeghi-Boroujerdi is a Lecturer in Comparative Political Theory at Goldsmiths, University of London, UK. He was previously a British Academy Postdoctoral Research Fellow at the University of Oxford, UK, and received his DPhil in Middle Eastern Studies at Queen's College, University of Oxford. He is the author of *Revolution and Its Discontents: Political Thought and Reform in Iran* (2019).

Lauren Banko is a Lecturer in the Department of History at Yale University, USA, teaching courses related to the history of the modern Middle East and North Africa, as well as Palestine and Israel. Her current research is broadly focused on the impact of colonialism before and during the interwar period of the twentieth century in the Arab Middle East and in pre-1948 Palestine.

Political Parties in the Middle East

Edited by
Siavush Randjbar-Daemi,
Eskandar Sadeghi-Boroujerdi
and Lauren Banko

LONDON AND NEW YORK

First published 2020
by Routledge
2 Park Square, Milton Park, Abingdon, Oxon, OX14 4RN

and by Routledge
52 Vanderbilt Avenue, New York, NY 10017

Routledge is an imprint of the Taylor & Francis Group, an informa business

First issued in paperback 2021

British Library Cataloguing in Publication Data
A catalogue record for this book is available from the British Library

ISBN13: 978-1-138-39096-6 (hbk)
ISBN13: 978-1-03-209046-7 (pbk)

Typeset in Myriad Pro
by Newgen Publishing UK

Publisher's Note
The publisher accepts responsibility for any inconsistencies that may have arisen during the
conversion of this book from journal articles to book chapters, namely the inclusion of journal
terminology.

Disclaimer
Every effort has been made to contact copyright holders for their permission to reprint material
in this book. The publishers would be grateful to hear from any copyright holder who is not here
acknowledged and will undertake to rectify any errors or omissions in future editions of this book.

Contents

Citation Information   vii
Notes on Contributors   ix

1 Introduction   1
   Siavush Randjbar-Daemi, Eskandar Sadeghi-Boroujerdi and Lauren Banko

2 Political parties in MENA: their functions and development   9
   Raymond A. Hinnebusch

3 Protesting gender discrimination from within: women's political
   representation on behalf of Islamic parties   26
   Mona Tajali

4 'We wander in your footsteps'—reciprocity and contractility in
   Lebanese personality-centred parties   44
   Christian Thuselt

5 The party, the *Gama'a* and the *Tanzim*: the organizational dynamics
   of the Egyptian Muslim Brotherhood's post-2011 failure   61
   Marie Vannetzel

6 Party and governance in the Arab republics   77
   Joseph Sassoon

7 The origins of Communist Unity: anti-colonialism and revolution in Iran's
   tri-continental moment   90
   Eskandar Sadeghi-Boroujerdi

8 Political Parties and Women's Rights in Turkey   117
   Zehra F. Kabasakal Arat

9 The historical emergence and transformation of the Moroccan political
   party field   132
   Khalil Dahbi

10 The Popular Front for the Liberation of Palestine during the First
    Intifada: from Opportunity to Marginalization (1987–1990)   145
    Francesco Saverio Leopardi

    Index   160

Citation Information

The following chapters were originally published in the *British Journal of Middle Eastern Studies*. When citing this material, please use the original page numbering for each article, as follows:

Chapter 2

Political parties in MENA: their functions and development
Raymond A. Hinnebusch
British Journal of Middle Eastern Studies, volume 44, issue 2 (April 2017) pp. 159–175

Chapter 3

Protesting gender discrimination from within: women's political representation on behalf of Islamic parties
Mona Tajali
British Journal of Middle Eastern Studies, volume 44, issue 2 (April 2017) pp. 176–193

Chapter 4

'We wander in your footsteps'—reciprocity and contractility in Lebanese personality-centred parties
Christian Thuselt
British Journal of Middle Eastern Studies, volume 44, issue 2 (April 2017) pp. 194–210

Chapter 5

The party, the Gama'a and the Tanzim: the organizational dynamics of the Egyptian Muslim Brotherhood's post-2011 failure
Marie Vannetzel
British Journal of Middle Eastern Studies, volume 44, issue 2 (April 2017) pp. 211–226

Chapter 6

Party and governance in the Arab republics
Joseph Sassoon
British Journal of Middle Eastern Studies, volume 44, issue 2 (April 2017) pp. 227–239

Chapter 7

The origins of Communist Unity: anti-colonialism and revolution in Iran's tri-continental moment
Eskandar Sadeghi-Boroujerdi
British Journal of Middle Eastern Studies, volume 45, issue 5 (December 2018) pp. 796–822

Chapter 8

Political Parties and Women's Rights in Turkey
Zehra F. Kabasakal Arat
British Journal of Middle Eastern Studies, volume 44, issue 2 (April 2017) pp. 240–254

Chapter 9

The historical emergence and transformation of the Moroccan political party field
Khalil Dahbi
British Journal of Middle Eastern Studies, volume 44, issue 2 (April 2017) pp. 255–267

Chapter 10

The Popular Front for the Liberation of Palestine during the First Intifada: From Opportunity to Marginalization (1987–1990)
Francesco Saverio Leopardi
British Journal of Middle Eastern Studies, volume 44, issue 2 (April 2017) pp. 268–282

For any permission-related enquiries please visit:
www.tandfonline.com/page/help/permissions

Notes on Contributors

Zehra F. Kabasakal Arat is a Professor of Comparative Politics, International Relations, and Political Theory in the Department of Political Science at the University of Connecticut, USA. She studies human rights, with an emphasis on women's rights, as well as processes of democratization, globalization, and development.

Lauren Banko is a Lecturer in the Department of History at Yale University, USA, teaching courses related to the history of the modern Middle East and North Africa, as well as Palestine and Israel. Her current research is broadly focused on the impact of colonialism before and during the interwar period of the 20th century in the Arab Middle East and in pre-1948 Palestine.

Khalil Dahbi is a PhD candidate in the Graduate School of Global Studies at Tokyo University of Foreign Studies, Japan.

Raymond A. Hinnebusch is a Professor in the School of International Relations at the University of St Andrews, UK. His work has focused on Middle East international relations and foreign policy, rural politics and agrarian development, elites, authoritarian regimes, political parties, and economic liberalisation in the Middle East.

Francesco Saverio Leopardi is a Postdoctoral Research Fellow in the Department of Political and Social Sciences at the University of Bologna, Italy. He deals with the contemporary history of the Middle East and North Africa with particular attention to the area of Eastern Arabia.

Siavush Randjbar-Daemi is a Lecturer in Modern Middle Eastern History in the School of History at the University of St Andrews, UK. His research interests lie in the evolution of the state in modern and contemporary Iran, and the contribution to the public sphere— particularly in periods of relative pluralism, such as the early 1950s or 1979–1981—of a variety of actors, from crowds formed by subaltern parts of society elites.

Eskandar Sadeghi-Boroujerdi is a Lecturer in Comparative Political Theory at Goldsmiths, University of London, UK. He was previously a British Academy Postdoctoral Research Fellow at the University of Oxford, UK, and received his DPhil in Middle Eastern Studies at Queen's College, University of Oxford.

Joseph Sassoon is an Associate Professor at Georgetown University, USA, and holds the al-Sabah Chair in Politics and Political Economy of the Arab World. He is also a Senior Associate Member at St Antony's College at the University of Oxford, UK.

Mona Tajali is Assistant Professor of International Relations and Women's Studies at Agnes Scott College, USA. Her research and teaching interests fall in the fields of comparative politics, Middle East studies, and women's studies.

Christian Thuselt is Chair for Politics and Society of the Middle East in the Department of Political Science at Friedrich-Alexander-University Erlangen-Nuremberg, Germany. His fields of research are Lebanon, Syria, Iraq, political theory, religion and politics, political parties in the Middle East, state-building and -failure, nationalism, and Christianity in the Middle East.

Marie Vannetzel is a Postdoctoral Researcher at the Centre for International Studies and Research at Sciences Po, France. Her current research focuses on the mutations of movement in the revolutionary process and on the recompositions of political identities and local forms of power in Egypt.

1   Introduction

Siavush Randjbar-Daemi, Eskandar Sadeghi-Boroujerdi and Lauren Banko

The evils of political parties are all too evident; therefore, the problem that should be examined is this: do they contain enough good to compensate for their evils and make their preservation desirable?[1]

Simone Weil

The first decades of the twenty-first century, like the previous one, have already witnessed protests, uprisings, rebellions, armed insurrections and calls for revolution, all of which forcefully underscore the ongoing and tumultuous re-negotiation of the relationship between state elites and societies in the Middle East and North Africa (MENA). From the major urban conurbations of Egypt to the more insular quarters of Morocco, from the Pearl Roundabout of Manama to the city squares of central Tehran, all have witnessed the concerted efforts of disaffected citizens aspiring to transform the prevailing relationship between government and the governed.[2] The erstwhile social compact, upon which state elites and apparatchiks had long counted and sought to preserve intact, found itself cast to the wind leaving many befuddled and bemused and at a loss of how to respond to or understand the current conjuncture. The current volume initiates an investigation into the various histories, disparate roles and political articulations of the political party in the Middle East over the last century and in light of these revolutionary (and counter-revolutionary) times.

Political parties are complex organizational machines which tend to escape easy categorization and elude any single explanatory framework.[3] A pervasive feature of modern political systems, they have long been regarded as an essential ingredient of representative parliamentary democracy and its cognates. This is even while the latter can hardly be said to exhaust political parties' multifarious roles, forms and functions. In modern Western political history, parties have generally been thought of as one of the key sites of organized political activity for antagonistic elites, and more recently the middle and working classes, and held to be essential in the process of defining the leading political issues of the day. In the words of Cavatorta and Storm: 'Parties, in short, aggregate and articulate the interests of the citizenry and formulate political programmes, thereby strengthening their voice'.

---

[1] Simone Weil, *The Abolition of All Political Parties*, trans. Simon Leys (New York: NYRB, 2013), Loc 95.

[2] Mehran Kamrava, ed. *Beyond the Arab Spring: The Evolving Ruling Bargain in the Middle East* (Oxford and New York: Oxford University Press, 2014).

[3] Cedric de Leon, *Party and Society: Reconstructing a Sociology of Democratic Party Politics* (Cambridge: Polity, 2014), Introduction.

Moreover, 'they are better at aggregating interests, coordinating decision-making in parliament, and at ensuring vertical accountability, that is, when power is necessarily delegated from the citizenry to a select group of representatives'.[4] But parties cannot and should not be viewed as passive reflections of a series of disembodied and unmediated interests, which they proceed to merely aggregate and represent. Thus, according to de Leon, Desai and Tuğal, clearly taking inspiration from the work of Laclau and Mouffe and their conception of 'political articulation', rather than inert reflections of extant social preferences and identities, political parties should be understood as crucial 'agencies that structure social cleavages'.[5] Or, alternatively, we might say, channelling Laclau and Mouffe in their classic work, *Hegemony and Socialist Strategy*, 'politico-hegemonic articulations retroactively create the interests they claim to represent'.[6]

In their myriad and diverse struggles, parties along with their representatives and members have fought for limitations to absolutism, the defence of private property and entrenched hierarchies, parliamentary representation and the extension of the franchise, workers' rights, and land and wealth redistribution, often transforming the institutions of political rule, social reproduction and societal cleavages in the process. Nevertheless, as should already be clear enough, the notion that parties are the standard-bearers of the ineluctable march of democracy has long ceased to be a convincing proposition.

In the aftermath of World War I, the states comprising the MENA region, both independent and under forms of colonial rule, began to increasingly experience patterns of political mobilization and participation that resembled those which had become commonplace in metropolitan centres, which had overseen the region's uneven incorporation into the world economy and had ensured its subordination to Europe's competing global empires.[7] Where people and social groups had previously pursued political activity by means of secret societies, or redress through traditional associations such as guilds, village elders, urban notables and the clergy,[8] with the advent of the modern era, the political party came to be viewed as an ever-more appropriate and efficacious means of orienting and channelling political action, dispensing patronage and articulating political demands.[9]

Following World War II and the gradual retreat of direct imperial tutelage in tandem with the onset of the global Cold War, this trend gathered pace and saw radical projects such as Arab nationalism, Ba'athism, Communism and Nasserism sharply rise in influence and transform their societies in the process.[10] The chief concerns of this epoch included the

[4] Francesco Cavatorta and Lise Storm, *Political Parties in the Arab World: Continuity and Change* (Edinburgh: University of Edinburgh Press, 2018), Loc 231.

[5] Cedric de Leon, Manali Desai, and Cihan Tuğal, *Building Blocs: How Parties Organize Society* (Stanford, CA: Stanford University Press, 2015), p. 2.

[6] Ernesto Laclau and Chantal Mouffe, *Hegemony and Socialist Strategy: Towards a Radical Democratic Politics* (London and New York: Verso, 1985), Loc 117.

[7] Roger Owen, *State, Power and Politics in the Making of the Modern Middle East* (Abingdon and New York: Routledge, 2004), Chapter 1.

[8] Ervand Abrahamian, *Iran Between Two Revolutions* (Princeton, NJ: Princeton University Press, 1982), Chapters 1, 2; Hanna Batatu, *The Old Social Classes and the Revolutionary Movements of Iraq: A Study of Iraq's Old Landed and Commercial Classes and of its Communists, Ba'thists, and Free Officers* (London: Saqi, 2004 [1978]), Part 2.

[9] For examples of how innovative politicians such as Abd al-Rahman al-Shahbandar moved from the Committee of Union and Progress structure of the late Ottoman Empire to their own fledgling political organisations under French mandate in Syria, see Michael Provence, *The Last Ottoman Generation and the Making of the Modern Middle East* (Cambridge and New York: Cambridge University Press, 2017), Chapters 1, 3 and 4.

[10] John Chalcraft, *Popular Politics in the Making of the Modern Middle East* (Cambridge and New York: Cambridge University Press, 2016); Joel Gordon, *Nasser's Blessed Movement: Egypt's Free Officers and the July Revolution*

quest for Arab unity, national independence and the overturning of the traditional sources of social power and elite rule which were often locked into a relationship of reciprocity or dependency vis-à-vis the imperial mandate and/or colonial state.[11] The region was changed irrevocably in an era which witnessed the flourishing of strong aspirations for decolonization and non-alignment, and enormous socio-economic and structural transformations upending the social power of traditional notables and the landed classes. These objectives often came to fruition through strong and charismatic leaders and the one-party states they led, all the while grounding claims to legitimacy in the mobilization of wide-ranging coalitions of groups enveloping the intelligentsia, members of the new professional classes and state bureaucracies, recent urban migrants and the peasantry.[12]

In the aftermath of the defeat of the Arab front in June 1967, the Palestinian cause for national liberation assumed a more independent line as evidenced by the early politics of Fatah,[13] while Israel's party system found itself forced to come to terms with a rapidly shifting demography and at times a capricious proportional representation system under the shadow of a military occupation penetrating virtually all facets of public and everyday life.[14] By contrast, following the Iranian Revolution of 1979 and the consolidation of the Islamic Republic, Iran saw the birth of intra-elite factional contestation labouring under the *imprimatur* of theocratic rule, and has subsequently struggled to institute a stable party political system. What we have often been faced with instead are loose electoral coalitions which, despite some degree of ideological and political coherence, tend to be heavily reliant on personal relationships and alliances which can change and disappear almost as quickly as they appeared.[15] Meanwhile, elsewhere in the MENA, Islamist organizations such as the Muslim Brotherhood, despite their longevity, sought to persevere in debilitating authoritarian contexts through the cultivation of welfare regimes and solidarity networks to permeate the population at the grassroots level.[16] In both cases, these varied proponents of political Islam eschewed the single-party model, which was abandoned in Iran after 1987, when the Islamic Republic Party fell prey to internal in-fighting and found itself unable to forge a centralized party and accompanying bureaucracy through which to

---

(Oxford and New York: Oxford University Press, 1992); Tareq Y. Ismael, *The Communist Movement in the Arab World* (London and New York: RoutledgeCurzon, 2005); Tareq Y. Ismael, *The Rise and Fall of the Communist Party of Iraq* (Cambridge and New York: Cambridge University Press, 2008); Elizabeth F. Thompson, *Justice Interrupted: The Struggle for Constitutional Government in the Middle East* (Cambridge, MA and London: Harvard University Press, 2013).

[11] Timothy Mitchell, *Carbon Democracy: Political Power in the Age of Oil* (London and New York: Verso, 2013), Chapter 3.

[12] Adeed Dawisha, *Arab Nationalism in the Twentieth Century: From Triumph to Despair* (Princeton, NJ and Oxford: Princeton University Press, 2009), Chapters 5, 7.

[13] Karma Nabulsi and Abdel Razzaq Takriti. The Palestinian Revolution. http://learnpalestine.politics.ox.ac.uk/. Oxford: Department of Politics and International Relations, University of Oxford, 2017.

[14] Eyal Weizman, *Hollow Land: Israel's Architecture of Occupation* (London and New York: Verso, 2012); Gershon Shafir, *A Half Century of Occupation: Israel, Palestine, and the World's Most Intractable Conflict* (Berkeley and Los Angeles, CA: University of California Press, 2017).

[15] Siavush Randjbar-Daemi, *The Quest for Authority in Iran: A History of the Presidency from Revolution to Rouhani* (London and New York: I.B. Tauris, 2018); Arang Keshavarzian, 'Contestation without Democracy: Elite Fragmentation in Iran', in Marsha Pripstein Posusney and Michelle Penner Angrist, eds., *Authoritarianism in the Middle East: Regimes and Resistance* (Boulder, CO: Lynne Rienner, 2005), pp. 63–88.

[16] Hazem Kandil, *Inside the Brotherhood* (Cambridge: Polity, 2014); Janine A. Clark, *Islam, Charity, and Activism: Middle-Class Networks and Social Welfare in Egypt, Jordan, and Yemen* (Bloomington and Indianapolis, IN: Indiana University Press, 2004).

rule.[17] This panoply of party systems, and their relationships with modern state institutions such as the civilian bureaucracy and army, as well as with the old and new social classes, has until very recently largely evaded comprehensive assessment or an integrative analytical framework.[18]

Needless to say, the wave of upheavals which swept across the MENA region following January 2011 has led to significant challenges concerning the place and the continued relevance of political parties. As social movements, both informal and highly integrated, take centre-stage in this profoundly networked information age,[19] the role and function of the political party as gatekeeper to the levers and trappings of power are often considered to have been eroded and markedly diminished. While the post-2011 Arab uprisings may well have marked the weakening of the party political form as it had hitherto stood, the counter-revolutions which almost invariably followed reaffirmed the importance of highly regimented, hierarchical and, often, militarized organizations to political outcomes in evolving social conflicts. The Green Movement of Iran and the Tahrir Square protests, commonly seen by participants and observers alike as shunning structured political organization and leadership, made them all the more unpredictable.[20] More sceptical voices were, however, quick to point out the inherent limitations and inability of such movements to overturn decades-long and deeply entrenched structures of political and economic domination confronting the popular-democratic upsurge.[21] The tenor of the ongoing debate over democratic confederalism and the political model and form of collective self-government inspired by the ideas of Abdullah Öcalan and Murray Bookchin, and embodied in the Democratic Union Party (PYD) in Rojava or northeastern Syria, despite its idiosyncratic nature, would appear to only confirm the suspicions of those who were doubtful so-called 'leaderless movements' could realize the larger and deeper structural changes aspired to by their participants and well-wishers.[22] Finally, the apparent sectarianization of several geopolitical conflicts in the region has been strongly linked to political groupings and mobilizations by identity entrepreneurs along confessional lines, in turn posing the question as to whether the 'sectarian party' is here with us to stay.[23] In short, the debates over the nature, function and efficaciousness of political parties, and their relationship to processes of democratization, authoritarian rule, ethnic and sectarian identity, class struggle and economic transformation, are a long way from being satisfactorily resolved.

[17]   H. E. Chehabi, 'Religion and Politics in Iran: How Theocratic Is the Islamic Republic?', *Daedalus*, 120(3) (Summer 1991), pp. 69–91.
[18]   See Cavatorta and Storm, *Political Parties in the Arab World: Continuity and Change*. This recent volume is one of the few systematic attempts to address the subject of political parties in the Arab world.
[19]   Asef Bayat's work on so-called "nonmovements" is perhaps the single most important contribution to this genre of literature. Asef Bayat, *Life as Politics: How Ordinary People Change the Middle East*, Kindle ed. (Stanford, CA: Stanford University Press, 2010, 2013).
[20]   'Matn-e kamel-e virast-e dovvom-e manshur-e sabz', *Kalameh* 3 Esfand 1389 [22 February 2011].
[21]   Morozov's well-known critique of cyber-utopianism in an age where social media activism and social movements have often come to be seen as interchangeable is pertinent on this score. Evgeny Morozov, *The Net Delusion: How Not to Liberate the World* (London and New York: Allen Lane, 2011).
[22]   Michael Knapp, Anja Flach, and Ercan Ayboğa, *Revolution in Rojava: Democratic Autonomy and Women's Liberation in Syria* (London: Pluto Books, 2016).
[23]   Nader Hashemi and Danny Postel, eds., *Sectarianization: Mapping the New Politics of the Middle East* (Oxford and New York: Oxford University Press, 2017).

These broad reflections on past and present forms of party political organization in the Middle East were the initial impetus for a conference supported by the Centre for the Advanced Study of the Arab World (CASAW) and convened at the University of Manchester on 28–29 January 2016. Several of the articles delivered at the conference have since been further developed and came to form the basis of a special issue of the *British Journal of Middle Eastern Studies* upon which this volume is based. They address a host of important issues ranging across comparative studies of party political systems, to one-party states, as well as nuanced case studies of the development of oppositional, revolutionary and clandestine party organizations, party political activism through the optics of sectarian identity, and women's activism within ruling parties. Thoughtful reflection on the history and contemporary modus operandi of political parties remains of crucial importance as traditional party-based formations and loyalties increasingly dissipate and are reshaped in response to, *inter alia*, internal and external struggles and conflicts over political power and economic capital, imperial interventions and military occupations, religious, ethnic and national identities, environmental degradation, urban space and the right to the city. This volume not only seeks to present several empirical case studies of political parties in the MENA, but also tries to address some of the underlying reasons for the persistence of political parties and demands for legal and constitutional reforms which would permit their institutionalization despite the flurry of diagnoses confidently declaring their decline in the present.

Raymond A. Hinnebusch opens the issue with a comprehensive survey of the development of party political organization and party systems in the MENA region from the early period of oligarchic pluralism to the era of mass single-party systems, and the later controlled attempts at liberalization and constrained multi-party systems in the 1990s. As he pertinently notes, party systems were also 'decisive for the changing character of regimes in the region. Party formation enabled the mass mobilization against colonial rulers that helped win independence for many Arab countries, with the Egyptian Wafd the prototype'.

His attention then turns to the present-day relationship between political party configurations and regime trajectories in the post-Arab Spring context. Importantly, he questions the charges of Middle Eastern 'exceptionalism', rejecting the notion that cultural factors have posed a unique obstacle to modern forms of political association, showing how political parties have in turn shaped the societies out of which they emerged.

Mona Tajali elaborates upon the role of elite women in Islamic political movements and organizations in contemporary Iran and Turkey. Through extensive ethnographic work, she shows how women activists from these putatively conservative organizations have sought to challenge prevalent discriminatory norms and practices and have thereby contributed to the struggle for gender equality in novel and unexpected ways. As she cogently argues, various forms of 'internal criticism' have been decisive to increasing women's representation and enhancing women's status within their respective organizations.

In his contribution, Christian Thuselt sets out to question the assumption that Lebanese parties comprising the state's confessional political system are little more than the clientelist instruments of their leaders and 'cults of personality' and offers a sharp rejoinder to those who have claimed the party structure to be wholly alien to Middle Eastern political culture. Instead, he delineates an 'informal social contract' defining their operation, expounding upon the consequent relationship of reciprocity between leaders and partisans, with particular reference to the dynamics of Lebanon's contemporary Christian political parties.

Marie Vannetzel provides a fascinating window into the complex workings of Islamic party politics through her examination of the longstanding Egyptian Muslim Brotherhood's first foray into party organization, the Freedom and Justice Party, which emerged in the early stages of the post-Mubarak era. She examines the profound challenges engendered by decades of 'forbidden yet tolerated' activism by the parent organization, and its accompanying apparatus, as well as the failure to adapt to new political realities demanding greater transparency regarding policy objectives and decision-making processes.

Joseph Sassoon undertakes a sweeping, comparative examination of the style and patterns of governance in the twentieth century's Arab republics, which included both one-party e.g. Iraq/Syria, and multi-party systems e.g. Egypt/Tunisia. He lays out the substantial role of ruling parties in perpetuating certain political regimes and achieves this through recourse to a vast and rich memoir literature which has become available to scholars in recent years, providing insight into several underappreciated aspects of these diverse political systems and providing clarity on the complex relationship between the regime and the single party in Arab autocracies.

Eskandar Sadeghi-Boroujerdi analyses the historical emergence of the Organization of Communist Unity, which coalesced out of the National Front of Iran and its Organizations abroad. In the aftermath of the MI6/CIA-orchestrated 1953 coup d'état, a new generation of political activists left Iran for Europe and the United States to pursue higher education. While politically active in the Organizations of the National Front Abroad, they gradually turned to revolutionary Marxism against the backdrop of the torrential waves of decolonization and resistance to imperial military interventions undulating across the Global South. This same constellation of activists was not only fiercely anti-imperialist, but also opposed any form of dependence on the U.S.S.R. or the People's Republic of China. They would move from Europe and the United States to establish themselves in several locations across the Arab world, and pursue political activism and their advocacy of guerrilla warfare, as part of their ambition to launch a national liberation struggle against the regime of Mohammadreza Pahlavi. By examining Communist Unity's predecessors and their manifold transnational ideological, political and logistical networks with like-minded revolutionary movements inside the Middle East, this chapter brings to the fore hitherto under-explored South–South connections and situates Iran's revolutionary opposition within the global moment of '1968'. It also highlights some of the political challenges faced by activists involved in a broad political coalition and transnational network, who subsequently decided to establish a revolutionary vanguard party, while aspiring to retain the mechanisms and wherewithal of internal organizational democracy.

Working at the juncture of human rights and gender, Zehra F. Kabasakal Arat undertakes a discourse analysis of Turkish political parties' political programmes and their approach to the question of women's rights between 1923 and 2007. Arat observes how the once neglected question of gender and women's rights has been taken up by political parties, even while the discourses of different parties continue to discernibly vary, and notes the importance of the emergence of autonomous women's organizations in this regard. Conservative and religious parties articulated what she terms a 'dualist approach', advocating traditionalism, but also conceding ground to the claims of gender equality, while a variety of left-leaning groups have come to increasingly propound positions that are identifiably feminist in orientation.

Khalil Dahbi explores the formation of the 'political party field' in post-independence Morocco. To achieve this aim, he draws upon the conceptual affordances of Pierre Bourdieu's field theory, calibrating it to the socio-historical specificity of his case study. Nevertheless, as he warns, it is important to avoid engaging with an 'assumed political entity such as "an authoritarian political system" and investigating its "ingredients" retrospectively'. The more appropriate approach consists of 'exploring and studying the processes which bring into existence this holistic entity, the role of various actors, how these actors were constrained by rules and positions of the very field that they are piecing together'. Dahbi's chief contribution lies in its attempt to furnish a novel approach to the study of political parties in Morocco, going beyond accounts which have tended to be elitist in character.

Finally, Francesco Saverio Leopardi tackles one of the foremost leftist political forces on the Palestinian political scene, the Popular Front for the Liberation of Palestine (PFLP), and its role during the First Intifada of 1987–1990. Through both an analysis of official PFLP ideology, publications, and interviews with former and current party members, and the adoption of the concept of policy fluctuation as a key theoretical underpinning, Leopardi attempts to unravel the reasons behind the PFLP's declining ability to impact the terms of the political settlement between the Israeli state and the Palestinian leadership. He examines the policies and practice of the PFLP against the backdrop of Fatah's adoption of a diplomatic agenda and strategy, the fragmentation of the Palestinian left, and the rise of the Islamist movement.

Together, it is hoped that these chapters will provide a modest contribution to the burgeoning literature on the history, contemporary practice, and modus operandi of political parties in the MENA region, and demonstrate the disparate methodological and thematic approaches, as well as empirical case studies available for scholarly enquiry and investigation. Far from providing the final word on the subject, these theoretically rigorous and empirically grounded articles are intended to spur further research into what has come to be recognized as an indispensable facet of political life and a key agent of socio-economic change and transformation.

Bibliography

Abrahamian, Ervand. *Iran Between Two Revolutions*. Princeton, NJ: Princeton University Press, 1982.

Batatu, Hanna. *The Old Social Classes and the Revolutionary Movements of Iraq: A Study of Iraq's Old Landed and Commercial Classes and of its Communists, Ba'thists, and Free Officers*. London: Saqi, 2004 [1978].

Bayat, Asef. *Life as Politics: How Ordinary People Change the Middle East*. Kindle ed. Stanford, CA: Stanford University Press, 2010, 2013.

Cavatorta, Francesco, and Lise Storm. *Political Parties in the Arab World: Continuity and Change*. Edinburgh: University of Edinburgh Press, 2018.

Chalcraft, John. *Popular Politics in the Making of the Modern Middle East*. Cambridge and New York: Cambridge University Press, 2016.

Chehabi, H. E. 'Religion and Politics in Iran: How Theocratic Is the Islamic Republic?' *Daedalus*, 120(3) (Summer 1991), pp. 69–91.

Clark, Janine A. *Islam, Charity, and Activism: Middle-Class Networks and Social Welfare in Egypt, Jordan, and Yemen*. Bloomington and Indianapolis, IN: Indiana University Press, 2004.

Dawisha, Adeed. *Arab Nationalism in the Twentieth Century: From Triumph to Despair*. Princeton, NJ and Oxford: Princeton University Press, 2009.

de Leon, Cedric. *Party and Society: Reconstructing a Sociology of Democratic Party Politics*. Cambridge: Polity, 2014.

de Leon, Cedric, Manali Desai, and Cihan Tuğal. *Building Blocs: How Parties Organize Society*. Stanford, CA: Stanford University Press, 2015.

Gordon, Joel. *Nasser's Blessed Movement: Egypt's Free Officers and the July Revolution*. Oxford and New York: Oxford University Press, 1992.

Hashemi, Nader, and Danny Postel, eds. *Sectarianization: Mapping the New Politics of the Middle East*. Oxford and New York: Oxford University Press, 2017.

Ismael, Tareq Y. *The Rise and Fall of the Communist Party of Iraq*. Cambridge and New York: Cambridge University Press, 2008.

Ismael, Tareq Y. *The Communist Movement in the Arab World*. London and New York: RoutledgeCurzon, 2005.

Kamrava, Mehran, ed. *Beyond the Arab Spring: The Evolving Ruling Bargain in the Middle East*. Oxford and New York: Oxford University Press, 2014.

Kandil, Hazem. *Inside the Brotherhood*. Cambridge: Polity, 2014.

Keshavarzian, Arang. 'Contestation without Democracy: Elite Fragmentation in Iran', in Marsha Pripstein Posusney and Michelle Penner Angrist, eds., *Authoritarianism in the Middle East: Regimes and Resistance*. Boulder, CO: Lynne Rienner, 2005, pp. 63–88.

Knapp, Michael, Anja Flach, and Ercan Ayboğa. *Revolution in Rojava: Democratic Autonomy and Women's Liberation in Syria*. London: Pluto Books, 2016.

Laclau, Ernesto, and Chantal Mouffe. *Hegemony and Socialist Strategy: Towards a Radical Democratic Politics*. London and New York: Verso, 1985.

'Matn-e kamel-e virast-e dovvom-e manshur-e sabz'. *Kalameh*, 3 Esfand 1389 [22 February 2011].

Mitchell, Timothy. *Carbon Democracy: Political Power in the Age of Oil*. London and New York: Verso, 2013.

Morozov, Evgeny. *The Net Delusion: How Not to Liberate the World*. London and New York: Allen Lane, 2011.

Owen, Roger. *State, Power and Politics in the Making of the Modern Middle East*. Abingdon and New York: Routledge, 2004.

Provence, Michael. *The Last Ottoman Generation and the Making of the Modern Middle East*. Cambridge and New York: Cambridge University Press, 2017.

Randjbar-Daemi, Siavush. *The Quest for Authority in Iran: A History of the Presidency from Revolution to Rouhani*. London and New York: I.B. Tauris, 2018.

Shafir, Gershon. *A Half Century of Occupation: Israel, Palestine, and the World's Most Intractable Conflict*. Berkeley and Los Angeles, CA: University of California Press, 2017.

Thompson, Elizabeth F. *Justice Interrupted: The Struggle for Constitutional Government in the Middle East*. Cambridge, MA and London: Harvard University Press, 2013.

Weil, Simone. *The Abolition of All Political Parties*. Translated by Simon Leys. New York: NYRB, 2013.

Weizman, Eyal. *Hollow Land: Israel's Architracture of Occupation*. London and New York: Verso, 2012.

2 Political parties in MENA

Their functions and development

Raymond A. Hinnebusch

ABSTRACT

This article provides an overview of the development of parties and party systems in the MENA region from early oligarchic pluralism to the mass single-party systems of the populist era and the limited multi-party experiments of the 1990s era of political liberalization. The survey shows how parties develop in parallel with the deepening of politicization and become nearly indispensable adjuncts in the construction of political order. The article then examines parties in the post-2010 period, with case studies of Turkey, Egypt, and Tunisia demonstrating how very different configurations of party development dramatically impact on regime trajectories, ranging from democratization to hybrid regimes.

Political parties are often said to matter little in the Middle East and North Africa (MENA), where monarchs or the military tend to subordinate or marginalize parties. Moreover, with a disproportionate number of no-party, one-party, or dominant-party states, the region suffers from a deficit of the *party competition* associated with democracy.

Bill and Springborg offered a 'political culture' explanation for this: the continued viability of traditional solidarity groups (kinship groups, shillas) and of clientalism and tribalism as alternative mechanisms of elite–mass linkage, both of which deter and colonize more inclusive forms of impersonal association. An alternative structural explanation points to the pre-emption of political space by the prior external imposition of (and subsequent channelling of oil 'rent' through) the bureaucratic and military arms of the state, allowing it to subordinate or corporatize political structures, including parties, which would otherwise have represented civil society or mobilized class constituencies.[1]

To the extent this is so, it may go far towards explaining the dysfunction of MENA political systems for it may be taken as one of the few 'laws' of political science that the healthy operation of modern polities requires political parties. Only parties, with their unique capacity to organize large numbers of citizens behind leaders with a governing programme, potentially give ordinary people a voice in governance that can balance the oligarchic minorities who wield monopolies of money, guns, or traditional status. Mass class-based parties were the main vehicles by which political participation was widened in the West. And it is parties that provide the consistent organized support needed if governments are to effectively govern.

---

[1] James A. Bill and Robert Springborg, *Politics in the Middle East* (New York: HarperCollins, 1994), pp. 84–105, 235; Fred W. Riggs, 'Bureaucrats and Political Development: A Paradoxical View', in Joseph LaPalombara, ed., *Bureaucracy and Political Development* (Princeton, NJ: Princeton University Press, 1967), pp. 120–167.

Why political parties in the Middle East matter

The Middle East is not, however, entirely 'exceptional' in respect to parties. Organizations with a family resemblance to parties exist in two-thirds of Arab states and while their roles may be more marginal than in developed states, similar *structures* are unlikely to perform wholly dissimilar *functions* in a political system. To be sure, MENA parties reflect the political culture of their societies: the power of sub-state identities and small group politics is manifest in the tendency of parties to form and fragment around personalities, clans, and sects. At the same time, however, culture is amenable to change and once traditional legitimacy eroded, newly emergent elites in MENA soon adopted a new 'political technology'—party ideology and organization—in order to mobilize support for their agendas.[2] Parties were major instruments for the spread of politicization further down in the stratification system—from oligarchy to middle class to masses—and, in the process they, in turn, evolved beyond the personal factions of notables though the adoption of the party organization needed to incorporate widening numbers of participants: in the first stage, branches appeared in the provincial towns dominated by educated professionals and civil servants, then later, cells in factories and villages brought in workers and peasants. In parallel, as party recruitment widened to include activists of middle- and then lower-class origin, the ideologies of parties came to appeal to wider constituencies, promoting more egalitarian and reformist programmes, potentially changing the balance of social class power in MENA societies.

Party systems were also decisive for the changing character of regimes in the region. Party formation enabled the mass mobilization against colonial rulers that helped win independence for many Arab countries, with the Egyptian Wafd the prototype. The potential of the liberal oligarchies that took power after independence to consolidate early fragile democracies through mass inclusion was aborted because their party systems were too fragmented or polarized to widen participation and manage peaceful change; the outstanding exception, the transformation to democracy achieved in 1950s Turkey, was dependent on the emergence of two relatively equal parties sufficiently close in ideology for each to accept democratic electoral competition over power. The failure of democratization in the Arab world opened the way for the 1960s dominance of populist authoritarian (PA) regimes which used ruling single parties, 'the modern form of authoritarianism',[3] to carry out revolution from above and mobilize the constituencies needed to consolidate themselves against the old oligarchy. Then, as single parties ran out of ideological steam, parallel to the 1980s shift from populist to post-populist versions of authoritarianism pursuing neo-liberal policies, elites turned single parties from instruments of mobilization into mechanisms of clientalism and demobilization, used to contain mass resistance to neo-liberal reforms. However, the political vacuum created was quickly filled by Islamist political movements seeking to mobilize the victims of post-populism and forcing further regime adaptation. In the 1990s, as part of strategies of 'authoritarian upgrading', regimes sought to co-opt increasing opposition, both Islamist and liberal, through limited pluralization of party systems, in which the ruling party was flanked by smaller opposition parties of the left and right. For this to lead to democratization, opposition parties had to become mass organizations, but their failure, with few exceptions, to do so, in this period and also in the brief opportunities opened by the Arab

---

[2]Manfred Halpern, *Politics of Social Change in the Middle East and North Africa* (Princeton, NJ: Princeton University Press, 1963), pp. 281–283.
[3]Samuel Huntington, *Political Order in Changing Societies* (New Haven, CT: Yale University Press, 1968), p. 398.

uprising, helps explain the Middle East's continuing democracy deficit. Crucial to the only successful democratization issuing from the post-2010 Arab Uprisings, that of Tunisia, was the emergence of a competitive two-party system.

The following discussion traces party development over several stages, namely, the eras of liberal oligarchy; populist revolution; post-populist authoritarianism; and Arab Uprising. The narrative will show both that party systems were shaped by the features of the stage, notably whether politicization and inclusion were widening or contracting, but also how parties were important factors both in the levels of consolidation of regimes at each stage and in the transitions to subsequent stages. Case studies of countries where parties played such important roles bridge the four stages to illustrate the interaction of regime formation and party systems over time. While the evolving pattern of party change was most pronounced in the authoritarian republics, comparing them to the somewhat different party trajectories of those monarchies that allowed party formation and with democracies (with Lebanon distinct from Turkey and Israel) underlines the intimate interrelation of regime and party development.

Party development

Early party pluralism under liberal oligarchies

This stage spanned a period beginning around 1900, when political contestation emerged within a small oligarchic political arena, and usually ended in the 1950s or 1960s when the mobilization of middle-class activism occurred.

The earliest precursors of political parties appeared in the late Ottoman period when groupings of officers, bureaucrats, or professionals formed to press for modernization, constitutional rule (The Committee of Union and Progress), or Arab rights within the empire (al-*Ahd*). The collapse of the empire led to a proliferation of nationalist parties seeking to fill the ideological vacuum, notably the *Fatat* party that backed the short-lived Faisal government in Damascus. Under Western imperialism and early independence, *parties of 'notables'* dominated; parties were the instruments of small groups of wealthy local leaders (*ayan, zuama*), normally great landlords or merchants, whose extended families controlled certain urban quarters or villages. These parties were precipitated by the creation of parliaments where factions of deputies grouped together in 'conservative' or 'liberal' blocs supporting or opposing the government but seldom able to hold it accountable. Linked more by personal ties than ideology, they were ephemeral and vulnerable to factionalism. Able to count on the dependants of the notables, such as peasants on their estates or clients in urban quarters, to win elections, notable parties had little need for party cadres or organization. Classic examples of such parties were the Liberal-Constitutionalists of Egypt, the various court parties in Morocco and Jordan, and the National and Constitutional blocs in Lebanon. In the early Iranian *majlis,* caucuses (maslaks) of royalists and liberals appeared.

The main initial opposition to the upper-class notable parties emerged as a still-small Westernized middle class emerged. New parties formed, led by intellectuals and professionals, often teachers and their students, professing liberal or radical ideologies, often organized around a political newspaper, and, in the 1930s, sometimes giving birth to fascist-inspired militant youth groups (Green Shirts, Blue Shirts). Such parties were often able to mobilize student demonstrations and influence educated political opinion but, lacking the great wealth to establish clientalist networks in a era prior to mass politicization, they remained relatively small urban groups and were seldom able to win elections. Mustafa Kamil's National Party in Egypt, the Iraqi Istiqlal party, the Democrat Iran party, and the early Ba'th party are good examples.[4]

Where nationalist agitation spurred political mobilization, certain early parties evolved into large-scale independence movements, normally combining coalitions of notables, groups of intellectuals, and students mobilized by nationalist ideology, with elements of the lower classes brought in through street agitation or the clientele networks of the notables. Some became formidable electoral machines, able to win parliamentary majorities through a combination of nationalism in the cities and clientalism in the villages. The Egyptian Wafd and the Moroccan Istiqlal, Mossadeq's National Front in Iran, and the Syrian Kutla (National Bloc) all came close to representing the whole nation against the imperialist power.[5] However, their mobilization of a socially heterogeneous base around the single issue of independence doomed most of them to fragment after independence when they tended to lose their intellectual activists and their mass bases (as happened to the Moroccan Istiqlal from which the National Union of Popular Forces seceded) or to factionalize (thus, the Syrian Kutla split into the Damascus-centred Watani and the Aleppo-centred Sha'b parties). The major exception was the Tunisian Neo-Destour Party whose charismatic leadership and exceptional organizational capacity enabled it to make the transition to a ruling single party.

As, from the 1940s to the 1960s, the educated middle class grew and politicization spread to the rural peripheries, several parties of intellectuals were able to develop and fill the vacuum left by the decline of notable parties. The key to this was an ability to bridge the middle class–mass and urban–rural gaps by propagating nationalist and populist ideology and developing formal organization with branches in the provincial towns. They included several secular nationalist parties such as Egypt's Misr al-Fatat (Young Egypt, later the Socialist Party of Egypt), the Syrian Social Nationalist Party (SSNP),[6] the National Democratic Party in Iraq, the National Socialists of Jordan, and the Arab Socialist Ba'th Party in Syria and Iraq. All combined ideologies mixing nationalism and reformist socialism and found support among middle-class professionals, army officers, and growing student populations with footholds in trade unions and peasant movements. At the same time, Communist parties attempted to organize the emerging working classes, achieving temporary successes in Iran, Egypt, and Syria; but they were quite vulnerable to ideological factionalism, state repression, and delegitimation on nationalist grounds and in some cases remained too rooted in certain ethnic minorities. Finally, widely imitated across the region was the Muslim Brotherhood of Egypt which, attracting activists from religious students and support from the petite bourgeoisie (small merchants, artisans, clerks) and recent migrants to the city, demonstrated the ability of Islamic ideology and militants to build a well-organized mass base, including cooperatives, charities, and paramilitary organizations.[7]

The ideological and organizational power of the Brotherhood, the communists, and the Ba'thists was demonstrated by their ability to spread across state boundaries. Although still

---

[4]Arthur Goldschmidt, 'The Egyptian Nationalist Party, 1892–1919', in P. M. Holt, ed., *Political and Social Change in Modern Egypt* (London: Oxford University Press, 1968); George Jabbur, *al-fikra al-siyasi al-mu'asir fi Suriya* [Contemporary Political Thought in Syria] (London: Riad El-Rayyes, 1987); James Jankowski, *Egypt's Young Rebels: "Young Egypt,": 1933-1952* (Stanford, CA: Hoover Institution Press, 1975).

[5]Marius Deeb, *Party Politics in Egypt: The Wafd and its Rivals, 1919–39* (London: Ithaca Press, 1979).

[6]Labib Zuwiyya Yamak, *The Syrian Social Nationalist Party: An Ideological Analysis* (Cambridge, MA: Harvard Center for Middle Eastern Studies, 1966).

[7]Richard Mitchell, *The Society of Muslim Brothers* (London: Oxford University Press, 1969).

partly leader-dependent (the Egyptian Ikhwan temporarily declined after the supreme guide was killed), their remarkable durability amidst state repression and generational change in leadership indicated considerable organizational and ideological institutionalization. However, in agrarian societies where notables and tribal chiefs kept much of the mass public encapsulated in their clientele networks, none of these parties were normally able to mobilize the electoral majorities needed to take power constitutionally (although some entered into coalition governments with parties of notables); and most therefore flirted with attempts to subvert and use the military to gain power.

Party development took somewhat different forms in different states. In the post-World War II period when the Iranian political system was rapidly liberalized, a number of significant parties were founded. The Democrat Party, a catch-all party including both landowners and intellectuals and centred around the personality of veteran politician Ahmad Qavam al-Sal-taneh, actually won a majlis majority in 1947. The Iran Party was a liberal grouping of intel-lectuals. The Marxist Tudeh Party, possessing both middle-class and worker activists and the most disciplined organization, led the trade unionization of Iran's emerging industrial work-ing class after World War II. Mossadeq's National Front (Jebhe-ye Melli), an umbrella move-ment of notable parties and middle-class parties of intellectuals rather than an organized mass party, nevertheless dominated the majlis in the early 1950s on the strength of its nationalist programme and charismatic leader.[8] This pluralism was cut short by the 1953 re-imposition of royal autocracy.

In Iraq, middle-class parties could not make breakthroughs into the notable-dominated parliament but developed outside and against it. These included the Istiqlal, followers of Arab nationalist veteran Rashid Ali al-Gaylani, and the liberal National Democratic Party, which grew out of the earlier Ahali group of intellectuals. After the 1958 revolution there was a dramatic expansion in participation as the now-tolerated Communist party, recruiting from intellectuals, the working class, and the Shi'a urban poor, rapidly grew to 25,000 mem-bers by 1959 while the Kurdish Democratic Party mobilized the Kurds, both tribal and intel-lectual, and the Ba'th Party incorporated lower-middle class Sunnis. The degeneration of this pluralism into near-anarchy invited unstable military rule until the consolidation of the Ba'th Party regime after 1968.[9]

Lebanon is a limiting case where pluralism survived beyond the 1950s—even into the post-Uprising period; yet communal fragmentation deterred the emergence of a mature party system in spite of the state's liberal political structures. Instead, earlier primitive pro-to-parties adapted and were later joined by mass movements with communal bases. The first proto-parties were the 'blocs' of notables (zuama), typically parliamentary caucuses linked to society through clientele networks rather than extra-parliamentary organization. To be sure, in parliamentary elections from 1951–1972, the representation of true party-af-filiated deputies climbed from 10% to 30% of the seats, but, where successful, parties were almost always clan-led and were only able to mobilize cross-class mass support by ideolo-gizing a sectarian appeal. The most durable such party was the Maronite Kataib (or Phalanges) led by the Gemayal clan, which mobilized the Maronite bourgeoisie, the petite bourgeoisie, and parts of the peasantry, in opposition to other sects but also often against the main

[8]Richard Cottam, 'Political Party Development in Iran', Iranian Studies, 1(3) (1968), pp. 82–95.
[9]Reeva Simon, 'Iraq', in Frank Tachau, ed., Political Parties of the Middle East and North Africa (London: Mansell, 1994), pp. 174–197.

Maronite zuama. Other similar but less organized parties included the National Liberals (of the Maronite Chamouns), the Druze-dominated Progressive Socialists (of the Junblatts), and the Dashnak party representing Armenian Christians. The Muslims were represented by zuama blocs inside parliament and outside it were regionally fragmented into urban quarter-based Nasserite or Sunni Islamic groups. Even the communist party factionalized along sectarian lines between Orthodox Christian and Shia factions. During the civil war from 1975, party militias, pushing aside the zuama, ruled 'cantons' and collected taxes, with the Lebanese Forces, a Kataib offshoot, controlling most Maronite regions and the Shia militias, Amal and Hizbollah, emerging to dominate the Muslim regions. In the post-Taif 1992 elections, however, zuama domination revived, with only 39 of 108 parliamentary deputies being party-affiliated; this election did, however, register the post-civil war change in the sectarian balance of power: the Shia Hizbollah and Amal movements, re-invented as parties, won 12 seats, the largely Orthodox Christian SSNP 4, the Dashnak 4, and the Progressive Socialists 4, with the Maronite parties self-excluding themselves.[10]

Single party systems and revolution from above

In a second phase (1950–1960s) of party development, middle-class political leaders, variously originating in middle-class parties and/or the military, established single-party systems as instruments of 'revolution from above in PA regimes'. Where this happened, many of the parties of the liberal period disappeared, although some, such as the Ba'th, reinvented themselves as ruling single parties. According to Huntington, the single-party system originates in a bifurcation between the revolutionary regime and 'traditional' society (or the old oligarchy), its function to both *concentrate* power in the hands of the revolutionary elite (and exclude the oligarchy from power) while *expanding* power by mobilizing a mass constituency. The revolutionary struggle substitutes for party competition in keeping the party dynamic and the ruling elite responsive; where there is little such struggle, the single party tends to be weaker and as conflict with the old oligarchy declines, so does the party's responsiveness to its mass constituency. Indeed, as the party elite becomes part of a new upper class, the party starts to change from an instrument of revolution into a patronage machine (through which clients seek favours and careerists upward mobility).[11]

Single parties aspired to be mass parties penetrating the peripheries and organizing the masses, but they varied widely in their ability to do so. What Owen[12] calls 'rallies and unions' were relatively weak parties established by military leaders from above (such as the Liberation Rally and National Union in Egypt, the Arab Liberation Movement of Syrian dictator Adib Shishakli, and the Arab Socialist Unions [ASU] established by military leaders in Egypt, Iraq, Sudan, and Libya). In these parties, ideological commitment was unimportant and nominal membership was extended to virtually the entire population except for active opponents of the regime; this made these organizations vulnerable to infiltration by many contradictory vested interests, even those unsympathetic to the regimes' reform programmes. Such parties

---

[10]Michael Suleiman, *Political Parties in Lebanon: The Challenge of a Fragmented Political Culture* (Ithaca, NY: Cornell University Press, 1967); John Entelis, *Pluralism and Party Transformation in Lebanon: al-Kataib, 1936-1970* (Leiden: E.J. Brill, 1975).

[11]Samuel P. Huntington, 'Social and Institutional Dynamics of One-Party Systems', in Louis J. Cantori, ed., *Comparative Political Systems* (Boston, MA: Holbrook Press, 1974), pp. 323–370.

[12]Roger Owen, *State, Power and Politics in the Making of the Modern Middle East* (London: Routledge, 1992), pp. 255–272.

were not elite recruitment mechanisms, with the military and bureaucracy remaining the career paths to the top. On the contrary, party offices at the centre and province were staffed by ex-military officers and bureaucrats 'on loan' rather than by political activists; the top layers of the party hierarchy were thus a mere auxiliary of the bureaucracy, incapable of channelling participation or aggregating interests. Harik calls this sort of organization a 'collaboration movement' because at the local level it co-opted notables (and their clientele networks) who were allowed a relatively free hand in their locales in return for acquiescence in the regime but had no say in national policy; as such, these parties were also crippled as mobilizational instruments. Those leaders who wanted to carry out a revolution in the village soon became dissatisfied with and tried to transform such organizations. Thus, Nasser tried to reinvigorate the ASU by recruiting a cadre of young militants on ideological grounds to displace or balance the village notables but abandoned the effort after the 1967 war. In Libya Muammar Qaddafi attempted to invigorate his mass organization by encouraging a 'cultural revolution' against the bureaucrats and tribal leaders and by recruiting ideological militants into 'revolutionary committees' meant to 'guide' the wider mass membership.[13]

Stronger single-party regimes resulted when the party, through a history of grassroots struggle, acquired a cadre of militants and some roots in the population prior to the assumption of power. Subsequently, party leaders normally adopted a 'Leninist' strategy of party building from top down, in which ideological militants recruited from plebeian strata established party cells in villages, factories, and schools, while creating or taking over labour, peasant, and youth unions. The ruling party acquired a full-time professional apparatus, and a pyramid of congresses, partly elected, partly co-opted, linked base and centre. The party might share power with a charismatic leader and/or the military, but the sign of its 'strength' was its greater centrality in the performance of political functions than in the 'rally' form of single party. Thus, the party organization was a major ladder of recruitment into the political elite, its top congress, representing the regime elite assembled, had some role in policy making, the party normally subordinated and supervised the government bureaucracy in the implementation of policy and, at the local level, party militants played a key role in social reforms, notably land reform. The Destour Socialist Party in Tunisia, the Yemen Socialist Party (previously National Liberation Front) in former Democratic Yemen, and the ruling Ba'th parties in Syria and Iraq approximated this model. The decline of the party tended to be accompanied by its displacement from policy making, by the ascendancy of the military over it (as in Syria under Asad), by its transformation into a creature of personal rule (as in Iraq and Tunisia), or by its degeneration into personal and tribal factions (as in former Democratic Yemen where the party violently self-destructed along such lines).

The Algerian FLN was mid-way between the weak and the strong types of single-party systems. Algeria's struggle for independence gave birth to a succession of mass parties that expressed the dominant nationalist and Islamo-populist political culture. The FLN (*Fronte Liberation Nationale*) began as a guerrilla organization mounting armed insurrection and evolved into an umbrella absorbing almost all pre-existing political groups. In this process, the FLN was factionalized and after independence, its constituent parts were absorbed into the army and bureaucracy or went into opposition, leaving it a moribund shell subordinated to the military. In the 1970s, President Boumediene revived the FLN as a bureaucratic apparatus with 10,000 party workers, controlling the mass organizations and charged with

---

[13]Iliya Harik, 'The Single Party as a Subordinate Movement: The Case of Egypt', *World Politics*, 26(1) (1973), pp. 80–105.

carrying out his 'agrarian revolution'. Its congress was, moreover, the formal arena in which the succession of President Chadli Ben Jedid was brokered.

None of the single-party systems succeeded in wholly eliminating opposition. Rather, Islamist parties, whether variants or offshoots of the Muslim Brotherhood or Shia analogues, such as the Dawa party in Iraq, representative of the marginalized merchants and *ulama*, tended everywhere to survive or emerge underground, from where, facing repression by regimes, some attempted—unsuccessfully—violent insurgency in the 1980s–1990s.

Limited party pluralism under post-populist authoritarianism

In the next phase of development beginning in the 1970s, the region was dominated by post-populist republics or monarchies under which a dominant president or monarch allowed limited scope for political pluralism. Such states were associated with two main types of party system, the 'dominant party system' (in which the ruling single party permits small opposition parties) and the 'palace-dominated multi-party system'.

The dominant party system was an outcome of the partial liberalization in the authoritarian republics beginning in the 1970s. As the populist consensus that accompanied single-party rule collapsed and rulers began to economically liberalize against the resistance of statist interests while populations threatened by this turned to political Islam, regimes sought to mobilize social forces favourable to liberalization, find ways to co-opt opposition, and trade limited participation rights for public acceptance of the gradual abandonment of the populist social contract. Their strategy, a limited pluralization of the party system was, arguably, an adaptation to the ideological pluralization of the political arena. This liberalization allowed some of the earlier parties marginalized under single-party rule to re-emerge, e.g. the Egyptian Wafd party was reborn as the 'New Wafd Party'.

Egypt after Nasser is the best case of the dominant-party system in the Middle East. As Egypt's Nasserite consensus dissolved, the all-embracing ASU was disbanded in 1976 and some of its fragments or the remnants of pre-revolutionary parties were allowed to constitute themselves as 'loyal' opposition parties. While the presidency remained the centre of authoritarian power and the new ruling party never failed to win a large parliamentary majority, opposition parties were allowed to compete, not for governing power, but for *access* to power (e.g. parliamentary seats). While the government party sought to straddle the centre of the political spectrum, opposition parties flanked it on the left and right. The ruling National Democratic Party (NDP) was a direct descendant of Nasser's ASU, incorporating the ruling alliance of senior bureaucrats, top police and army officers, businessmen, and the provincial landed notables, albeit shorn of the leftwing intellectuals and politicized officers who briefly dominated the ASU. The NDP's ideology of a mixed economy was compatible with both the public sector in which many bureaucrats and state managers had a stake and the growing role of private and foreign capital from which both officials and pro-regime businessmen were being enriched. A stream of initiatives and responses to government from its parliamentary caucus sought to defend or promote the particular interests of elements of its largely bourgeois constituency while providing its MPs with access to patronage.

More an appendage of government than an autonomous political force, the NDP enjoyed little loyalty from its members, had few activists, and was hence only a primitive organization. This reflected its lack of interest in mass mobilization; if anything, its function was to enforce demobilization. As such, it had to depend on village headmen and local notables to bring out the vote; it also lacked financial resources to back its candidates who depended on personal resources to run their campaigns and on their ability to deliver government patronage to attract votes. Nevertheless, by way of the clientele networks of the notables it co-opted, the NDP brought a portion of the village and urban masses into the regime camp, denying the opposition access to them; it also nominally incorporated large numbers of government employees and, an instrument of corporatism, placed its partisans in the top posts of many of the professional and labour syndicates.

An array of opposition political parties seemed to give expression to different interests and values than those of the ruling party. More than personalistic factions, they either revived some pre-Nasser political tradition or were rooted in a major societal or issue cleavage, and the rough correspondence between their ideologies and their social bases seemed for a while to be moving Egyptian politics beyond a mere competition of patrons and shillas without social roots. Two liberal parties grouping landlords and wealthy professionals positioned themselves to the 'right' of the ruling party: the tiny Liberal (*Ahrar*) Party and the New Wafd, the voice of the old aristocracy excluded from power by Nasser and of the wing of the private bourgeoisie still antagonistic to the state. On the left, the National Progressive Unionist Party (NPUP) or *Tagammu* brought together, behind an ideology of nationalist populism, a coalition of Marxist and Nasserite intellectuals and trade union leaders under the leftwing ex-Free Officer, Khalid Muhy ad-Din. It had a small but well-organized base of activists, but the regime, in intimidating trade unionists into distancing themselves from it, robbed it of its putative mass constituency and it later degenerated into a government-aligned faction opposed to political Islam. The Socialist Labour Party (SLP), a descendant of the radical nationalist pre-1952 Misr al-Fatat, began as a defender of the public sector and critical of Western alignment, but, lacking a mass base, moved into close alignment with the Muslim Brotherhood under the slogan 'Islam is the solution'. The Brotherhood itself, never legalized as a party, nevertheless stood candidates as independents or under the SLP banner. Led by *ulama* and wealthy merchants, it was silent on the regime's economic liberalization but highly critical of its Western alignment. While the movement was weak among industrial workers and peasants, it was strongly attractive to more 'marginal' elements such as educated unemployed rural migrants and the traditional mass of small merchants and artisans who wanted an 'Islamic economy' that accepted private property and profit but sought to contain their inegalitarian consequences by a moral code and a welfare state. The Brotherhood was differentiated from smaller, more radical Islamic groups by its willingness to proselytize peacefully within the political system.

The representative potential of a dominant-party system required opposition parties to become 'parties of pressure' representing constituencies left outside the ruling coalition in order to pressure the government to adopt parts of their programmes. The potential for such a system peaked in the most open and competitive elections of 1984 and 1987. In 1984 the New Wafd and the Muslim Brotherhood formed a joint ticket that captured 58 of 448 seats with 15% of the vote and emerged as the main opposition forces; in 1987 the New Wafd, competing alone, got 35 seats, while the small Liberal and Labour parties, joined with the Muslim Brotherhood in the Islamic Alliance, won 60. Thus, while the government majority remained unchallengeable, the liberal and Islamist interests emerged as a significant opposition presence in parliament where, however, instead of combining against the government, the first advocated economic and political liberalization and the second won Islamization concessions from the secular regime.

However, the regime stopped short of allowing (and even reversed) the political freedoms needed to expand party pluralization to the level of the mass public and make the opposition parties effective parties of pressure. The government's manipulation of electoral laws, its monopoly of the broadcast media, restrictions on the opposition's ability to campaign and associate, intimidation of opposition activists, and the often fraudulent administration of elections all enforced the message that the opposition would not be allowed to translate its potential support over issues into votes and seats in parliament. The low turnout for elections indicated that many Egyptians were unconvinced that voting under these conditions made any difference to political outcomes; those who did vote, behaving rationally, voted according to a candidate's perceived ability to deliver patronage, a resource largely controlled by the regime.

In this situation, the government party was able to co-opt the local notables with the best personal followings and family alliances who, knowing they had to deliver government patronage to retain their seats, were deferent towards it. Because opposition parties also needed to deliver patronage they too tended over time to mute their opposition. The one exception to the enervation of the opposition parties was the Muslim Brotherhood which alone possessed a significant cadre of activists, independent financial resources, and real organization; precisely for this reason it became the main target of government repression, suffering massive arrests of its cadres at election time, which effectively contained its electoral potential. In general, thus, the pluralization of the party system actually reinforced the regime: elections functioned to co-opt and channel political activity that might otherwise have taken a covert, even violent, anti-regime direction into more tame, manageable forms. Additionally, the divisions in the opposition generally allowed the regime to play off secularists against Islamists, left against right.[14]

Limited republican pluralism took country-specific variations in Yemen and Iran. The unification of the two Yemeni single-party states resulted at first in a unique co-habitation between the two ruling parties, the conservative-tribalist People's General Congress of the north and ex-Marxist Yemen Socialist Party of the south, later joined by the Islamic Islah party; before long however they fell out in a violent civil war in which the socialists were marginalized.[15] Different again was post-revolutionary Iran where the single party, the Islamic Republican Party, never more than an umbrella for disparate groups, dissolved into several clergy-led networks each of which expressed the views of distinct societal constituencies: 'reformists', 'centrists', and 'conservatives'. In this proto-multi-party system, electoral competition was real and came to turn on issues: first the struggle between populist radicals and economic pragmatists; then that between cultural conservatives and liberals. The impact of the electorate on outcomes has, however, been filtered by the 'checks and balances' of the non-elected theocratic part of the political system—the religious leader and the council of guardians which vets electoral candidates.

The transformation of a single-party system into a dominant-party system was by no means easy or inevitable. In Algeria, the ruling FLN failed to maintain its dominance and the opposition FIS (Front Islamique du Salut) won the first liberalized elections by mobilizing all those excluded from state patronage networks. Based on thousands of mosques, its cadre

---

[14]Raymond Hinnebusch, *Egyptian Politics under Sadat* (Boulder, CO: Lynne Rienner, 1988), pp. 158–170, 186–222, 302–304; Maye Kassem, *In the Guise of Democracy: Governance in Contemporary Egypt* (Reading: Ithaca Press, 1999).
[15]Renaud Detalle, 'Les parties politiques au Yemen: paysage après le bataille', *Revue des Mondes musulmans et de la Mediterranee*, 81(2) (1996), pp. 341–396.

of imams preached against government corruption, appealing to the commercial strata (who financed the organization), and to the educated unemployed and recently urbanized. The military's repression of the FIS after it won the 1991 elections left Algeria without an effective party system and opened the door to civil war. Tunisia's move towards pluralism similarly failed, with the repression of the Islamists resulting in continued near-single-party rule.[16] Where the single party was particularly strong, as in Iraq and Syria, it left even less room for associational activity outside its corporatist institutions and the Ba'th regimes therefore made only cosmetic concessions to pluralization—sacrificing the opportunity to fully incorporate new social forces, such as crony capitalists and Islamist movements, via 'authoritarian upgrading'.

A second type of limited pluralism is the palace-dominated fragmented party system. In the liberal era, constitutional monarchy appeared to be evolving in Morocco, Jordan, Iran, and Kuwait. Parties competed for parliamentary seats; however, when they challenged royal authority to pick and dismiss governments, kings dissolved parliaments, even closed down party politics, and assumed 'personal rule'. Indeed, parallel with the 1960s regional move away from pluralism, this happened in all these monarchies. However, this actually provoked greater instability: attempted coups in Morocco, riots in Jordan, and revolution in Iran. In reaction, and along with the post-populist re-pluralization across the region in the 1990s, monarchies reintroduced a 'palace pluralism' in which multiple-party competition was arbitrated by a monarchy 'above' partisan politics.

Monarchic pluralism is most authentic in Morocco. More than in Egypt, the main parties have programmes, organizations, and substantial constituencies. In the 1950s the Istiqlal, the mass independence party led by veteran nationalist Allal al-Fassi, had 250,000 active members, branches at the grassroots level, and full-time party officials; if, at its core, it was the party of the traditional urban bourgeoisie, its vague nationalist ideology allowed it to incorporate a broad societal cross-section, including the urban poor. Its main weaknesses, typical of such independence parties, were an urban centredness that left the rural (and Berber) hinterland in the hands of conservative notables who tended to support the monarchy, and its inability to prevent the post-independence breakaway of many of its more radical activists and trade union cadres who formed the National Union of Popular Forces (NUPF).

Above the parties, the monarchy, having stood up to the French, had a nationalist legitimacy unique among monarchs, while also controlling the levers of state patronage and of repression (including an army disproportionately recruited from Berber tribes). The king, possessed of these resources and exploiting the Istiqlal's weaknesses, was able to avoid a choice between repression of all party pluralism and letting a majority party or coalition control the government. Rather, he was able to preserve the right to make and unmake governments while allowing enough party pluralism to satisfy participatory pressures.

The king sustained royal power by dividing parties and forcing them to compete for his favour. To be played off against the urban-centred opposition parties, there was always a party of the 'king's men', recruited from the high bourgeoisie and the traditional rural Berber tribes. Ironically, the main parties fragmented precisely over whether to play the king's game, with the NUPF splitting from the Istiqlal over its refusal to play and it was itself later eclipsed by breakaway elements that were willing to do so (which formed the Socialist Union of

---

[16]Cecil Jolly, 'Du MTI a la Nahda [en Tunisie]', *Cahiers de l'Orient*, 38 (1995), pp. 19–40.

Popular Forces). Thus, Morocco's party evolution has been away from a single mass party towards increasing party fragmentation and weakness, a reflection of the declining mobilizational capacity of the parties and the divide-and-rule policy of the king.

Under this system, the parties do have a role in providing the ministerial elite and in mediating between the king and people. The king tolerates this limit on royal sovereignty because he found the narrowing of his support under personal rule invited instability (attempted coups), and because limited pluralism actually helped, as Zartman argued, to consolidate the regime. Their participation in the system not only co-opts the party elite but, because their inclusion requires they moderate the demands of their constituencies, also it tends to weaken their societal support to the king's benefit. Yet, parties have regularly demonstrated sufficient electoral support that the king has felt obliged to include them in government or, alternatively, to take the wind out of their sails by co-opting their demands as his own; in this sense they function as 'parties of pressure' serving as crucial safety valves by ensuring some responsiveness to interests outside the establishment. Even when the parties have turned radical and resorted to strikes that have degenerated into urban insurrection over economic deprivation, they have been useful to the king in that examples are made of them: jail terms for their leaders, followed by amnesty and possibly co-optation. Thus, the Moroccan monarchy has been able to simultaneously tolerate partisan activity and remain in control of it by an assiduous exploitation of the societal cleavages expressed by the fragmented party system.[17] Party pluralism in Kuwait and Jordan was also tolerated as part of monarchs' co-optation strategies.

The region's experiments in controlled party pluralism produced hybrid regimes that, rather than being a transitional period on the road to democratization, were a substitute for it. Limited party pluralism, wherein some were included and others excluded, allowed regimes to play a more sophisticated form of divide and rule.[18] But the opposition parties, not just the regimes, were themselves part of the problem in that their dependence on personalities, un-democratic internal life, and rapid proliferation and fragmentation rendered them unable to promote, support, or hold accountable democratic governments.

An alternative trajectory: democratization via mass competitive party systems

Parallel to the hitherto described developments in most MENA states, the Middle East's most socio-economically 'advanced' societies, Turkey and Israel, advanced along a different trajectory of democratization, in which mass-incorporating competitive party systems played central roles. The two cases also illustrate how the alternation in power of ruling and opposition parties is central to the formation and accountability of governments and how the party configuration is crucial to governments' effectiveness.

Turkey's transition from a single- to a two-party system in the 1950s remains the prototype for democratization in the region. Each of the two rival parties that emerged incorporated distinct social constituencies: the formerly ruling Republican People's Party (RPP) centred on retired military officers, urban bureaucrats, and intellectuals, while the new opposition Democrat Party (DP), led by businessmen and rural notables, appealed to the rural majority.

[17] I. William Zartman, 'Opposition as Support of the State', in A. Dawisha and I. William Zartman, eds., *Beyond Coercion: The Durability of the Arab State* (London: Croom Helm for Instituto Affairi Internazionali, 1988), pp. 61–87.
[18] Ellen Lust-Okar, 'The Decline of Jordanian Political Parties: Myth or Reality?', *International Journal of Middle East Studies*, 33(4) (2001), pp. 545–571.

Competitive elections made a difference, for example, in allowing peasant voters to force governmental responsiveness to formerly neglected rural interests. Societal and parliamentary support enabled the majority DP to sustain stable government for a decade.[19]

The two main parties proved remarkably institutionalized, surviving leadership and ideological changes and forced reconstructions during periods of military intervention. The RPP survived the transition to a two-party system, a long period in opposition in the 1950s, and a transformation in its leadership to professionals and intellectuals and of its base to urban white- and blue-collar workers, becoming, under Bulent Ecevit, a social democratic party. The Democrat Party, although mutating into several new incarnations, notably the Justice Party (JP), could be said to have survived several leadership changes while still representing the same broad business–rural coalition.

After 1960, the two-party system evolved into a multi-party system, reflective of the deepening mobilization and polarization of society, with smaller, more radical parties emerging on the left and right and speaking for those dissatisfied by the two main centrist parties. In addition, periodic military interventions, that briefly banned parties and forced them to reconstitute themselves, weakened the parties. After the 1960 intervention, the Islamic National Salvation party, mobilizing imams and religious students as grassroots activists, built an effective organization that incorporated a constituency among small businessmen and artisans, becoming the third largest party. The National Action party, an authoritarian nationalist Pan-Turkist party with some middle-class and youth support, exercised disproportionate influence owing to its pivotal role in making up centre-right coalitions in the 1970s. In this period, the JP and RPP alternated pluralities but the JP was more successful in forming governing (centre-right) coalitions. Intensified party competition and the accompanying scramble for state patronage led to ineffective coalition governments and fiscal deficits that opened the door to political instability and the 1970 and 1980 military interventions.

After the 1980 intervention, the party system became increasingly fragmented. The centre-right split into the Motherland party (neo-liberal, Anatolian-based) and the True Path party (descendant of the Justice Party). The centre-left was divided by rival personalities between the Democrat Left Party of Ecevit, Erdel Inonu's Social Democratic Populist Party, and Deniz Baykal's Republican People's Party. Thus was ushered in another period of weak coalition governments, increasingly discredited in public eyes, which ended in the implosion of all the parties except the Islamic Justice and Development Party (AKP; descendant of the Islamic Salvation, for a period the Refah Party) that won a parliamentary majority in the 2002 elections. Its successful formation of a government, in the face of the Islamophobia of the military, was a test of the power of political parties.

In Israel, party development took a similar course. Two strong parties, the dominant left-wing Mapai (later Labour), incorporating the trade unions, and the rightist Herut (later Likud), were initially permanent ruling and opposition parties. By the 1980s, they were alternating in power or occasionally joining in national unity governments. Simultaneously, however, the polarization of society led to fragmentation of the vote and the party system, hence a disproportionate weight was acquired by small extremist parties in unstable coalition governments. The result was an on-going paralysis in foreign policy that obstructed the prospects for Middle East peace. Party weakness was paralleled by the increasing co-optation

---

[19]Kemal Karpat, *Turkey's Politics: The Transition to a Multi-Party System* (Princeton, NJ: Princeton University Press, 1959).

of ex-generals into party leadership.[20] The Israeli and Turkish cases show that, as mass politicization turns into democratization, party capacity determines the effectiveness and stability of government and where party capacity does not keep up with political mobilization, weak governance results.

Party systems and the Arab Uprising: between democratization, restoration, and state failure

In the decade beginning in 2000, de-stabilization swept the Middle East, beginning with the 2003 US invasion of Iraq and culminating in the Arab Uprisings, starting in 2010, that challenged authoritarian regimes in the name of democracy.

Party systems alone did not determine whether regimes were vulnerable to the Uprising; thus, in Morocco and Egypt dominant-party systems led to dissimilar outcomes and single-party systems gave way to democratization in Tunisia and to civil war in Syria. But states' party systems nevertheless had some bearing on the trajectories—democratization, old regime restoration, or civil war—that they took.

Thus, in Syria, Bashar al-Asad debilitated the Ba'th party, seen as a hindrance to his power consolidation and economic reforms; this inadvertently weakened his regime's organized connection to its constituency, making it vulnerable to anti-regime mobilization. Still, the reconfiguration of the loyalist Ba'th party remnants as armed militias helped prevent regime overthrow, resulting instead in civil war. In Iraq, the US 'de-Bathification'—dissolution of the Ba'th party, hence also of the intertwined army and bureaucracy—was the direct cause of state failure and ex-Ba'th cadres played a role in subsequent insurgencies against the new anti-Ba'th Baghdad regime, including that of ISIS. By contrast, Qaddafi's no-party system ended in total regime collapse. Party debilitation was a factor in state failure.

Further, the configuration of party systems was decisive in determining whether democratic transitions were consolidated or reversed, producing dramatically different outcomes in three iconic cases: Turkey, Egypt, and Tunisia. Democratization faltered when individual parties were *either* too strong (Turkey) at the expense of the *party system* or too weak (Egypt). Only in Tunisia did the makings of a two-party system have the potential to consolidate democratization.

In Turkey, the party system since the 1970s had been notoriously weak, producing fragmented parliaments and coalition governments that allowed the military to dominate until the AKP won majorities in several successive elections in the 2000s. The causes of AKP success were its conservative yet democratic version of Islam, combined with neo-liberal policies such as privatizations of state-owned enterprises, that appealed to a cross-class constituency, linking the Anatolian capitalist class to the pious provincial middle and lower classes. Economic growth after several economic crises consolidated the party's position as a dominant party within a multi-party system.

The consequences were in one respect positive for democracy: government that could govern and enjoyed popular support, but had, nevertheless, regularly to face accountability to the electorate; and the ability of a strong ruling party to marginalize the endemic military intervention in politics. On the other hand, the AKP party leader, Erdogan, gradually assumed a majoritarian notion of democracy in which he interpreted electoral mandates as enabling

---

[20]Samuel J. Roberts, *Party and Policy in Israel* (Boulder, CO: Westview Press, 1990).

him to curtail opposition criticism, liberties, and press freedoms. Turkey seemed to slide into electoral authoritarianism in which the ruling party abused its power; yet, even as the economy faltered and Erdogan's policy of intervention in the Syrian Uprising generated damaging blow-back, the party escaped electoral reverses largely because the rest of the political spectrum was so sharply divided, with opposition parties on the right and left of the AKP having little capacity to act together as an effective loyal opposition. Even when the AKP lost its overall majority in the 2015 election, it was able to exploit public fears of instability (which it had helped foster) to call a new election and recover its absolute majority. If Turkey's democracy was initiated by a balanced two-party system and came close to failure amidst fragmented multipartism, it was now threatened by regression to a semi-democratic dominant-party system.

Meanwhile, in Egypt the opposite outcome—a very weak party system that emerged in the post-uprising period—opened the door to a restoration of the old regime under overt military leadership. In initial elections, the Muslim Brotherhood, organized in the Justice and Development Party, and the salafists, organized in the Nour party, proved themselves to be the most effective vote-getters, possessing electoral machines or networks constructed under Mubarak's limited pluralist opening, that penetrated mass neighbourhoods (while the remnants of the old NDP—local notables and their clientele networks—chose to lay low at this time). By contrast, the secular older-generation parties such as the NPUP, Nasserites, and Wafd had, over time, shrunk and splintered and initially played little role in the uprising while the new youth movements that had spearheaded it likewise splintered in its aftermath; both lacked the organizational capacity to mobilize mass voters. As a result, they could not compete with the Islamist parties who dominated the first post-Mubarak assembly or match, in the post-Mubarak presidential elections, the Muslim Brotherhood's Muhammed Morsi and the old regime candidate Muhammed Shafiq who delivered the remnants of Mubarak's constituency. Unable to compete with the Islamists, the liberal secularists chose to join ranks with General al-Sisi to oust Morsi, the democratically elected president. After Morsi's over-throw, loose pro-Sisi coalitions delivered votes using the networks and techniques of the old NDP to produce a parliament filled with 'president's men'. Counter-revolution had triumphed owing to the inability of the revolutionary factions and secular parties to organize themselves into an effective party coalition able to mobilize the mass followings that might have allowed them to balance the military and the Islamists.

In Tunisia, two major parties competed for power in the post-Ben Ali era. The moderate Islamist an-Nahda won the first election, ruling in coalition with a liberal party, an ability to share power that contrasts sharply with the other two cases. Its rule precipitated a broad counter-coalition, Nidaa Tounes, of disparate forces united by secularism, including remnants of the old ruling party and the trade union movement. An apparent two-party system seemed emergent, giving the electorate a choice between two parties capable of governing. The subsequent electoral victory of the Nidaa Tounes allowed the electorate to push the Islamists from power without destroying the democratic transition, as had happened in Egypt. The features of the party system were arguably pivotal to this outcome, namely the existence of two parties, each representative of a large segment of society, yet able to contain ideological polarization and equal enough to feel confident they could defend their interests within an electoral system.[21]

---

[21]Michelle Penner Angrist, 'Party Systems and Regime Formation in the Modern Middle East: Explaining Turkish Exceptionalism', *Comparative Politics*, 36(2) (2004), pp. 229–249.

Table 1. The Evolution of MENA Political Parties.

Stages	Arab Republics	Democracies: Turkey and Israel	Lebanon	Monarchies
Early oligarchic liberalism (1930–50)	Parties of notables or intellectuals and middle-class branch parties fail to incorporate middle classes	Single- and dominant-party systems in Turkey and Israel	Notable proto-parties dominate	In Moroccan, Iranian, and Jordanian constitutional monarchies, notable and mass parties compete in multi-party systems
Populist revolution from above (1952–80)	Ruling single parties in Egypt, Iraq, Syria, Algeria, Libya, and Tunisia consolidate populist authoritarianism; but also stimulate underground Islamist movements among the excluded	Mass two-party systems in Turkey and Israel enable democratization; multi-party fragmentation undermines it, enabling periodic military intervention or military-based politicians	Parties of notables persist; emergence of mass militias and Islamist movements	Monarchic absolutism and de-pluralization in Morocco, Iran, and Jordan
Post-populist era (1980–2010)	Post-populist authoritarian 'upgrading' via dominant-party systems: ruling single parties flanked by re-emergent notable or middle-class parties	Fragmented party systems in Turkey and Israel	Parties of notables, mass militias, and Islamist movements co-exist	Revolution overthrows Iran's monarchy; monarchic re-pluralization in Morocco, Kuwait, and Jordan
Post-Arab Uprising (2010–)	Weak party system in Egypt congruent with authoritarian restoration; in Iraq, Syria, and Yemen violent competition between remnants of ruling and opposition Islamist movements spells state failure; in Tunisia emergent two-party system enables democracy	Unbalanced competitive party systems in Turkey and Israel	Parties of notables, mass militias, and Islamist movements co-exist	Monarchic pluralism proves immune to Arab Uprising

Conclusion: parties in Middle East politics

The important role played by parties in the Middle East challenges 'exceptionalist' claims that political culture deters wide-scale association there. Modernization changes culture, widening politization and reshaping the balance between impersonal (rational-legal /ideological) association and traditional forms of *asabiyyah*; thus, the spread of literacy, industrialization, and class formation propelled politicization and the consequent development of large-scale parties, even if factional *shillas* and clientelism persisted inside formal party organizations. At the same time, parties had *agency* and were pivotal factors in the evolution of politics in the region, with party evolution paralleling regime formation. Table 1 summarizes this parallel regime and party development.

In the early pluralist period, parties allowed individuals and groups to cooperate on a less asymmetric basis by comparison to the age-old clientele networks of the politics of notables. But early pluralism remained relatively limited to the upper and middle classes and seldom penetrated the rural areas. Party systems were debilitated by the extreme inequality in the distribution of wealth, notably land, and their failure to incorporate middle-class support for the liberal order opened the door to the era of populist revolution from above. In Lebanon where, exceptionally, no such revolution marginalized the notability, the old party pattern persisted while in Turkey and Israel, a very different scenario—the emergence of mass-incorporating two-party systems—paralleled democratization.

With the 1960s rise of populist-authoritarian regimes, party organization proved an indispensable new 'political technology' in the launching of 'revolutions from above' that mobilized and organized large sectors of the middle and lower classes; authoritarian republics that did not develop an effective ruling party proved unstable, such as North Yemen and Iraq from 1958 to 1968. To be sure, party association by itself proved unable to consolidate these states and the resort of leaders to charisma and clientalism as supplementary political cement inside or parallel to formal institutions tended to debilitate political life within ruling parties; moreover such single parties always excluded the significant portions of the population damaged by revolution from above; these were the natural constituents of the underground Islamist movements that threatened to destabilize populist authoritarian (PA) regimes. In parallel with republican authoritarianism, monarchies in Morocco and Jordan also sharply contracted the party pluralism of the earlier era.

Populist authoritarianism gave way, in the period of economic liberalization and 'authoritarian upgrading', to 'post-populist' regimes that initiated limited liberalization. In the republics, authoritarian presidents conceded opposition party formation within the ambit of dominant-party systems that served as instruments of co-optation, clientelism, and of divide and rule in the transition towards crony capitalism; in certain monarchies party pluralism played a similar role.

The failure of such limited party pluralism to satisfy more complex mobilized societies opened the door to the Arab Uprisings, but party configurations shaped subsequent outcomes. Where democratization advanced, as in Turkey and post-uprising Tunisia, its consolidation depended on the emergence of a mass-incorporating two-party system and was threatened in Turkey by a seeming decline into a dominant-party system. The contraction of the incorporative capacities of single parties in Syria and Iraq made them vulnerable to combinations of external intervention and internal revolt, but loyalist Ba'th party rumps or remnants prevented victory by anti-Ba'th opponents, leading to civil war and state failure. In Egypt party system weakness opened the door to restoration of a variant of the old regime. It is, therefore, apparent that party development is inextricably bound up with—and cannot be ignored in any convincing analysis of—political development in the Middle East.

Disclosure statement

No potential conflict of interest was reported by the author.

3   Protesting gender discrimination from within

Women's political representation on behalf of Islamic parties

Mona Tajali[†]

ABSTRACT

In recent decades, Islamic political movements, and their subsequent political parties, have been increasingly recruiting and nominating women to high-level decision-making positions despite the fact that the ideology they espouse often acts to dissuade women from assuming positions of political leadership. My ethnographic research on religious women's activism in Iran and Turkey helps explain this unexpected trend by shedding light onto the role of Islamic party women in challenging the gender discriminatory attitudes and behaviours of their male party leaders. In particular, I highlight the role that a number of high-ranking Islamic party women with close ties to the ruling elites played in pressuring their male party leaders to address women's political underrepresentation in formal politics. Women's close ties to the ruling elites consisted of formal ties with key Islamic leaders that evolved thanks to women's long-term devotion to the Islamic movement or learning at Islamic seminaries. I demonstrate that such close ties to the leaders, as well as the presence of a public discourse in favour of women's increased access to politics, enabled influential Islamic women to leverage a form of 'internal criticism' as an important strategy to enhance women's political rights and status from within the Islamic movements.

Introduction

In many Muslim-majority countries, Islamic movements and parties tend to negatively view women's access to political decision-making positions since their dominant gender discourse often emphasizes women's domestic duties over their public roles.[1] Despite this patriarchal

---

[†] The author's current affiliation is Assistant Professor of International Relations and Women's Studies, Agnes Scott College, Decatur, Georgia, USA.

[1] For the purpose of this study, the term 'Islamic movements' refers to ideologically and politically motivated movements that advocate living according to Islamic social mores. While many Islamic movements are presented as revivalist movements that arise in response to extreme secularization, Westernization, and suppression of religious expression, it is important to note that there is great ideological and practical variety among Islamic movements in different contexts and times. Despite significant ideological shifts however even within the same particular movement, it can be argued that the dominant gender discourse of most Islamic movements is patriarchal, in which women hold subordinate positions. For more on Islamic political movements see: Lihi Ben Shitrit, 'Women, Freedom, and Agency in Religious Political Movements: Reflections from Women Activists in Shas and the Islamic Movement in Israel', *Journal of Middle East Women's Studies*, 9(3) (2013), pp. 81–107; Saba Mahmood, *Politics of Piety: The Islamic Revival and the Feminist Subject* (Princeton, NJ: Princeton University Press, 2005). This is the case with the Islamic movements in Iran and Turkey. Although the Islamic discourse is constructed differently in each country (one a theocracy and the other a secular state which is currently governed by a pro-religious party), the dominant gender discourses of both movements advocate non-gender-equal agendas.

gender ideology, in recent decades increasing numbers of Islamic parties have been recruiting and nominating women to high-level decision-making positions, sometimes even in higher proportions than their secular and more liberal counterparts. In countries such as Yemen and Jordan,[2] Tunisia,[3] Morocco,[4] and Egypt and Palestine,[5] scholars are finding either that Islamic parties are at the forefront of increasing women's political representation, or that they fully implement and even publicly justify the legislated quota measures of their countries by nominating women candidates for major elections. With the increasing rise to power of Islamic parties in various Muslim countries, it is of significance to witness that women's political representation is increasing rather than decreasing, which is unexpected given the negative stance of these parties on women's public roles.

This ethnographic research aims to contribute to our understanding of the recent rises of women's political representation on behalf of religious political parties through an analysis of two case studies of Iran and Turkey, both of which have witnessed these trends. In 2009, Iran's neo-conservative president Mahmoud Ahmadinejad's bold move of nominating three women as members to his cabinet surprised many.[6] This move was particularly surprising since unlike his more reformist and liberal counterparts, Ahmadinejad never campaigned on women's access to high-level decision-making positions, but also because the gender ideology of his party renders women primarily to the domestic sphere. It has been similarly puzzling to witness that in Turkey, women's rate of representation in the parliament rose notably under the watch of the pro-religious and conservative Justice and Development Party (*Adalet ve Kalkınma Partisi—AKP or AK Parti*).[7] Indeed, within the past decade AKP leaders have been strategically nominating token amounts of women in electable positions at a higher rate than their secular counterparts of the previous decades.[8] In 2013, due to

---

[2]Janine Astrid Clark and Jillian Schwedler, 'Who Opened the Window? Women's Activism in Islamist Parties', *Comparative Politics*, 35(3) (2003), pp. 293–312.

[3]Monica Marks, 'Women's Rights before and after the Revolution', in Nouri Gana, ed., *The Making of the Tunisian Revolution: Contexts, Architects, Prospects* (Edinburgh: Edinburgh University Press, 2013), pp. 224–251; Mona Tajali, 'Women's Rise to Political Office on Behalf of Religious Political Movements', *Project on Middle East Political Science (POMEPS) Studies*, 19 (2016), pp. 17–21.

[4]Hanane Darhour and Drude Dahlerup, 'Sustainable Representation of Women through Gender Quotas: A Decade's Experience in Morocco', *Women's Studies International Forum*, Democratization and Gender Quotas in Africa, 41(2) (2013), pp. 132–142.

[5]Lihi Ben Shitrit, 'Authenticating Representation: Women's Quotas and Islamist Parties', *Politics & Gender*, 12(4) (2016), pp. 781–806.

[6]Scholars have argued that President Ahmadinejad represents a new rank among the conservative faction in Iranian politics, referred to by some as 'neo-conservatives' or 'revolutionary hardliners', whose populism, drive for revolutionary ideals, militarism, and social justice distinguish them from old guard conservatives and clerical elites. See: Said Amir Arjomand, *After Khomeini: Iran under His Successors* (New York: Oxford University Press, 2009); Naghmeh Sohrabi, 'Conservatives, Neoconservatives and Reformists: Iran after the Election of Mahmud Ahmadinejad', *Middle East Brief: Crown Center for Middle East Studies* no. 4 (2006), pp. 1–5.

[7]Turkey's *Justice and Development Party (Adalet ve Kalkınma Partisi—AKP or AK Parti)* was founded in 2001 by members of former Turkish Islamist parties such as the *Welfare (Refah)* and *Virtue (Fazilet)* parties. Since its landslide victory in 2002, AKP, which identifies itself as a 'conservative democratic' rather than 'Islamist' party, has steadily increased its percentage of popular votes in general elections. See: Yalcin Akdogan, 'The Meaning of Conservative Democratic Political Identity', in M. Hakan Yavuz, ed., *The Emergence of a New Turkey: Democracy and the AK Parti* (Salt Lake City: University of Utah Press, 2006), pp. 49–65. Due to AKP's support of a secular system in which public displays of religion have a place, I identify this party as 'Islamic' or 'pro-religious'.

[8]An important exception among all of Turkey's political parties is the pro-Kurdish rights parties, which put particular emphasis on women's political representation. The 2015 parliamentary elections were the first time however that a pro-Kurdish party, the HDP (*Halkların Demokratik Partisi*) or the People's Democracy Party, entered the parliament as a party, gaining 59 seats from 550 total seats. Women constituted close to half of HDP candidates, and about 40% of those who entered the parliament on behalf of the party in November 2015. For more on HDP's efforts towards gender parity see: Mona Tajali, 'The Promise of Gender Parity: Turkey's People's Democratic Party (HDP)', *openDemocracy*, 28 October 2015, https://www.opendemocracy.net/5050/mona-tajali/promise-of-gender-parity-turkey-s-people-s-democratic-party-hdp.

women's pressuring, AKP also removed the decades-long headscarf ban for women serving in state institutions, including parliaments.[9] Removal of this restriction further contributed to women's political representation as it enabled headscarved women, who constitute more than 70% of the female population in Turkey, to also be able to access the parliament.[10]

The recent rise of women to political office on behalf of Islamic political movements and parties remains an understudied topic.[11] The assumption of many feminist scholars that these parties are 'bad' for women, in addition to the puzzle of why women even participate in movements that seem to limit their freedom and equality in the first place, has hindered a thorough analysis of Muslim women's political participation and representation[12] within and on behalf of these parties.[13] The limited research that has taken place on women's participation in Islamic parties has mostly focused on women's roles as grassroots organizers and voter-recruiters, and rarely addresses women's own aspirations and activism to reach high-level political office on behalf of these parties.[14] Given the absence of such analysis, the recent rises of women to political office are often unjustly credited to their male party leaders for their wiliness to recruit and nominate women to these positions, with little attention on the decades of women's organizing and pressuring of their party leaders to address women's political underrepresentation.

It is the purpose of this article to shed light onto the role that women activists of Islamic political movements have played in the two Muslim-majority countries of Iran and Turkey in relation to the recent modest expansion of women's political representation. It argues that, in addition to the presence of important political and discursive opportunity structures that facilitated women's rise to political office on behalf of these pro-religious parties,[15] another important factor has been the increasing outspokenness of Islamic women's rights activists themselves against the gender discriminatory party behaviours and attitudes that keep women out of politics. Islamic women's recent outspokenness is largely credited to women's own mobilization and politicization within the Islamic movement for decades, and their eventual frustration with their ruling elites' inaction in addressing women's political underrepresentation. Realizing that they have public sympathy on their side, a number of high-ranking Islamic women's rights activists with close ties to the ruling elites have been

[9]Mona Tajali, 'Women's Dress and the Politics of Access to Political Representation in Contemporary Turkey', *Anthropology of the Middle East*, 9(2) (2014), pp. 72–90.

[10]Dilek Cindoglu, *Headscarf Ban and Discrimination: Professional Headscarved Women in the Labor Market* (Istanbul: TESEV Publications, 2011).

[11]Indeed, academic analysis of women's political roles in religious political movements in various Western countries is also a recent phenomenon, thanks to the realization that these women also pose a powerful political force, despite the patriarchal and gender-unequal ideologies of their parties. For instance, see: Rosie Campbell and Sarah Childs, '"To the Left, to the Right": Representing Conservative Women's Interests', *Party Politics*, 21(4) (2013), pp. 626–637; Ronnee Schreiber, *Righting Feminism: Conservative Women and American Politics* (New York: Oxford University Press, 2008).

[12]By women's *political participation*, I am referring to women's involvement in grassroots politics, such as voting and campaigning, while women's *political representation* refers to women's presence in political decision-making positions. See: Anne Phillips, *The Politics of Presence*, Oxford Political Theory (Oxford: Clarendon Press, 1995). This article only concerns women's descriptive representation, or the rate of women present in political office, versus their substantive representation, or the actual representation of women's interests and demands.

[13]Ben Shitrit, 'Women, Freedom, and Agency'; Mahmood, *Politics of Piety*.

[14]Yesim Arat, *Rethinking Islam and Liberal Democracy: Islamist Women in Turkish Politics* (Albany: State University of New York Press, 2005); Humeira Iqtidar, *Secularizing Islamists?: Jama'at-E-Islami and Jama'at-Ud-Da'wa in Urban Pakistan*, South Asia across the Disciplines (Chicago, IL: The University of Chicago Press, 2011); Jenny B. White, *Islamist Mobilization in Turkey: A Study in Vernacular Politics*, Studies in Modernity and National Identity (Seattle, WA: University of Washington Press, 2002).

[15]Mona Tajali, 'Demanding a Seat at the Table: Iranian and Turkish Women's Organizing for Political Representation' (PhD diss., Concordia University, 2014), http://spectrum.library.concordia.ca/978565/.

at the forefront of demanding women's greater access to political leadership. Hence these women activists have been leveraging a form of internal criticism to enhance women's political rights and status from within the Islamic movements.

Similar to most other shifts in the rate of women's political representation, the recent rise of women to political office on behalf of Islamic parties in Iran and Turkey is not monocausal, and rather credited to a number of factors. For the purpose of this article, I focus on the role of Islamic party women, and the dominant factors that assisted their efforts. I demonstrate that Iranian and Turkish Islamic party women's actions to be included in decision-making were largely assisted by (1) exceptional political experience and devotion of key women activists to the Islamic political movement which enabled them to establish close ties to male elites and gain leverage, and (2) the presence of a public discourse and interest around women's political representation which had already been championed by women's rights groups in each country. These two factors together empowered key Islamic party women to eventually address women's political underrepresentation in the public sphere and through the usage of media. I demonstrate that their decision to publicize this demand came after they had exhausted negotiations with their male party elites behind closed doors, and having recognized the public's support.

To document Islamic women's discourses and strategies towards the expansion of women's presence in political leadership roles, I made multiple visits to Iran and Turkey between 2009 and 2015 to research the organizing and framing efforts of the most vocal and active Islamic women's groups in each country. I define Islamic women's groups as those who support a religious way of life and public expressions of piety, but at the same time demand women's active participation in the public sphere. Hence, despite the fact that the majority of such women have risen out of the larger Islamic movements of their countries, they do not see a contradiction between their faiths and women's access to positions of leadership. In fact, many are disillusioned by the fact that the Islamic political movements in which they have invested so much time and effort, have failed to deliver on the promise of 'Islamic justice', including the promise to restore women's rightful place in an Islamic society.[16] Hence, there are currently a number of Islamic women's groups that are engaged in reformulating or reinterpreting the dominant patriarchal gender discourses of their male counterparts and that advocate gender equality, including in accessing positions of authority.[17]

In Iran these groups consist of the Zeinab Society (*Jameh Zeinab*) and the United Front of Conservative Women (*Jebheh Mottahed Zanan-e Usulgera*), both of which are influential conservative women's organizations and registered women's parties that are linked to the conservative faction. In Turkey, I include the voices and efforts of women activists of the ruling pro-religious AKP, many of whom have been particularly active on the expansion of headscarved women's access to the parliament, which has been very controversial in Turkey's secular context. Through a close analysis of media and state reports, as well as in-depth interviews with influential Islamic party women in Iran and Turkey, this article analyses the ways that Islamic women's rights activists tackle the conservative gender ideology espoused by the religious political movements in which they are involved.[18]

---

[16]Arzoo Osanloo, *The Politics of Women's Rights in Iran* (Princeton, NJ: Princeton University Press, 2009).

[17]This research is not about the many women within the Islamic movements in Iran and Turkey who, similarly to many of their male counterparts, oppose gender equality and are silent on the issue of women's political representation.

[18]I use pseudonyms for the women I quote, except for those outspoken women campaigners in the media who consented to forgo anonymity.

The findings of this research help fill a gap in the literature on Islamic party women by deconstructing various assumptions that have persisted about this group. By highlighting Islamic party women's own activism and campaigning efforts to be included in political decision-making positions, this research challenges the previous portrayals of female activists of such parties as subjects of male control or as mere 'foot-soldiers' for the party.[19] While it acknowledges that for decades women activists of Islamic parties were intentionally marginalized from politics by their party elites, it also emphasizes the fact that many women, particularly those who secured the most legitimacy with their parties, eventually pushed back against gender discrimination in their parties, and demanded change from within.

Internal criticism as a means to deliver lasting reform

Scholarship on women and politics has identified 'internal criticism', understood as when members of a party or organization criticize the discriminatory practices of their own leadership or structure, to be an important factor towards reform.[20] This is because institutions that are competing for political influence often resist criticisms that are waged externally, regardless of their rationale and objectivity. Such resistance for reform tends to be fiercer when outsiders challenge the ideological tendencies of a political movement. In particular, given the sensitivity and controversy surrounding women's rights and status, religious political movements tend to show the most resistance when challenged by outsiders on their gender ideology.[21] However, criticism that is internal, in that it uses resources and discourses from inside of the movement in order to criticize certain aspects of that movement, tends to generate reforms with lasting effects.[22] Hence an effective tactic for reform is when criticisms are raised internally, from what are perceived to be inconsistencies between rhetoric and reality within the movement, or from discriminatory attitudes that unjustly deny certain rights and opportunities from a particular section of the movement.[23]

Islamic party women's increasing outspokenness constitutes a form of internal criticism, with the potential to deliver lasting change, including institutional reform. The articulation of this demand by Islamic women activists, who have devoted their lives to the Islamic movement in their countries, highlights the extent to which it is internally driven rather than externally influenced. This is particularly significant in the case of the Islamic Republic of Iran, whose conservative factions are quick to dismiss any demands for women's rights and gender equality as a Western import that should be confronted. Yet the Islamic party elites, who are eager to appeal to voters, often cannot afford to disregard women's internally driven demands when articulated in the public sphere, and by the movement's most recognized female members. Significantly, the Iranian and Turkish Islamic women activists, who are now

---

[19]Arat, *Rethinking Islam and Liberal Democracy*; Iqtidar, *Secularizing Islamists?*; White, *Islamist Mobilization in Turkey*.

[20]Abdullahi Ahmed An-Naim, 'Toward a Cross-Cultural Approach to Defining International Standards of Human Rights: The Meaning of Cruel, Inhuman, or Degrading Punishment', in Abdullahi Ahmed An-Naim, ed., *Human Rights in Cross-Cultural Perspectives: A Quest for Consensus* (Philadelphia: University of Pennsylvania Press, 1992), pp. 19–43; Jennifer Curtin, 'Women, Political Leadership and Substantive Representation: The Case of New Zealand', *Parliamentary Affairs*, 61(3) (2008), pp. 490–504; Anne Phillips, *Gender and Culture* (Oxford: John Wiley & Sons, 2013).

[21]Roxanne D. Marcotte, 'How Far Have Reforms Gone in Islam?', *Women's Studies International Forum*, 26(2) (2003), pp. 153–166.

[22]Martha Nussbaum and Amartya Sen, 'Internal Criticism and Indian Rationalist Traditions', *WIDER (World Institute for Development Economics Research) of the United Nations University Working Papers* no. 30 (1987).

[23]Anne Phillips, 'Multiculturalism, Universalism and the Claims of Democracy', *Democracy, Governance and Human Rights Programme Paper* no. 7 (2001).

at the forefront of challenging the dominant gender ideology of the Islamic political movements, are themselves the products of these movements.

This article outlines instances of Islamic women's organizing from within the Islamic movements in Iran and Turkey to address women's political underrepresentation, and the impact of such internally driven efforts on women's eventual increased access to political office. These examples include when a number of influential Islamic women in Iran with close linkages to the Islamic regime put out a women's-only list for the 2008 parliamentary elections to protest their exclusion from the main party list of the conservative faction. This move of Islamic women, who had devoted their activism to the Islamic regime and its objectives, was a public denouncement of the Islamic party elites' discriminatory attitudes against women in candidate selection. Such efforts of the Islamic party women in combination with their extensive lobbying campaign of Iran's male elites eventually resulted in the appointment of the first-ever female minister in 2009 from this conservative women's party. Similarly, in Turkey, in a novel move, a high-ranking member of AKP, and herself one of its founders, threatened to resign from her post to protest her party's unwillingness to nominate headscarved women as candidates for the parliament. This bold and public form of internal criticism eventually resulted in action from the ruling AKP to remove dress-code limitations on headscarved women's access to the parliament in 2013.

In what follows, I briefly review the main factors that the literature on women and politics has identified as leading to the recent rises of women to political office in Muslim contexts. I argue that in much of such analysis, Islamic women's own roles as important political actors who have been organizing for their increased access to political office have been largely ignored. I address the evolution of some Islamic women's rights activism since their initial involvement with Islamic movements, with attention to particular factors that empowered women to publicly protest gender discrimination from within these conservative and male-dominated institutions. I end with two instances of internal criticism launched by influential Islamic women activists in Iran and Turkey in demand of women's increased access to political leadership positions.

Factors that have contributed to the recent rise of Islamic women in politics

Scholars have identified a number of different internal and external factors that have contributed to the recent expansion of women's access to political office in various Muslim countries. Among the most prominent internal reasons are the recent political and social shifts that have been unfolding in the region in demand for democracy, human rights, and gender equality. The recent pro-democratic uprisings in the Muslim world—in which women also played key roles—provided unique opportunities for public discussion and legislative and political reforms towards strengthening of gender equality provisions, including the passage of gender quota laws, in various Muslim countries.[24] Despite the rise to power of a number of Islamic political parties across the region, such popular uprisings have motivated

---

[24]Darhour and Dahlerup, 'Sustainable Representation of Women'; Marks, 'Women's Rights before and after the Revolution'; Ellen McLarney, 'Women's Equality: Constitutions and Revolutions in Egypt', *Project on Middle East Political Science (POMEPS) Studies*, 19 (2016), pp. 22–26; Nayereh Tohidi, 'Women and the Presidential Elections: Iran's New Political Culture', *Informed Comment*, 2009, http://www.juancole.com/2009/09/tohidi-women-and-presidential-elections.html (accessed 26 January 2017).

some Islamic political elites to expand women's political roles, though mostly in token amounts, to appeal to voters as well as the international community by appearing more democratic and moderate.[25] In addition to these internal factors, various scholars have also identified the impact of external pressure, including the spread of international norms, and pressure from donors, as important motivations for enhancement of women's political representation.[26] But in much of such analysis, the role of Islamic women and their organizing efforts to reach high-level decision-making positions have been absent. The limited scholarly attention on Islamic women is despite the fact that many studies have highlighted the large number of women members and supporters of Islamic political movements, as well as studies that have demonstrated that women's organizing efforts helped many such parties to rise to power.[27]

Having been mobilized and politicized by the Islamic political movements in their countries decades prior, many Islamic party women feel that the time has come for them to have a share in political decision-making and contribute to their societies.[28] Although many were hopeful that their male party leaders would eventually expand women's access to positions of leadership, the persistence of systematic discrimination against women within their parties has led some to become outspoken against it. Hence, despite their party's insistence and official stance on women's activism at the lower party echelons, many Islamic party women evolved from grassroots organizers to aspirants for political office.

Here, I outline the key elements that assisted Islamic party women's increased outspokenness against their leaders, namely the role of influential and devoted Islamic women activists who had gained enough legitimacy and leverage to pressure their male party elites, as well as the presence of a public discourse around the issue of women's political representation thanks to the awareness-raising efforts of women's rights advocates in each country.

Influential Islamic women activists: from grassroots organizers to aspirants for political office

The dominant gender ideology of Islamic political movements, which is often based on patriarchal interpretations of religious texts, views women's proper place to be within the domestic sphere as mothers and wives, and largely denies women's active presence in the public sphere, including in political decision-making. Scholarly analysis of women's activities and involvement in political parties that arise out of Islamic political movements has persuasively argued that despite the high level of women's political participation on behalf of such parties, women tend to have low levels of political representation. For instance, a number of scholars have pointed to the fact that many Islamic political parties have mobilized and politicized women to merely serve as voter-recruiters and grassroots organizers to help bring the party to power, or have utilized women's bodies and dress as public markers of

---

[25]Ben Shitrit, 'Authenticating Representation'; Tajali, 'Demanding a Seat at the Table'.

[26]Sarah Sunn Bush, 'International Politics and the Spread of Quotas for Women in Legislatures', *International Organization*, 65(1) (2011), pp. 103–137; Mona Tajali, 'Gender Quota Adoption in Post-Conflict Contexts: An Analysis of Actors and Factors Involved', *Journal of Women, Politics, and Policy*, 34(3) (2013), pp. 261–285; Aili Mari Tripp and Alice Kang, 'The Global Impact of Quotas: On the Fast Track to Increased Female Legislative Representation', *Comparative Political Studies*, 41(3) (2008), pp. 338–361.

[27]Arat, *Rethinking Islam and Liberal Democracy*; Iqtidar, *Secularizing Islamists?*; White, *Islamist Mobilization in Turkey*.

[28]Personal interview with various Islamic party women in Iran and Turkey 2011–2015.

their identity claims.[29] For instance, in the case of Iran, researchers have argued that the 1979 revolution would not have been successful without women's active participation in the demonstrations and organizing efforts that toppled the Pahlavi monarchy.[30] Veiled women also became a global symbol of Iran's Islamic revolution. Regarding Turkey, Arat[31] and White[32] highlight the significant role that women played in the electoral success of Islamist political parties in Turkey in the mid-1990s as they engaged in extensive voter-recruitment and grassroots organizing efforts as members of the party's women's branch.

But once in power, the male elites of such parties have often denied women any real power or influence in formal politics.[33] Despite politicizing and mobilizing the previously marginalized female sections of the society to enter the political sphere, the Islamic political leaders never expected women's political engagement and experience to eventually translate into women political leaders. This is evident by the fact that, for instance, soon after the success of the Iranian revolution in which women's participation was greatly encouraged by its founders, Islamic political and religious leaders restricted women's access to a number of positions of authority, including the presidency and judgeship.[34] Similarly, in Turkey, while women party activists have played a decisive role in enabling Islamist political parties—such as the Welfare (*Refah*) party, the predecessor to AKP—to achieve continuous electoral victories since the mid-1990s, women have been largely absent in decision-making positions, whether in the party structure or in the government.[35]

Additionally, the absence of democratic features, such as democratic candidate recruitment mechanisms for major elections, has also closed many doors for hopeful female party activists as Islamic party leaders blatantly discriminate against women in candidate recruitment. For instance, in Iran, a very energetic and passionate Islamic woman activist from a conservative party shared her experience of being nominated onto a party's open list in a highly contested district for local elections. After passionately campaigning throughout the district, the party's leadership however suddenly replaced her with a male candidate just days before the election without any explanations.[36] Gender discrimination is also apparent in Turkey, when Islamic parties, similar to most other parties, often place women low on the

---

[29]Arat, *Rethinking Islam and Liberal Democracy*; Lara Deeb, *An Enchanted Modern: Gender and Public Piety in Shi'i Lebanon*, Princeton Studies in Muslim Politics (Princeton, NJ: Princeton University Press, 2006); Homa Hoodfar and Shadi Sadr, 'Islamic Politics and Women's Quest for Gender Equality in Iran', *Third World Quarterly*, 31(6) (2010), pp. 885–903; Iqtidar, *Secularizing Islamists?*; Mahmood, *Politics of Piety*; Elora Shehabuddin, *Reshaping the Holy: Democracy, Development, and Muslim Women in Bangladesh* (New York: Columbia University Press, 2008); Tajali, 'Women's Dress and the Politics of Access'; White, *Islamist Mobilization in Turkey*.

[30]Homa Hoodfar, *The Women's Movement in Iran: Women at the Crossroads of Secularization and Islamization* (Grabels Cedex, France: Women Living Under Muslim Laws, 1999); Parvin Paidar, *Women and the Political Process in Twentieth-Century Iran* (New York: Cambridge University Press, 1995).

[31]Arat, *Rethinking Islam and Liberal Democracy*.

[32]White, *Islamist Mobilization in Turkey*.

[33]Arat, *Rethinking Islam and Liberal Democracy*; Paidar, *Women and the Political Process*; White, *Islamist Mobilization in Turkey*.

[34]Mehranguiz Kar, 'Women's Political Rights after the Islamic Revolution', in Lloyd Ridgeon, ed., *Religion and Politics in Modern Iran: A Reader*, International Library of Iranian Studies (New York: I. B. Tauris, 2005); Nikki R. Keddie, 'Iranian Women's Status and Struggles since 1979', *Journal of International Affairs*, 60(2) (2007), pp. 17–33; Paidar, *Women and the Political Process*.

[35]Arat, *Rethinking Islam and Liberal Democracy*; Nuray Gol, 'Women's Participation Issue and Analysis of Woman Organization Structure in Turkey: A Comparison of KA.DER (Association for Supporting and Training Women Candidates) and Türk Kadinlar Birligi (Turkish Women Union)', *Thinking Gender Papers, UCLA Center for the Study of Women* (2009), http://escholarship.org/uc/item/2jc4v0hs (accessed 26 January 2017).

[36]Personal interview, June 2015.

party's closed-lists in unelectable positions, yet encourage them to campaign actively on behalf of the party in hopes for election.[37]

As Islamic party women are increasingly vocal against gender discrimination in their parties, my research finds that those who have close ties with party leaders are often better equipped to protest women's exclusion from political decision-making. Women's close ties to the ruling elites consist of formal ties that have evolved thanks to women's long-term devotion to the Islamic movement or learning at Islamic seminaries. Decades of women's activism within the Islamic movement has not only provided them with exceptional political experience and insight, but has also won them the support of key male political figures. Male Islamic leaders, having realized women's devotion to the movement as well as their potential in mobilizing supporters, established close linkages with a select number of Islamic women, and even recruited them to key posts or entrusted them with important responsibilities.

In Iran, for instance, in the lead-up to the 1979 Iranian revolution many Islamic women actively organized their local mosques, universities, and neighbourhoods in support of Ayatollah Khomeini and the establishment of an Islamic state. Many women, on par with their male colleagues, were imprisoned and tortured by the Pahlavi regime. Many also enrolled in religious seminaries of key Islamic leaders, and held their own religious classes and sermons for women to attend.[38] In the wake of the revolution's victory, the founders of the Islamic Republic, recognizing that they cannot marginalize women from all spheres of political life, recruited just a select few of these 'revolutionary' women to key political decision-making posts, including in the post-revolutionary Iranian parliament.[39] Among such women were Maryam Behrouzi, a pre-revolutionary female preacher, who was among the first few women to enter the Iranian parliament after the revolution, and eventually leader of the most important Islamic women's party, the Zeinab Society; Azam Taleghani, the daughter of renowned Ayatollah Mahmoud Taleghani and also a female parliamentarian during the first four post-revolutionary parliaments; and Monireh Gorji, a learned woman who served as the only woman in Iran's first Assembly of Experts responsible for drafting the Islamic Republic's constitution. In the years that followed, being branded as a 'revolutionary woman' entailed close linkages to the Islamic regime and its founder, Ayatollah Khomeini. While similar to their male peers, Islamic women were also subject to the eventual factional divides between reformists and conservatives; here, I mostly focus on women activists who identify with the conservative faction. This is because the conservative leaders have demonstrated greater resistance to women's inclusion in politics, while reformist leaders have at least paid lip service to this demand, hence decreasing women's outspokenness against them.[40]

In Turkey, Islamic women's extensive activism and voter-recruitment in support of the Islamist *Refah* Party in the 1990s, resulted, in the early 2000s, in a number of highly politicized and active women constituting several of the founding members of the pro-religious AKP, signalling these women's close linkages with the key male leaders of the party, including

---

[37]Tajali, 'Demanding a Seat at the Table'.
[38]Personal interview with an Islamic woman activist, July 2011.
[39]Paidar, *Women and the Political Process*.
[40]Hoodfar and Sadr, 'Islamic Politics and Women's Quest'.

Recep Tayyip Erdogan himself. Among these influential Islamic women activists were Ayse Böhürler, one of AKP's headscarved founders and a renowned journalist and filmmaker; and Fatma Bostan, another headscarved founder of AKP and long-term member of the religious women's organization Capital City Women's Platform. Close ties between influential women activists and the male leaders of the Islamic political movements privileged women to derive from their political experience and devotion to the Islamic movement the authority to increasingly demand certain reforms to the movement's gender ideology. In the case of Turkey, Islamic women were particularly outspoken surrounding the expansion of head-scarved women's access to the parliament, which many felt was not sufficiently prioritized by the party leadership, despite the fact that headscarved women constituted an important base for Turkey's pro-religious parties, including AKP. Significantly, while most of the Islamic women's public protests against their marginalization from political leadership were resisted and even criticized by the Islamic party's leadership, they nonetheless had the important impact of highlighting to the public women's discontent with their party's leaders, and in effect shaming them into action.

'Where are the women in politics?' Raising public awareness about women's political rights and roles

For the past few decades, in both Iran and Turkey, women's rights movements have launched important public campaigns in support of women's increased access to political deci-sion-making. These efforts were initiated around the same time as the global discourse on the significance of women's increased rate of representation in politics of the mid-1990s, as highlighted during the 1995 Fourth UN Conference on Women and its Platform for Action.[41] The backing of the international community particularly legitimated and empowered Iranian and Turkish women's rights groups who supported gender equality and women's increased presence in politics, to take their demands more forcefully to the public sphere. My analysis of the major women's campaigns launched to address women's political underrepresentation in Iran and Turkey demonstrates that most were geared towards raising public awareness of the significance of women's access to political office, while at the same time pressuring political elites to increase women's access to such positions. Targeting the public is funda-mental for such campaigns given the realization that party elites depend on the electorate's support to win votes. Even in undemocratic contexts, as in Iran, high voter turnout and support are a major indication of legitimacy for the Islamic regime and its parties.[42]

A great example of women's initiatives to enter the issue of women's political representa-tion into the public sphere is the foundation and organizing efforts of the feminist women's organization in Turkey, KA-DER (Association for the Support and Training of Female Candidates). Founded in 1997 by mostly secular women activists, this organization's main strategies include: utilizing the media to highlight the discriminatory attitudes and behav-iours of Turkish political parties often through provocative billboards; organizing workshops and conferences to train potential female candidates for political office; and advocating for the adoption of gender quotas and lobbying political elites to take measures that ensure

---

[41] The Beijing Platform for Action highlighted the need for government measures to increase women's political power and access to decision-making positions (United Nations, 1995).

[42] Hoodfar and Sadr, 'Islamic Politics and Women's Quest'; Mehdi Moslem, *Factional Politics in Post-Khomeini Iran*, vol. 1, Modern Intellectual and Political History of the Middle East (Syracuse, NY: Syracuse University Press, 2002).

women's inclusion in politics.[43] In the years since its foundation, KA-DER's effective usage of the media to underline the significance of women politicians as well as women's intentional exclusion from politics by male party leaders during major elections resulted in major public discussions and debates on women's public roles and candidacy in Turkish society. In the words of Fezal Gulfidan:

> we are pleased that (at the time of elections) there is often much public discussion around the proportion of women candidates nominated by each party, and the mainstream media increasingly scrutinizes which parties nominated the least and the most women candidates on their lists, and why.

Indeed, KA-DER's media success increasingly forced major party leaders, including AKP's Recep Tayyip Erdogan, to publicly comment on women's political recruitment to political office and the need for gender quotas in the media and other gatherings.[44] Women's continuous pressuring of male leaders who are the main gatekeepers to women's political representation, has led to gradual increasing of the number of female candidates on major party lists in Turkey in recent elections, as each party is attempting to increase their electoral appeal.

While an organization such as Turkey's KA-DER, with the specific objective of addressing women's political underrepresentation, has been absent in Iran, women's rights groups have nonetheless sought to enter the issue of women's political rights and roles into the Iranian public discourse. A major venue to outline such demands for the larger public, while also indirectly pressuring political elites, was popular women's magazines, such as *Zanan* (Women), *Payam-e Hajar* (Hajar's Message), and *Huquq-e Zanan* (Women's Rights). Although managed by religious women, these magazines created the space for both secular and religious women's rights activists to highlight the systematic discrimination that women face in politics, as well as ways of tackling it. In 1994, for instance, *Zanan* magazine devoted an entire issue to 'Women's political rights in Iran: From the Islamic Revolution until today', the main article for which was penned by the renowned lawyer and secular women's rights activist, Mehrangiz Kar. In this piece, Kar highlights the gaps that exist in terms of women's political rights and roles as outlined by international human rights documents, such as CEDAW (The Convention on the Elimination of All Forms of Discrimination against Women), and what is granted to women under post-revolutionary Iranian law.[45] Another instance of women's publication on their intentional marginalization from politics is Azam Taleghani's[46] problematizing of the ambiguous condition of '*rijal*' that Iranian elites utilize to ban women from the office of presidency in her periodical, *Payam-e Hajar*.[47] Although all of these women's magazines are now banned, during their active years, they helped influence Iranian public opinion on women's political representation and the unjust discrimination that women face.

The effectiveness of Iranian and Turkish women's media and campaigning efforts, which aimed at raising public awareness while shaming key political elites for marginalizing women

---

[43]Personal interview with Fezal Gulfidan, KA-DER board member and former trainer, June 2011.
[44]Ibid.
[45]Mehranguiz Kar, 'Women's Political Rights in Iran: From the Revolution until Today' (In Persian), *Zanan Magazine*, 1994.
[46]'Can a Woman Become President?' (In Persian), *Payam-E Hajar*, 1997.
[47]Article 115 of the Iranian constitution lists the term '*rijal*' (as opposed to men) as one of the required conditions of the presidency, with the sole intention to keep women's access to this office ambiguous and up to the interpretation of key religious elites. Thus far, Iranian elites have interpreted this term to mean 'men', hence denying women the right to even compete for the presidency, while women's rights activists, such as Taleghani, argue that it is gender neutral. See: Mona Tajali, 'Notions of Female Authority in Modern Shi'i Thought', *Religions*, 2(3) (2011), pp. 449–468.

from politics, is evident from the increasing public discussions on women's political roles, particularly at the time of elections, as well as the overwhelming electoral support that women candidates at times receive. For instance, the Turkish electorate has repeatedly demonstrated its support for parties that are inclusive of women candidates, despite their size and influence, as they have been for small pro-Kurdish parties. Also Iranian voters in 1996 exhibited that they have no problems with women's political leadership when a renowned woman candidate, Faezeh Rafsanjani, daughter of Ayatollah Rafsanjani, received the second highest votes in the country for the fifth parliament, and almost became the parliament's speaker.[48] I argue that such public support for women's increased access to positions of political authority, which is thanks to various women's rights groups' organizing, has been an important motivating factor in the campaigning efforts of Islamic women to pressure their own party leaders on this demand.

Protesting gender discrimination from within: the women-only candidate list of conservative Islamic women in Iran

The Zeinab Society (*Jameh Zeinab*) is Iran's largest and the most influential Islamic women's political organization, as well as a registered women's political party with close linkages to the conservative faction in Iran. This entity was founded just years after the 1979 Iranian revolution with the blessing of Ayatollah Khomeini to organize women's religious seminaries and educate women in accordance with the ideals of the Islamic regime. Khomeini entrusted this responsibility to none other than Maryam Behrouzi, one of his few female students, who had devoted much of her time to holding religious sermons for women in major cities across Iran prior to the revolution. The fact that Behrouzi was imprisoned by the Pahlavi regime due to her activism in support of the Islamic movement, further exemplified her status as a true revolutionary woman in the eyes of key Islamic leaders. As a result of the support that she received from Khomeini, Behrouzi was one of a few women to enter the 270-seat post-revolutionary parliament for four consecutive terms from 1980–1996. Although Behrouzi lacked any familial linkages to leaders of the Islamic regime, her commitment to the Islamic regime led to the formation of strong personal ties to key religious and political figures, including Khomeini himself. This status privileged her to at times follow her own ideals regarding women's roles in an Islamic society, even if they might be at odds with the dominant stand of the conservative Islamic leadership in Iran.

As director of Zeinab Society—an entity which not only managed eight women's religious seminaries across the nation, but also functioned as one of Iran's rare women's political parties—Behrouzi actively sought to increase women's access to positions of both religious as well as political authority. Hence, while in full support of a theocratic regime and the office of the Supreme Leader, Behrouzi, as a learned woman, advocated women to reach the level of *ijtihad* (independent reasoning) through extensive religious training, as well as their rise to political decision-making positions.[49] However, her extensive organizing on expanding women's access to positions of authority often faced fierce opposition from conservative male religious figures who in general opposed women's greater access to political leadership.

---

[48] Ziba Mir-Hosseini, 'The Rise and Fall of Fa'ezeh Hashemi: Women in Iranian Elections', *Middle East Report* no. 218 (2001), pp. 8–11.
[49] Personal interview with Maryam Behrouzi, July 2011.

In a personal interview, Behrouzi expressed the challenges she faced when she met party elites to lobby them on substantially increasing the number of female candidates on their party lists from Zeinab Society:

> I would ask [conservative party leaders] to include at least 10 women onto their Tehran candidate lists, from a total of 30 parliamentary seats; but even to add one woman's name [in addition to the few token women whom the party had itself chosen], I would face much struggle.

When I inquired about the type of struggles that Behrouzi faced from the parties, she mildly laughed and responded:

> They would tell me, 'Khanoom [lady], 10 women for a 30-member district list is too much, five or khoms is enough'; hence adding only about 4–5 maximum women on Tehran's candidate list, all of whom would get elected to the parliament.[50]

The party elites' utilization of the term 'khoms', which refers to an Islamic obligation to contribute one-fifth of a certain type of income to charity, illustrates their mindset that nominating women to party lists is similar to doing women's groups, like Zeinab Society, a favour and an act of charity. Women's groups' insistence on women's inclusion in party lists, instead of running as independent candidates, is due to women's limited financial resources to campaign outside of party lists.

However, Behrouzi was aware that such resistance against women's leadership did not extend to the Iranian electorate, including those who support the conservative faction in Iran. As a long-term leader in the Islamic women's movement, Behrouzi was familiar with the increasing rate of women's enrolment in her religious seminaries and participation in political organizations, with the support of their families. Indeed, after decades of organizing there were many qualified and passionate women whom Behrouzi had mentored to contribute to the Islamic regime through their religious training and political experience.[51]

Realizing that the Iranian electorate, in particular Iran's female voting bloc, sympathizes with her attempts to recruit more women to leadership positions, Behrouzi made her demands of Iran's ruling elites public. Failing to convince her male colleagues to nominate a sufficient number of women on candidate party lists behind closed doors, she became increasingly vocal in the media and on women's websites about the discriminatory practices of conservative party leaders. In preparation for the 2008 parliamentary elections, Behrouzi in collaboration with a number of other influential conservative women activists formed the United Front of Conservative Women (jebhe motahed zanan usulgara, or the Front). Using the media and women's websites, the Front publicly threatened that if at least 10 women were not included in the major candidate list of the conservative faction for Tehran's 30-member list, they would put forth a women-only candidate list.[52] Behrouzi's interviews with the media on the Front's decision to produce this list were widely circulated. Given the fact that this women-only list would be composed of renowned Islamic women activists, this was a bold move of pressuring conservative male elites to give into women's demands, or risk losing votes for the conservative faction. In the end, when the conservatives announced their final candidate list for Tehran, which did not reflect the Front's demands, conservative women

---

[50]Ibid.
[51]Ibid.
[52]Bultannews, 'Conservative Women put forth a new list' (in Persian), 2008, http://www.bultannews.com/fa/news/70538/%
D8%B2%D9%86%D8%A7%D9%86-%D8%A7%D8%B5%D9%88%D9%84%DA%AF%D8%B1%D8%A7-%D9%84%
DB%8C%D8%B3%D8%AA-%D8%AC%D8%AF%D8%A7-%D9%85%DB%8C-%D8%AF%D9%87%D9%86%D8%AF

activists announced their own 10-women-only party list under the banner of the United Front of Conservative Women.[53]

According to one of the Islamic women who appeared on this list, putting forth a women-only list was a bold move to merely protest the discriminatory actions of conservative party leaders, as none of the women expected to get elected without the party's financial support for campaigning:

> I know that I can serve better than most men in my party, and even they know that. The only reason that I am not on the main [party] list is because men do not want to give up their place for a woman.[54]

All of the women financed their own campaigns with their limited budgets. Although none of the women from the Front managed to enter the parliament, they are certain that they took some votes away from the main conservative party lists in Tehran. Hence, women's primary intention was to shame their party leaders by highlighting their gender discriminatory attitudes in the public sphere. In an effort to save face, and recognizing that Behrouzi was the mastermind behind this move, male conservative leaders pressured Behrouzi to refrain from putting forth a women-only list. Although Behrouzi was forced to officially remove herself from the list, the other women whom she had mobilized as part of the United Front of Conservative Women were still firm in their stance to shame their male party leaders.

A year later, in 2009, the United Front of Conservative Women, with the support and leadership of Maryam Behrouzi, managed to successfully lobby neo-conservative president Ahmadinejad to nominate women as members of his cabinet. Ahmadinejad, who following the contentious 2009 presidential elections that seriously challenged his legitimacy was eager to appeal to the Iranian public, nominated three conservative women to seem moderate and to distance himself from the ultra-conservative forces. Eventually, one woman nominee, Marzieh Vahid-Dastejerdi, a long-term member of the Zeinab Society and current director of the United Front of Conservative Women, became Iran's minister of health.[55] Although a modest achievement, the appointment of the first female Iranian post-revolutionary minister was largely thanks to Islamic women's extensive lobbying of conservative male leaders, many of whom oppose women in positions of authority.[56] The public's demands for democracy in their demonstrations in 2009 further encouraged Ahmadinejad to give in to Islamic women's calls for more inclusive political bodies.

Overall, the internal criticisms as articulated by high-ranking Islamic women from within the conservative faction in Iran sent a strong message to their male political figures that they cannot continue to marginalize women. In their public media campaigns, Islamic women activists expressed their disillusionment with the Islamic political movement in Iran in having failed to create a just Islamic society, in which women and men have a share in all spheres of domestic and public life. Realizing that they have public sympathy on their side,

---

[53]Personal interview with an Islamic woman activist, June 2015.

[54]Ibid.

[55]Although Maryam Behrouzi passed away in 2012, the Zeinab Society continues to be active, though to a lesser extent. In June 2015, in preparation for the 2016 parliamentary elections, the United Front of Conservative Women registered itself as a political party under the leadership of Marzieh Vahid-Dastjerdi, post-revolutionary's Iran's first woman minister and long-term member of the Zeinab Society. Vahid-Dastjerdi, who ran on the conservative list for Tehran, however failed to enter the parliament in the 2016 elections, as the reformist list of 'Hope' won all of Tehran's 30-member seats, enabling unknown women from the reformist faction to enter the parliament instead.

[56]Nazanin Shahrokni, 'All the President's Women', *Middle East Report* no. 253 (2009); Tajali, 'Notions of Female Authority'.

Islamic women publicly responded to and challenged the gender discriminatory statements of key clerical figures in Iran. In such statements, Islamic women activists often emphasized women's significant contributions during the 1979 revolution and the eight-year Iran–Iraq war, as evidence of their commitment to the ideals of the Islamic regime and their political experience. As learned women, these influential Islamic women also pointed to egalitarian Islamic precepts to highlight the patriarchal misinterpretations of various clerics on the issue of female authority.[57] However, the effectiveness of such public protests to resonate with the public and pressure elites into action depends on whether they are voiced by high-profile Islamic women with enough leverage and legitimacy to avoid being sidelined.

The headscarf ban in Turkey and Islamic women's lobbying efforts of AKP leaders

A major concern of Turkish Islamic women's rights activists has been the removal of the ban on headscarved women's right to access state buildings, including the national parliament. With the rise of political Islam in Turkey in the 1990s and the secular elites' subsequent attacks on and forceful closures of Islamist parties, women's dress and body became the battlefield in which male Islamist and secularist elites figuratively fought for control over the state and its institutions. This is apparent by the repeated election campaign promises of Turkey's Islamic elites to remove the headscarf ban, and the secular elites' responses of pursuing party closures and implementing even stricter bans on headscarved women's access to state facilities, including universities and the parliament. The secular elites' shadow over pro-religious parties persisted even after AKP's landslide rise to power in 2002. Indeed when, in 2008, AKP attempted to remove the headscarf ban only for university students, it was rejected by the secularist-dominated Constitutional Court, and AKP narrowly escaped party closure.[58]

Frustrated with feeling powerless, AKP prioritized decreasing the secular establishment's influence in Turkish politics, before addressing the headscarf ban. The AKP government led an extensive campaign of legal, institutional, and structural reforms using the rhetoric of democratization, justice, and making Turkey compatible for EU membership. With the backing of the public in a constitutional referendum in 2010, AKP succeeded in consolidating much of the institutional power in its own hands. With AKP's increased power and popularity, Islamic women activists, who had for decades actively supported the party and the larger Islamic movement in Turkey, now expected AKP leaders to deliver on the implicit promise of pious women's political inclusion and fair treatment. Indeed, the promise to address the headscarf ban in Turkey was among the central reasons why many women initially joined the Islamic political movement in Turkey, and actively campaigned on behalf of the Islamist *Refah* party and its successor parties, including the AKP.

Therefore, for the 2011 parliamentary elections, some party women began to express the demand that the time had come for AKP to nominate headscarved women and represent the majority of its female supporters and members. However, when these women did not

---

[57]Tajali, 'Notions of Female Authority'.
[58]Dilek Cindoglu and Gizem Zencirci, 'The Headscarf in Turkey in the Public and State Spheres', *Middle Eastern Studies*, 44(5) (2008), pp. 791–806; Merve Kavakci Islam, *Headscarf Politics in Turkey: A Postcolonial Reading*, vol. 1 (New York: Palgrave Macmillan, 2010).

see any sincere efforts from AKP to address headscarved women's marginalization in accessing parliamentary seats, they took matters into their own hands. Consequently, a number of influential Islamic women activists launched major campaigns to protest the discriminatory actions of AKP party leaders against headscarved women. They argued that headscarved women not only face discrimination against other men, but also against non-headscarved women, many of whom were recruited from outside of the party structure to stand as parliamentary candidates.[59]

Fatma Bostan was among those who took matters into her own hands rather than continuing to remain patient for male elites to acknowledge her 'right' to political representation as a headscarved woman. In the months prior to the 2011 elections, Bostan, herself one of the founding members of AKP, had gone public about the need for the party to finally nominate headscarved candidates. Her outspokenness against her own party led her to become a controversial figure as the Turkish media either considered her as a 'brave or outspoken headscarved woman' or as a 'provocateur' for threatening AKP's existence.[60]

Despite Bostan's long history of involvement with the party, including her membership in the AKP's Central Decision and Administration Board, her headscarf prevented her from reaching important political decision-making positions. While her husband, who had a shorter history of party involvement, had served as an AKP parliamentarian from 2002 to 2007, Bostan was not even considered as a potential parliamentary candidate by party leaders. She opposed such discriminatory behaviour, as she believed it violated her individual *right* to access the political sphere, a right which is also supported by international human rights documents, such as CEDAW.

To raise public awareness of AKP's discriminatory stance, Bostan tactfully made her application to AKP for candidacy for the parliament public, along with a threatening statement that if party leaders were not ready or willing to nominate her, she would run as an independent, signalling her resignation from the party that she had helped found back in 2001.[61] This public threat and her insistence on 'rights' and 'anti-discrimination' caused fury in the ruling party, which was being attacked by one of its high-ranking members in the public sphere. In a personal interview, Bostan emphasized the reasoning behind her public move, which was motivated by the AKP party's unwillingness to nominate headscarved women for the 2011 elections, despite a large section of the public's readiness for this move:

> During last year's *istişare toplantısı* [a closed Consultative Meeting of the party] held in October 2010, I raised the issue that two-thirds of Turkish women are not represented in the Parliament. At that meeting I also pointed out that in July the CEDAW Committee had asked Turkey to do something about its headscarf ban and address the problem of women's low political representation. So as a signatory to CEDAW, it is time that we [the AKP] respond to this demand and show headscarved candidates in the next elections.[62]

However, the Prime Minister's response to her views and hopes that headscarved women would have access to the parliament in 2011 (which she chose not to disclose to me) encouraged her to take this public action. Along with her, a total of about 50 other headscarved

[59]Personal interview with an Islamic party woman, May 2011.
[60]Mustafa Akyol, 'Veiled Women versus Conservative Men', *Hürriyet Daily News*, 2011, http://www.hurriyetdailynews.com/Default.aspx?pageID=438&n=veiled-women-versus-conservative-men-2011-04-05 (accessed 16 January 2017).
[61]Fatma Zibak, 'Is Turkey Ready for a Headscarved Deputy?', *Today's Zaman*, 27 March 2011, http://www.trdefence.com/is-turkey-ready-for-a-headscarved-deputy/ (accessed 26 January 2017).
[62]Personal interview with Fatma Bostan, June 2011.

women applied for candidacy for the AKP, 10 of whom were close colleagues of Bostan, including another headscarved AKP founder. 'Although all of these women were qualified, I was 99% sure that AKP was not going to nominate any headscarved candidates.' She further continued:

> My main objective of registering for candidacy was mostly to put pressure on the party rather than to get elected. Hence, I only registered with the AKP so that I can talk about it later when they don't show me [on the party candidate list].[63]

To Fatma Bostan's surprise, while her outspokenness was attacked by many of her AKP colleagues and Islamic leaders, she found new allies within the secularist camps, including women's rights groups such as KA-DER that had been organizing for women's greater political presence in Turkey. KA-DER invited Bostan to their public events and, given the public's interest in headscarved women's rights, for the first time included headscarved women in their media campaigns. Bostan discussed this important transformation in secular women's rights groups to finally accept headscarved women's right to political representation by stating, 'Generally, these women viewed headscarved women as being obedient and stereotypically weak, but when they saw us raising our voices, we gained their respect.'[64] The important convergence of Islamic and secular women in Turkey for the 2011 elections strengthened the decades-long demand of the Turkish women's rights movement on more inclusive legislative bodies, while publicly shaming parties that discriminate against highly qualified and experienced women merely because of their gender.

Given the public's receptiveness to the issue of women's political rights, Islamic women were willing to be outspoken against injustice and discrimination, even if such criticisms were against their own leadership. In the end, the coalition of diverse women's groups against gender discrimination and in support of freedom of expression, including freedom in how to dress one's body, resulted in the official lifting of the headscarf ban in 2013. For the first time, Turkish women could finally claim their seats at the decision-making table regardless of their dress. The 2015 parliamentary elections were the first time that AKP nominated headscarved candidates. In a notable move, 44% of AKP's total female candidates were headscarved, most of whom were recruited from inside the party's structures, namely from its women's branches.[65]

Conclusion

The recent rise of women to political office on behalf of Islamic political movements and parties has been puzzling for many, except perhaps for the women who devoted years of activism and organizing to these parties, and today consider themselves equally qualified to reach decision-making positions. But when opportunities rose to claim their rightful place at the table, many faced fierce resistance and gender discrimination from their party leaders. Although the Islamic political movements in both Iran and Turkey had politicized women and encouraged their public support of the Islamic movement, they rarely sought for women's politicization and participation in grassroots politics to translate into women's active presence in political leadership.

---

[63]Ibid.
[64]Ibid.
[65]Personal interview with an AKP woman parliamentary candidate, May 2015.

This article addresses Islamic women's own initiatives to publicly challenge the conservative gender ideologies espoused by the religious political movements in which they are involved. It argues that in combination with a number of other important factors, the level of Islamic party women's own preparedness to address and publicly criticize the gender discriminatory actions and attitudes of their party leaders, played a key role in pressuring Islamic elites to recruit more women to office. Indeed, decades of women's activism on behalf of Islamic political movements in Iran and Turkey led to the maturation of Islamic women activists who refused to be sidelined from political decision-making positions by their male Islamic leaders. Realizing the public's increasing support for women's access to positions of authority, high-ranking Islamic women's outspokenness against women's political marginalization constitutes a form of internal criticism, which can potentially instigate more lasting reform given that it is internally driven and articulated by those with the most legitimacy in the eyes of the conservative movement. It remains to be seen, however, whether women's internally driven pressures will help transform their male-dominated parties to recruit and nominate women beyond token amounts, despite both Islamic men and women party members' continued resistance to 'gender equality' and 'feminism' for the time being.

Acknowledgements

I would like to thank Sarah Childs, Kimberley Manning, Melinda Adams, and Homa Hoodfar for their valuable feedback on earlier versions of this article. I am also grateful to the support that I received from Oxford University and Sasakawa Peace Foundation in researching and writing of this subject.

Disclosure statement

No potential conflict of interest was reported by the author.

4   'We wander in your footsteps'—reciprocity and contractility in Lebanese personality-centred parties

Christian Thuselt

ABSTRACT

This contribution questions the widespread assumption of Lebanese parties being mere 'instruments' in their leaders' hands by asking what partisans see through their chairmen. It describes an informal social contract between partisans and leaders, outlining reciprocity in interpreting the 'cause', being symbolized by the latter. The core of this contract is made up by a particular interpretation of a global normativity of the modern nation-state and reciprocity. Whereas the latter might be deeply felt, it often lacks institutionalized control within the party. Finally, the contribution highlights some noticeable restrictions of this informal contractility.

Introduction: are Lebanese parties meaningless?

Despite the fact that Lebanon has had a pluralistic and competitive multiparty system since the 1920s, parties are limited by political confessionalism.[1] This system goes hand in hand with sectarianism, regionalism and familism—all determined by patronage structures. Scientific literature therefore often deals with Lebanese parties by considering them to be almost exclusively focused on a narrow political elite. This elitism is said to lead to them becoming sclerotic, exhibiting a 'gelatinous identity',[2] being only clad 'in the clothes of a modern party',[3] constituting an 'aesthetical framework, touching the social reality, but not being able to emanate from the society in question'[4] and thereby functioning as 'propaganda machines' for their leaders,[5] as 'non-ideological political machines' without a 'credible programmatic content',[6] or at least only with an outdated one.[7] Arguably the most questionable

---

[1] This contribution has been taken from parts of my PhD thesis submitted in 2017. It has been supported by a research grant of Deutsches Orient-Institut Beirut.

[2] Shawkat 'Ishti, 'al-'Ahzab as-Siyasiyya fi Lubnan: 'Afkar 'Awwaliyya li-Maraja'at-t-Tajriba', in al-Markaz al-Lubnani li-d-Dirasat, ed., *al- 'Ahzab as-Siyasiyya fi-l- 'Alam al- 'Arabi* (Beirut: al-Markaz al-Lubnani li-d-Dirasat, 2006), p. 84.

[3] Ibid.

[4] Idem. [Chawkat Ichti], 'La place du leadership traditionel dans les partis politiques modernes: le cas de la za'āma des Arslans', in Franck Mermier and Sabrina Mervin, *Leaders et partisans au Liban* (Paris/Beirut: Karthala/Ifpo, 2012), p. 476.

[5] Rola el-Husseini, *Pax Syriana. Elite Politics in Postwar Lebanon* (Syracuse, NY: Syracuse University Press, 2012), p. 38.

[6] Daniel Corstange, 'Vote Trafficking in Lebanon', *Journal of Middle East Studies*, 44(3) (2012), pp. 483–505, here p. 488.

[7] Farid al-Khazin, *al- 'Ahzab as-Siyasiyya fi Lubnan: Hudud ad-Dimuqratiyya fi Tajribat-l-Hizbiyya* (Beirut: al-Markaz al-Lubnani li-d-Dirasat, 2002). But obviously not every party is outdated: the author, one of the best Lebanese political scientists, currently sits in parliament for the FPM.

opinion on them is certainly the one that does not even acknowledge political parties having any roots at all in the Middle East's political culture.[8] An otherwise rather deliberative author, Samir Khalaf, assumes that even the staunchly ideologically motivated Ba'thi ar-Rifa'i, the Nasserite Najjah Wakim[9] or the Gemayels[10] are (or were) only an incoherent 'pseudo-ideological variety'.[11] A well-known handbook on political systems in the Middle East claims that parties in Lebanon are mere 'tools of recruitment' in the hands of traditional leaders.[12]

I consider all these suggestions severely flawed. More precisely, it has rarely been asked whether these alleged traditional narratives are not modern—and many are—or what their recipients think about them.[13] When doing research on political socialization in Lebanon I observed how desperate the respective party members were to establish meaningful political biographies: not one of them ever understood himself as an instrument of anyone, not of a leader and not of some foreign influence.

Of course, one of the most prominent factors that make political parties more or less traditional and/or instrumental is certainly their domination by respective leaders or their families. There are, to be sure, purely parochial networks called 'parties', where we could safely assume the party has no or at least very limited mobilizing qualities; its main function is to transfer the family's hitherto purely local political capabilities onto a national level.[14] How important the mobilizing narrative actually is can be clearly highlighted by comparing the Miqati and the Hariri families: both are similarly wealthy, but only the latter has managed to be seen by many Lebanese Sunnis as symbolizing, so to say, them themselves.[15] Especially in times of crisis, Lebanon has therefore indeed brought about considerably influential political parties.

My hypothesis is that political mobilization as brought about by identities transgressing the parochial could also be brought about by parties that are largely centred on single persons if they allow for fully fledged modern political identities.

I will argue that in the three parties I researched, these personalities are portrayed as individuals but not as individualists: they are not part of a bizarre hero cult, but the symbolization of a 'cause', i.e. a political identity.[16] This personalization of a 'cause' matches a social contract. A social contract is not necessarily to be understood in a formalized, liberal way; it

---

[8]Bertrand Badie, 'L'Analyse des partis politiques en monde musulman: la crise des paradigmes universels', in Yves Meny, ed., *Idéologies: Partis politiques et groupes sociaux* (Paris: Presses de la fondation nationale des sciences politiques, 1991), pp. 327–343; Peter Pawelka, 'Funktionen politischer Parteien in nicht demokratischen Regimen des Vorderen Orients', in Gero Erdmann, Patrick Köllner, and Joachim Betz, eds., *Die gesellschaftliche Verankerung politischer Parteien. Formale und informelle Dimensionen im internationalen Vergleich* (Wiesbaden: VS, 2004), pp. 35–54.

[9]Both won seats in the Lebanese parliament in 1972. This caused some upset as it represented two of the rare major surprises in the country's elections. Their election could be considered an important sign of the old elite's loss of influence on its clientele. The Gemayels lead the Phalanges party.

[10]With regard to Arab names, I chose the versions employed most in Western news coverage and at times by their bearers alike: thus, al-Jumayyil becomes Gemayel, Ja'ja' Geagea, Ḥubayqa Hobeika, etc.

[11]Samir Khalaf, *Lebanon's Predicament* (New York: Columbia University Press, 1987), p. 86.

[12]Nassif Hitti, 'The Republic of Lebanon', in Tareq Y. Ismael and Jacqueline S. Ismael, eds., *Politics and Government in the Middle East and North Africa* (Miami: Florida International University Press, 1991), p. 219.

[13]One of the most refreshing contributions to the debate might be the rich volume by Mermier and Mervin which will hopefully help to give a more balanced view on Lebanese parties: Franck Mermier and Sabrina Mervin, eds., *Leaders et partisans au Liban* (Paris/Beirut: Karthala/Ifpo, 2012); see also: Myriam Catusse and Karam Karam, eds., *A Return to Partisan Politics? Partisan Logics and Political Transformations in the Arab World* (Beirut: Lebanese Centre for Policy Studies, 2010).

[14]Ishti, 'La place du leadership traditionel', pp. 461–480.

[15]Hannes Baumann, 'The "New Contractor Bourgeoisie" in Lebanese Politics. Hariri, Mikati and Fares', in Are Knudsen and Michael Kerr, eds., *Lebanon after the Cedar Revolution* (London: Hurst & Company, 2012), pp. 125–144.

[16]Identity means here the self-locating within the framework of institutionalized meanings; cf. Peter L. Berger and Thomas Luckmann, *The Social Construction of Reality. A Treatise on the Sociology of Knowledge*, Reprint (Garden City, NY: Doubleday, 1967).

might also work out informally. In that case, the personalized symbol allows his partisans to identify themselves. The individual is thereby an active interpreter.

Here I will deal with the three most important Christian parties in Lebanon, the Ḥizb al-Katāʾib al-Lubnāniyya (or: Phalanges), the al-Quwwāt al-Lubnāniyya (Lebanese Forces, LF), and the Tayyār al-Wataniyy al-Ḥurr (Free Patriotic Movement, FPM). The Kataʾib were founded in 1936 as a nationalist shirt-party, soon evolving into the country's leading Christian party. It has been headed, with interruptions, by members of the Gemayel family: notably Pierre Gemayel, the party's founding president. The LF were originally a war-militia largely staffed by these Phalangists. But when their original leader Bashir Gemayel was assassinated shortly after becoming president in 1982, they developed more and more into an organiza-tion of its own right. Since 1985 it has been headed by Samir Geagea, who had waged a coup against Bashir's older brother and successor Amin. The FPM stems from a civic move-ment against the militias among Lebanon's Christian bourgeoisie in the late 1980s. It was until 2015 led by Michel ʿAoun, a former army chief and newly elected president of Lebanon. Whereas the latter party is associated with the Hezbollah-dominated '8th of March' bloc, the two others are integral parts of the rivalling '14th of March'.[17]

I will proceed as follows. In the first section I explain how I understand democracy. I will argue it should be understood as a concept bound on a structural notion of modernity, based upon the concept of having an articulating public. Thus, the often-heard criticism, that Lebanese parties are not sufficiently democratic, results mostly from the assumption that one's own respective normativity equals 'democracy'. At least this is a questionable assumption, perpetuating a normative version of modernization theory. Thus, the usage of 'democratic' in Khalaf's aforementioned study[18] tells us only if *he* felt comfortable with the narratives of the Nasserite Wakim or the Phalangist Gemayels (obviously not) but nothing if they did fulfil functions of a party for their respective *adherents*.

Using a structurally informed history-of-ideas approach allows for dropping the wide variety of adjectives to categorize all those systems characterized by electoral competition that do not—either in their competitive openness, or in the election's actual results—match *our* respective expectations.[19]

Instead, I will argue all politics evoking the normativity of the articulating *demos* are 'democratic'. I will then argue that the notion of a social contract is at the centre of modern democratic power-relationships, although these contracts might also not always be as insin-uated by the liberal origins of the notion as such. Rather they might, as in my sample, resem-ble a charismatic relationship. After having clarified these assumptions, I will show how the

---

[17] The 8th March alliance is formed of the two Shiite parties Hezbollah and ʾAmal, the pan-Syrian Syrian Social Nationalist Party (SSNP), the Marada, a smaller Christian party from the north, and several less important organizations. The alliance focuses on an Iranian–Syrian axis but would conceive that as trying to build a sustainable 'regional surrounding' that would allow for a perspective in the region that is not based upon 'exclusivist' identities by either emphasizing 'citizenship' or—via anti-imperialism—a common base beyond these particularisms. The 14th March alliance comprises the Sunni-dominated Mustaqbal bloc, the Phalanges, the LF, and several smaller parties, all united by a pro-Western foreign policy and a rather liberal-conservative outlook. The two Christian organizations among them could probably be described as articulating a decidedly Lebanese but Christian identity, often with a considerable distance to the region at large, fearing for their political and cultural autonomy. The FPM sees itself largely as a liberal party and aims to tie the Lebanese Christians to the region by downsizing their exceptionalism in favour of a more citizenship-based identity. The socialist, Druze-dominated Progressive Socialist Party (PSP) has allied itself with both camps.

[18] 'pseudo-ideological variety', Khalaf, *Lebanon's Predicament*, p. 86.

[19] For example: Steve Levitsky and David Collier, 'Democracy with Adjectives: Conceptual Innovation in Comparative Research', *World Politics*, 49(3) (1997), pp. 430–451; Larry Diamond, *Developing Democracy towards Consolidation* (Baltimore, MD: John Hopkins University Press, 1999); Guillermo O´Donnell, 'Illusions about Consolidation', *Journal of Democracy*, 7(2) (1996), pp. 34–51; Wolfgang Merkel, 'Embedded and Defective Democracies', *Democratization*, 11(5) (2004), pp. 33–58.

three parties in question try to establish such a charismatic leadership between the persons dominating them and the rank and file.

I use thereby in a triangulating manner material from various online mediums of these parties, their official self-presentation, material published by their wider *Vorfeld*, written testimonies (former) members penned down, as well as interviews with functionaries and sympathizers I conducted in Lebanon and experiences I got from encounters when doing fieldwork.[20] My argument is that there are, unsurprisingly, dysfunctionalities with regard to the expectations the parties evoke themselves with their narratives. Yet, they have a modern and credible content, allowing for a social contract between the leader and the partisans which is based upon the leader embodying the 'cause'.

Democracy and modernity

First, I will assume that Lebanese parties are indeed a meaningful expression of modernity. They are neither 'imported' nor 'superficially employed'.

The central point in being modern is the 'articulation' of a *demos*, indissolubly bound to 'reflectivity' on the basis of living together,[21] since 'order' is no longer given,[22] and the emergence of a public. Now everyone is forced to communicate with others, even if he consciously decides to opt out of this modernity as a justification of his very own cause—as would be the case with Catholic Ultramontanists, Evangelical Christians, Salafists or Ultra-Orthodox Jews. Consequently, dialogicity becomes a core element of politics, towards all other conceptions around what Peter L. Berger called 'the heretic imperative'. This means that there is always someone else out there to whom one has to refer in his own belief.[23] But the dialogicity is also towards 'the people', which is turning from a passive audience into the evoked normative base of politics. One has to act *in the name* of 'We the people'. A society living under these conditions is called 'modern'. Such a dialogue might be formal—offering institutionalized channels of communication—or informal. The first variant would be the liberal solution, but there are other versions of modernity and democracy. Even deeply authoritarian concepts of 'We the people' could be evoked, as did all Arab Republican regimes at least temporarily.[24] Additionally, even liberalism is not only about the language of contractility: we just need to consider the number of social identities to which one belongs even in a deeply liberal society where enforceable rights are not really at the core: family, church, ethnic groups, friends, etc.[25]

---

[20]Twenty-seven semi-structured qualitative interviews conducted in 2010 and 2012 in Lebanon among partisans. Additionally I use material from a variety of informal everyday conversations, mostly with people within parties or close to them.

[21]Shmuel N. Eisenstadt, 'The Construction of Collective Identities and the Continual Reconstruction of Primordiality and Sacrality – Some Analytical and Comparative Indications', in *Comparative Civilizations & Multiple Modernities* Vol. 1 (Leiden: E. J. Brill, 2003), p. 105.

[22]Claude Lefort, *Democracy and Political Theory* (Cambridge: Polity Press, 1988), esp. pp. 9–20.

[23]Peter L. Berger, *The Heretical Imperative: Contemporary Possibilities of Religious Affirmation* (Garden City, NY: Doubleday, 1979).

[24]Christoph Schumann, 'Liberalization and Democratization in the Arab World: A Conceptual Critique', in Christoph Schumann and Meir Hatina, eds., *Arab Liberal Thought after 1967: Old Dilemmas, New Perceptions* (Basingstoke: Palgrave Macmillan, 2015), pp. 23–62.

[25]In addition, the FPM sees itself as a liberal party.

As Eric Voegelin[26] and Claude Lefort[27] point out, symbols of its existence enable a social group to perceive itself; so, anyone who manages to produce a set of symbols referring to the condition of dialogicity towards the 'others' and the *demos* might possibly be considered democratic, although he is not necessarily a liberal by the book.

The result might describe contractility. But in contrast to the original intention of this term, I will not argue in the language of game theories to develop a consensus on procedural mechanisms on what is 'reasonable' for society as a whole.[28] Nor am I trying to develop some criticism of Universalist ethics out of it,[29] or to lament contractualism's inability to provide for them.[30] Rather, my argument starts from the notion of the individual, the foremost point in every 'social contract',[31] present in all historiographies I consulted, as well as in all my interviews with Lebanese partisans. This individuality is very much different from the pre-modern ideas of a *corpus mysticum* and its loyalty. The traditional Islamic oath of loyalty (*bay'a*), for example, did not explicitly necessitate individual consent. Rather, if those capable of recognizing the rightful caliph had chosen a ruler, the *umma*'s oath would simply have been presupposed and imagined as having been already done by the *khassa*, the elite. Whereas the belief in God and his revealed true order was an individual necessity, a *conditio sine qua non*, the oath to the caliph as a ruler was seen as an acclamation rather than as a prerequisite to establish domination, based on reciprocity.[32]

Domination and reciprocity

Unlike other authors who emphasize the repressive, heavy-handed nature of power,[33] I devote more attention to the *limited but existing* possibilities of evasion or conceptual reinterpretation that limit every power holder's capabilities.[34] There are basically three of these limitations: dissidence, 'acting as if', and deviance by retreating into the niches of private life.

First and foremost, Lebanon is not a dictatorship—one can leave a party as a dissident. In fact, I met several former partisans. Most remained remarkably loyal to what they could

---

[26]Eric Voegelin, 'The New Science of Politics', in Manfred Henningsen, ed., *Modernity Without Restraint: The Collected Works of Eric Voegelin*, Vol. 5 (Columbia, MO: Missouri University Press, 2000 [orig. 1951]).

[27]Claude Lefort, *The Political Forms of Modern Society. Bureaucracy, Democracy, Totalitarianism*, ed. John B. Thompson (Cambridge: Polity Press, 1986).

[28]Most influential on the current debate is certainly: John Rawls, *A Theory of Justice*, Reprint, (Cambridge, MA: Harvard University Press, 2005); Idem, *Political Liberalism*, Expanded ed. (New York: Columbia University Press, 2005).

[29]See Helmut Kliemt, 'Die gefährliche Fiktion eines Gesellschaftsvertrages', *Aufklärung und Kritik*, 7(Special Issue on Contractualism) (2003), pp. 84–94.

[30]Robert Deinhammer, 'Gesellschaftsvertrag? Kritische Bemerkungen zur kontraktualistischen Ethik', *Rechtstheorie*, 36 (2005), pp. 402–415.

[31]Charles Taylor, *Sources of the Self. The Making of the Modern Identity* (Cambridge: Cambridge University Press, 1989), pp. 194–195.

[32]See Roswitha Badry, *Die zeitgenössische Diskussion um den islamischen Beratungsgedanken (šūrā) unter dem besonderen Aspekt ideengeschichtlicher Kontinuitäten und Diskontinuitäten* (Stuttgart: Franz Steiner, 1998), p. 131.

[33]Classically: Michel Foucault, 'Lecture on Governmentality', in Graham Burchell, Colin Gordon, and Peter Mille, eds., *The Foucault Effect. Studies in Governmentality* (London: Harvester Wheatsheaf, 1991); relating these ideas on Middle Eastern parties: Pierre Robert Baduel, 'Les partis politiques dans la gouvernementalisation de l'État des pays arabes', *Revue du monde musulman et de la Méditerranée*, 81–82 (1996), Les partis politiques dans les pays arabes, pp. 9–51.

[34]Basically, I understand power as something that could not be void of legitimacy, cf. Max Weber, *Economy and Society: An Outline of Interpretive Sociology*, ed. Guenther Roth and Claus Wittich, 2nd ed. (Berkeley: University of California Press, 1978). That encompasses compulsion as well as fitting into symbolisms thought to be plausible and thereby engaging in a process of objectifying their meanings by institutionalizing them, see: Berger and Luckmann, *The Social Construction of Reality*, p. 92.

single out as being their former party's narrative. As a written example, there is a book in Lebanon, widely read by partisans of every political current, ʾAqni ʿat-l-Mukhallis,[35] in which former adherents of Michel ʿAoun speak out against their former leader, whom they accuse of having betrayed their formerly common convictions. Reinhard Koselleck has rightfully insisted that every social relationship is reciprocal, especially narratives of legitimacy being actively interpreted by the respective recipients.[36] This interpretation results in a specific dynamic, as Lefort argued, since every legitimating ideology lives permanently between its reality and the tensions produced by its promises.[37] It will never fulfil it fully, but cannot risk not fulfilling anything at all. The interpretation of what ʿAoun's most frequently employed symbolic *topos* of the 'legal state' actually meant was very much dependent on the recipient's pre-existing political conceptions. There was obviously a high degree of reciprocity involved in interpreting these symbols—ʿAoun did not do it alone and the disappointed left his party. That is especially important since the FPM lost in 2009 many of the voters it still had in 2005.[38] I also met a former communist who recommended the Communist Party as the sole choice for a laic vote, but who left the party itself due to its authoritarian structure.[39] The former LF ideologue, Antoine Najm, also left the Forces as he no longer felt represented by Samir Geagea.

The next option, 'acting as if',[40] might be most closely related to approaching a party only to use its financial benefits. This is closely connected to the dependency on intermediate actors between the individual and the state[41]—and very typical for dysfunctional states.[42] 'Acting as if' might be also attributed to the de facto state militias established during the war, when it became dangerous to question the LF's narrative in the so-called 'Eastern Region'. But not everyone who uses the financial assets offered by Lebanese parties does so out of compliance. An FPM functionary expressed fear of Hezbollah, but lauded it for its 'social engagement' and for 'defending the country'.[43] A Shiite from the south who introduced me to the 'Wardieh' gas stations' concept (their surplus goes to the Fadl-Allah Foundation, not officially within Hezbollah's own network, but located within the same societal milieu) emphasized exactly their welfare function.[44]

Deviance, finally, might be located in retreating back to the private sphere and preying upon public resources.[45] Thus, whereas the World Value Survey (WVS)[46] shows a surprisingly high trust in political parties in Lebanon (in fact higher than in Germany, Denmark or the US), it also indicates a high degree of disappointment, in short: a highly polarized society.

---

[35]Muḥammad ʾAbi Samra and Waddah Sharara, ʾAqni ʿat-l-Mukhallis. Shahadat fi Shiʿat-l-ʾAwniyya wa ʾImamiha (Beirut: Dar an-Nahar, 2009).

[36]Reinhart Koselleck, *Critique and Crisis. Enlightenment and the Pathogenesis of Modern Society* (Cambridge, MA: MIT Press, 1988).

[37]Lefort, *Political Forms of Modern Society*, p. 189.

[38]See the results in: ʾIntikhabat Lubnan 2009: Taḥalil ʾIḥsaʾiyya wa-r-Raqmiyya li-n-Nataʾij fi Dawaʾir wal-l-ʾAqlam, Krunulujiyya al-ʾAḥdath, ath-Thuhur al-ʾIʿalamī, ed. Statistics Lebanon, (Beirut: Statistics Lebanon Ltd., 2009).

[39]Interview, 21 May 2012.

[40]Lisa Wedeen, *Ambiguities of Domination. Politics, Rhetoric, and Symbols in Contemporary Syria* (Chicago, IL: University of Chicago Press, 1999).

[41]Melani Claire Cammett, 'Partisan Activism and Access to Welfare in Lebanon', *Studies in Comparative International Development*, 46(1) (2011), pp. 70–97.

[42]Suad Joseph, 'Political Familism in Lebanon', *The Annals of the American Academy of Political and Social Science*, 636(1) (2011), pp. 150–163.

[43]Informal conversation in Jounieh, October 2010.

[44]Informal conversation, September 2012.

[45]Cilja Harders, *Staatsanalyse von Unten. Urbane Armut und politische Partizipation in Ägypten. Mikro- und mesopolitische Analysen unterschiedlicher Kairoer Stadtteile* (Hamburg: DOI, 2002).

[46]http://www.worldvaluessurvey.org/WVSOnline.jsp, rev. 8 May 2015.

Seventy-four per cent of the WVS's Lebanese respondents suspected that voters are very or at least fairly often bribed, while 64% assumed the 'elites' rig elections by buying votes.[47] This tells us a great deal about the widespread frustration among Lebanese regarding the shortcomings of their country's political system. However, these frustrations are not always quite honest: many Lebanese whom I talked to shared a general mistrust with regard to Lebanon's leading politicians, but when it came to the crucial questions of politics several revealed rather strong sympathies for one of the two blocs now dominating the scene (the 8th March alliance and 14th March alliance). For example, a young Christian denied having any political ambitions, generally suspecting that politicians do not care too much for the country, assuming them grimly to be thieves rather than heroes. Later on, it turned out he had very strong sympathies for the FPM, at times even attending the party's meetings and running for them in elections for his profession's union.[48]

Charisma

If the party succeeds in establishing a contractual relationship between a leader and his base, the result might be best described as a charismatic one. The very notion itself has been proposed to me several times by the parties and their members alike; and several publications have tried to apply the term to Lebanese parties.[49]

Charisma, therefore, has to be understood as a reciprocal relationship between a leader and those 'masses' willing to approve.[50] This concept departs considerably from Max Weber's version of it, which was highly indebted to the early-twentieth-century genius cult,[51] to which he also owed his questionable admiration of charisma as being inherently revolutionary.[52] So I could follow Michael Günther in claiming that charisma is nothing other than a social relationship, established on a cause that addresses the desire for an *emotionally* constituted community.[53] Thus, the charismatic effect is not brought about by the 'genius' and his specific 'heroic' characteristics, but by the cause, i.e. what is perceived by an addressee as allowing for a community, which could be characterized as: '[…] the epitome of vital, direct […] relations between humans. Authenticity and unreservedness are her genuine traits […]'[54] This communitarization is personalized in a single person, whereby this person as such is inseparably bound to something that far transcends their status as a person. Consequentially, it tends to be a personalized mask of a state or a cause that helps to deal with times of flawed stability.[55]

---

[47]WVS, 2010–14.
[48]Informal conversation in 2012.
[49]For example, several contributions in: Mermier and Mervin, *Leaders et partisans au Liban*.
[50]Hans-Ulrich Wehler, *Deutsche Gesellschaftsgeschichte. Vol. 4: Vom Beginn des Ersten Weltkrieges bis zur Gründung der beiden deutschen Staaten 1914–1949* (Munich: C. H. Beck, 2003), p. 598.
[51]For an insightful critique see Michael Günther, *Masse und Charisma. Soziale Ursachen des politischen und religiösen Fanatismus* (Frankfurt/Main: Peter Lang, 2005), pp. 127–267.
[52]Weber, *Economy and Society*, pp. 1115–1120.
[53]Günther, *Masse und Charisma*, pp. 212/220–224.
[54]Helmuth Plessner, *Grenzen der Gemeinschaft. Eine Kritik des sozialen Radikalismus*, Reprint (Frankfurt/Main: Suhrkamp, 2002), p. 44. (My own translation.)
[55]Günther, *Masse und Charisma*, pp. 249.

This stands contrary to the liberal ideal of 'society' as an interaction group based on juridical terms regulating it.[56] This is not the place to discuss this tendency in detail; I might only hint cautiously at the simmering doubt of whether the liberal state could, in its empiric manifestation, guarantee those motivations to act in exactly the manner it needs to reproduce itself.[57] The problem is, of course, the inherent tendency to overcome the Lebanese state's dysfunctionalities by transforming the nation from a community of regulated conflict into one of mutual consent by fitting into the respective conceptions of the 'right' Lebanese.

What fosters this personalism?

The Lebanese parliament actually exercises a certain degree of control, but in times of crisis it is left 'completely crippled'.[58] Thus, since the founding of the country in 1920, the political heavyweights have had to step in to restore 'order' through round table talks.[59] This consociationalism is deeply elitist: rather than bringing the coalition parties to the table, their leaders perform important tasks of intermediating not only between the different partners in government but also between themselves and their respective societal bases.[60] Thus, in contrast to those in other Arab countries, Lebanese parties ironically benefit from never having merged totally with the state apparatus; therefore their 'dream of a republic' remains a promise set apart from the tristesse of state failure.

According to a survey conducted in 2013, 66% of all Christians surveyed felt endangered in their very existence as a community; 83% of those polled claimed they were worried about the country's security situation, weapons owned by individuals and the Lebanese Army's obvious weakness. Seventy-nine per cent named the economic situation, including unemployment and the unusually high cost of living, as a major concern for them. And slightly less than half of all respondents (47%) feared for their personal safety and that of their family.[61] Thus, a mix of a potential physical threat and the sometimes harsh economic conditions enforced by a state incapable of fulfilling functions normatively ascribed to it provides the background for political apathy as well as for its optimistic opposite: enthusiasm for something better to come.

The structure of the parties in question also has to be mentioned here as a prerequisite for personalism. In fact, all of them are shaped by hierarchies. Their leadership is made up mostly of the better-educated. This indicator of legitimate cultural capital's relative scarcity, of course, has much to do with the cost of education in Lebanon.[62]

---

[56]See Jürgen Habermas, *The Theory of Communicative Action*, 2 vols. (Boston, MA: Beacon Press, 1987). As Taylor (*Sources of the Self*) and Sandel (Michael J. Sandel, *Liberalism and the Limits of Justice*, 2nd ed. (Cambridge: Cambridge University Press, 1998)) have elaborated, this assumption is not a given or based on relinquishing a substantial order altogether. Quite the contrary, the idea of how things should be ordered stipulates that society should be ordered by this typical liberal proceduralism.

[57]Helmut Dubiel, 'Unzivile Gesellschaft', *Soziale Welt* 52 (2001), p. 141; Taylor, *Sources of the Self*, p. 508; further: Margaret Canovan, *Nationhood and Political Theory* (Cheltenham: Edward Elgar, 1998).

[58]Abdo Baaklini, Guilain Denoeux, and Robert Springborg, *Legislative Politics in the Arab World: The Resurgence of Democratic Institutions* (Boulder, CO: Lynne Rienner, 1999), pp. 79–109.

[59]Michael W. Suleiman, *Political Parties in Lebanon. The Challenge of a Fragmented Political Culture*, (Ithaca, NY: Cornell University Press, 1967), pp. 50–51.

[60]Arend Lijphart, *Democracy in Plural Societies. A Comparative Exploration* (New Haven, CT: Yale University Press, 1977), pp. 49–50.

[61]*The Daily Star*, 9 January 2013.

[62]A single credit point at the American University at Beirut costs no less than USD 500.

All three parties discussed here are 'reformist', not 'revolutionary'.[63] Consequently, they tend to adapt to pre-existing mechanisms and the ability to potentially exercise power, in particular, arises from established symbolisms of a person-based patrimonialism.

Finally, media coverage everywhere tends to personalize political themes.[64] This is even more the case in a country like Lebanon, where several parties have succeeded in establishing their own media networks.[65]

Embodiment

In 2010, the Phalanges and the Forces alike put up multitudes of posters in eastern Beirut showing Bashir Gemayel's portrait captioned with the slogan *ḥulm jumhūriyya* (dream of a republic). '*Ḥulm*'—'dream'—in remarkable contrast to the mere earth-bound banalities of materialism, is probably the most widely used term associated with the former president, assassinated shortly after being elected in 1982, in the personality cult that developed around him. *Ḥulm jumhūriyya* is not only the caption of a poster, it is also the title of an MTV documentary on him, contrasting somewhat demagogically selected quotations of the 'martyr president' on his 'dream state' with pictures of menacing present-day Islamist fighters to document the unaltered actuality of Bashir's discourse.[66] *Le Réveil*, his brother Amin's newspaper, lamented after the bomb blast that killed Bashir Gemayel the death of Lebanon's dream; others considered the Lebanese as 'orphans, amputated of their chief, their dreams, their hope' from then on.[67] Pierre Gemayel, his father, is described in one of his biographies as having been the 'leader' who 'did not work for the fatherland with appropriate wishes but with ardent dreams'.[68] A hagiographic book on Michel 'Aoun is titled: 'Dream or illusion'.[69] The former army chief succeeded in the last phase of the civil war in the late 1980s in establishing himself as the leader of a civic protest movement. He claimed to stand for the 'legitimate state' against foreign influences and the militias. He was considered by one of his adherents to 'embody a promising dream for those people agreeing with the state and domination of the legitimate' against the 'predatory militias', as part of a whole chain of dreams of a strong state.[70] Taking up the position left vacant by others, one former adherent perceived him as nothing less than 'the leader and promised saviour ... he was the prudent fortune teller',[71] for whom 'especially the Christians, [but also] the Lebanese in general were yearning'.[72]

'Hope' is another word that is widely used in the official iconographies that the LF and Phalangists have written on Bashir Gemayel.[73] This 'hope' later exalts him to a 'myth', nothing

---

[63]See Shawkat 'Ishtī, *ash-Shuyu'ayun wa-l-Kata'ib. Tajriba at-Tarbiyya al-Ḥizbiyya fi Lubnana* (Beirut: al-'Intishar al-'Arabī, 1997), pp. 449–472; Idem, 'al-'Aḥzab as-Siyasiyya', p. 66.

[64]Shanto Iyengar, *Is Anyone Responsible? How Television Frames Political Issues* (Chicago, IL: University of Chicago Press, 1991).

[65]Sarah El-Richani, 'The Lebanese Broadcasting System: A Battle between Political Parallelism, Commercialization and de facto Liberalism', in Tourya Guaybess, ed., *National Broadcasting and Policy in Arab Countries* (Basingstoke: Palgrave Macmillan, 2013), pp. 69–82.

[66]http://www.youtube.com/watch?v=uVEn5sNd-VU, rev. 17 December 2013.

[67]Selim Abou, *Bechir Gemayel ou l'Esprit d'un Peuple* (Paris: Éditions Anthropos, 1984), p. 24.

[68]Rafiq Ghanim, *Pierre Gemayel: Qa'id wa Mu'assasa* (Beirut: Ḥizb al-Kata'ib al-Lubnaniyya, 1987?), p. 10.

[69]Sarkis Na'mun, *Michel 'Aoun: Ḥulm am Wahm* (Beirut: al-Mu'allif, 1992). This title inspired Antoine Najm, the former LF intellectual, to write a publication of his own, bearing the name 'with a dream against the illusion': Antoine Najm: *Ma'a Ḥulm dhid al-Wahm*, Afaq Mashriqiyya No. 9, Reprint, no place given (Beirut or Fanar?: Afaq Mashriqiyya, 2009 [orig. 2000]).

[70]'Abi Samra and Shararah, *'Aqni'at-l-Mukhallis*, pp. 37–38.

[71]The word 'qār'i' means also reader or reciter (of a holy scripture).

[72]'Abi Samra and Shararah, *'Aqni'at-l-Mukhallis*, p. 39.

[73]See for example Abou, *Bechir Gemayel ou l'Esprit*, p. 14.

less than the 'spirit of a people', bringing with him the 'promise of change' as a 'torch of res-
urrection'.[74] Lebanon as a compromise, a 'boutique', a 'broker', some ambivalent 'bridge'
(between cultures),[75] a country without a clear-cut identity but with a consociational system
said to be a mere 'theatre',[76] is exemplarily contrasted by Bashir Gemayel. He stands for the
desire for 'a modern society', 'a Second Republic', no less than 'the state of the year 2000', a
'united nation, confident of its identity'[77]—in short, for the normativity of the modern nation
state against the deficiencies of the current one.

The leader is described as acting as a symbol of 'the people'. He thus invokes a democratic
normativity. He acts for them, but seems to be indissolubly bound to a common will that is,
to be sure, never questioned: 'popular will' finds its limitations in untouchable *topoi*. Although
that might sound undemocratic, it is not necessarily: modernity claims human agency, but
seemingly untouchable resources are necessitated or at least invoked.[78] Within these limitations the respective leader is the 'incarnation of the collective will' ('Aoun),[79] 'the symbol
of vitality for all audacity, pride, steadfastness, youth, and hope which is in these proud
mountains'[80] (Pierre Gemayel), representing 'the Christian street' and in 'perfect harmony'
with the party base[81] (Samir Geagea). They are all introduced as being *sha 'bī*, i.e. stemming
from the ordinary people whom they are intended to represent and whom they evoke as
the base of their politics.

The leader occupies an exceptionally large space in party historiographies, but he is never
discussed as a person. All his personal characteristics (of course only positive ones) are
explained and introduced to the reader in the context of exactly this political life and the
'projects' he stood for. Psychology is not offered. He is not charismatic as a specific person,
but in his official function, by what he stands for.

For example, Pierre Gemayel, the Phalanges' founder, is portrayed as a man who is entirely
devoted to the country. His favourite lessons at school were allegedly history and geography,
two subjects central to his organization's highly modernist[82] understanding of Lebanon as
an objective entity with its 'own character'. He developed a special interest in exceptional
'heroes' in Lebanese history, instilling in him 'love for the fatherland', 'vigour' and 'pride', and
resulting in a picture of them in his mind which he tried to emulate. In his free time, young
Pierre imitated these national heroes together with his friends.[83] Later on as a student, like
many of his contemporaries, he discovered his passion for sports. This is said to have not
just been a leisure activity but instead these exercises were to express 'his love for organizing

---

[74]All quotations in: Ibid., p. 46.

[75]Ibid., p. 49.

[76]Sa'id al-Laḥham, *Ḥizb-l-Kata 'ib al-Lubnaniyya, min Pierre al-Mu 'assis 'ila Pierre ash-Shahid,* Vol. 6: *Bashir Gemayel: min al-Quwwat al-Lubnaniyya ila Riyasat-l-Jumhūriyya wa 'Ightialihi* (Beirut: Dar al-'Ittiḥad ath-Thaqafi al-'Arabi, 2007), p. 121.

[77]See Abou, *Bechir Gemayel ou l'Esprit,* p. 49.

[78]Hans Vorländer, 'Demokratie und Transzendenz. Politische Ordnungen zwischen Autonomiebehauptung und Unverfügbarkeitspraktiken', in *Demokratie und Transzendenz. Die Begründung politischer Ordnungen* (Bielefeld: tran-script, 2013), pp. 11–37. Here transcendence means to refer to interpretations transgressing specific situations and providing for axiomatic invocations of a common good to enhance its validity; see Ibid., pp. 20–21.

[79]Jean-Paul Bourre, *Génération Aoun. Vivre libre au Liban* (Paris: Éditions Robert Laffont, 1990), p. 181.

[80]Ibid.

[81]*Mawsuw 'at-l-Quwwat al-Lubnaniyya: Min Bashir Gemayel 'ila Samir Geagea.* Vol. 5: *al-Ḥakim: as-Sira wa-l-Masira* (Beirut: Dar al-'Ittiḥad ath-Thaqafi al-'Arabi, 2008), pp. 27–28.

[82]See Zygmunt Baumann, *Intimations of Postmodernity* (London: Routledge, 1992), pp. 1–25.

[83]All in: Jean Charaf, *Tarikh Ḥizb-l-Kata 'ib al-Lubnaniyya,* Vol. 1: *1936–1940* (Beirut: Dar al-'Amal li-Nashr, no date given), p. 97.

and discipline'.[84] Furthermore, scouting as related to Gemayel's passion for sport is narrated as having 'activated [in him] the love for the cheerful life out in the open, the humble spirit towards the norms, the loyalty to the leaders, and the shared life in common camps'.[85] There is no doubt allowed for, and no ambiguity tarnishes the heroic steadfastness—all is 'fi khidma Lubnān', serving the Lebanon defined by the Phalanges as a nationalist party, which started out as a paramilitary organization.

Glimpses into private life are allowed only rarely. If they are, then not beyond the narrow margins of those private issues that do not risk washing dirty linen in public.[86] Thus, the leader is not discussed as an *individualist* person, but in a specific community of intellectuals in a place and century, among teachers and surrounded by those he influenced.[87] But despite all references to what and who influenced him, it seemed important to depict the leader as an *individual* person: he is emancipated and recognizable. Where genealogy is used, it is intentionally 'popularized', i.e. desperately separated from the family as such, but brought down to 'the cause' for which family *members* had stood. The family alone is not considered to be in line with the normativity of the democratic nation-state; thus, an often harsh break with 'feudalism' is included in the narrations. Furthermore, all my interviewees and all written biographical sketches root themselves in some temporal and societal surroundings, but all emphasized their active role in finding their own place in politics and society. Geagea's biography narrates him as a boy from the north determined to break with feudalism and to reduce it as much as possible.[88] Elie Karamé, Pierre Gemayel's long-time deputy, felt attracted by the will to counter 'everyone who was against Lebanon's independence', predominantly opposing any merging with the 'Arabic surrounding'. Only then did the 'social question', i.e. the Phalanges as a *sha'bi*-organization, step in. But despite having an older brother already in the party and his father having been befriended by Pierre Gemayel, he claimed confessional and family-related aspects had played only a marginal role in his decision to enter the party.[89] This goes even to a point where it sounds exaggerated: a young Phalangist functionary insisted that he decided alone to join in, not knowing his father served in the party's militia during the war.[90] This is unconvincing: a father who comes home from work in a uniform, probably even holding a weapon in hand, is most likely not a solicitor or a baker. But obviously that point was important to the narrator—he wanted to hammer the message

---

[84]Ibid., p. 98.

[85]Ibid.

[86]In addition, the LF chronicle offers us a minuscule glimpse into the likeable though harmless field of everyday banalities when dealing with Samir Geagea: we are told that he loves art, listens to classical music or traditional rural Lebanese songs (especially those from Naji Karam); literature preferred by him is characterized as being politically, socially, or philosophically oriented. We learn that he cherishes Lebanese food without being picky in this regard, and chocolate, particularly 'chocolate foam kisses' with 'Pepsi'; see *Mawsuw'at-l-Quwwat al-Lubnaniyya*, vol. 5, pp. 21, 35. This also fits into his 're-invention' after 1990 which aimed to erase his former role of militia leader. The martyr status of Bashir Gemayel would simply not allow for his status to be de-politicized at all: Abou only calls him, for example, 'a devil' during his childhood, a good-hearted but unruly pupil tearing down his father's posters in Achrafieh in anger at him; Abou, *Bechir Gemayel ou l'Esprit*, p. 37.

[87]Not untypical for *traditional* Arab biographies: Judith E. Tucker, 'Biography as History: The Exemplary Life of Khayr al-Din al-Ramli', in Mary Ann Fay, ed., *Auto/Biography and the Construction of Identity and Community in the Middle East* (New York: Palgrave, 2001), p. 11.

[88]Joseph Wadi'a ash-Shartuni, *'Innahu huwwa...Samir Geagea: min al-Wilada 'ila...-l-Wilada*, 3rd ed. (Beirut: Wide, 2008), pp. 87–91.

[89]Shawkat 'Ishti, 'al-Iltizam al-Hizbī wa Wadh'a al-Multabis: Hizb al-Kata'ib wa Hizb ash-Shuyu'aï', in Joseph Bahout and Chawqi Douayhi, eds., *La vie publique au Liban. Expresssions et recompositions du politique* (Beirut: CERMOC, 1997), p. 61.

[90]Interview in Beirut, 18 June 2012.

of 'individuality' home—and individualism is less about empirical evidence than normativity.[91]

Official party-narration on the leader indulges in the *res gestae* of what he has already done as a kind of application letter for future jobs to come: the LF alone published an *encyclopaedia* of 24 volumes, the Phalangists took for their pendant 25 volumes, the FPM contented itself with only 4.[92] Hardly anything is omitted. With an unsurpassable passion for administrative detail, for example, the LF portray their 'de facto state' which they controlled as a Christian militia during the official Lebanese state's breakdown in the civil war (1975–90) in these volumes as an eternal promise of the *ḥulm jumhūriyya*. In consequence, even the committee of the merchants of Achrafieh is of Bashir Gemayel's, their commander's, personal concern, since the chronicle tells us that this issue interested him most.[93] What seems to the Western observer a somewhat profane act is raised to a level of unexpected importance before the backdrop of a rather existential experience with politics in Lebanon. The leader as a symbol of the respective political identity is the personalized mask of a political project intending to bring about a state well above the dysfunctionalities of the current one.

This becomes very evident when the cause for one's own existence is explained. An important narrative for the LF is, to be part of the al-Kataʾib as an *idea*, but having broken away due to being more radical, more determined, constituting a generation with a 'reformist character'.[94] Amin Gemayel, having been elected president after his brother Bashir's death, represents for them a breaking point by allegedly being *only* a part of a family, not representing a 'real party'. The 'real party' was an expression I encountered quite often during fieldwork to describe the respective own party. By not embodying anything—or better: the wrong things—one cannot head a 'real party'. A former member of the militia considered Amin Gemayel 'much weaker' than his brother. Claiming a patriotic mission for 'his' LF, the fighter denounced him as 'a leading candidate in pro-Syrian Moslem eyes'.[95] This notion obviously denies the upcoming president a 'patriotic' stand of his own. Samir Geagea, the Forces' new strong-man, likewise accused the new president of standing for 'the concept of heredity' (fikra al-warātha)[96] and having reduced the Phalanges party and its armed men to a mere 'submissive' instrument, a 'burnt offering'.[97]

This narrative is even told where it is highly implausible: Elie Hobeika, who never succeeded in turning from a warlord into a successful party leader, used Amin Gemayel as one of his primary arguments to legitimate his own move towards Damascus and against his former comrades Samir Geagea and Karim Pakradouni at the LF's head. Ostensibly highly indignant, he claimed to have had found back in 1984 a letter from the other two members

---

[91]See Taylor, *Sources of the Self.*

[92]*Mawsuwʿat-l-Quwwat al-Lubnaniyya: Min Bashir Gemayel ʾila Samir Geagea*, 24 vols. (Beirut: Dar al-ʾIttihad ath-Thaqafi al-ʿArabī, 2008); Saʿid Lahham, *Mawsuwʿah Hizb-l-Kataʾib al-Lubnaniyyah: Min Pierre al-Muʾassis ʾila Pierre ash-Shahid*, 25 vols. (Beirut: Dar al-ʾIttihad ath-Thaqafi al-ʿArabī, 2007); *Mawsuwʿah Michel ʿAoun. al-Jiniral alladhi tasaʿa ʾilayhi ar-Riʾiasa*, 4 vols. (Beirut: Dar ar-Rafidain, 2007). Besides, there exist virtually hundreds of clips, booklets, leaflets, books, etc. especially among the Phalangists.

[93]*Mawsuwʿat-l-Quwwat al-Lubnaniyya: Min Bashir Gemayel ʾila Samir Geagea*, Vol. 2: *Bashir Gemayel: as-Sira wa-l-Masira* (Beirut: Dar al-ʾIttihad ath-Thaqafi al-ʿArabī, 2008), pp. 33–39.

[94]ash-Shartunī, *ʾInnahu huwwa*, pp. 134–167.

[95]Robert Hatem, 'From Israel to Damascus', PDF document, neither date nor place indicated, p. 33.

[96]*Mawsuwʿat-l-Quwwat al-Lubnaniyya*, vol. 5, p. 11.

[97]ash-Shartunī, *ʾInnahu huwwa*, p. 120.

of the triumvirate[98] that then still existed, to the president, in which the two stated readiness to agree to whatever the president wished for. Therefore, he argued: 'we did not start the Intifada on this basis [... just] to remain paper-Forces in Amin Gemayel's pocket.'[99] No matter whether this letter ever existed, wilful submission to the so-called 'feudalist' who is not living up to the normativity of the democratic modern nation-state does not seem to be a legitimating narrative in this context. It does not sustain a possibility of establishing a credible narrative to allow for a charismatic relationship.

Wandering in one's footsteps

The most important fact here seems to be that the man at the helm stands for something, or as an admirer wrote on a *Facebook* fan page:

> How many times can you hear Sheikh Bashir Gemayel and get enough of it? I witness[ed] in real life most of his speeches and still hear them as if it was yesterday. I lived the worst and the best of these times, and still can't get over it. His words were part of our soul, we were part of his force, and till today I will not hesitate to give it all. Tell me how many leaders in the past [have] gone and kept their ideology alive? Show me if those leaders make you cry and laugh at the same time. I only know one.... Thank you Lord for that beautiful gift you gave Lebanon.[100]

There are millions of posters of leaders and martyrs in the country, martyr shrines, mausoleums, video clips, speech collections, films, pictures in private households and portraits in shops. Recently, coming along with the global fashion of the tattoo, some young Eastern Beirutis even have a tattoo of Bashir Gemayel on their bodies. When I was travelling by bus to Jounieh, the (Christian) bus driver set his vehicle's aging, creaking radio to full volume to entertain his passengers with fervid 'Bashir speeches'. Many of my interlocutors had photos of their respective party leaders at home. And as Rivoal[101] has observed for the Druzes in Australia, they were quite often positioned in a very private and intimate way: between or next to the family photos, on the desk, in the living room, etc. Even the Gemayel family, quite strongly entering the more traditional realm of rendering charisma something inherited, were always described as having—as a collective—'given' much to Lebanon and for 'our cause'.

The—in a Weberian sense—extraordinary qualities of the charismatic are occasionally ascribed to a divine blessing, but they are also seamlessly connected to a very real, mundane, immanent vision of a certain political order which is thought to serve one's own community most: 'Your martyrdom terminated our hope of a Lebanon we dreamt of. May God protect us, we follow you. We are loyal to the free Lebanon, sovereign and independent, over an area of 10,452 km².'[102] Well-known slogans of Phalangists and Forces alike are: 'And the journey continues' (wa-l-masīra mustamirra), 'Bashir lives in us' (Bashīr hayy fīnā), 'I want you, oh Sheikh' (biddī yāk ya Sheikh). His adherents write about him: 'Give us strength', 'Bashir hasn't died, help us', because his charisma is 'God's gift to Lebanon', the ideology is said to still be

---

[98]Established after the coup against Amin Gemayel in 1985 at the LF's top. It consisted of Samir Geagea, Elie Hobeika, and Karim Pakradouni. It held no longer than a few months.

[99]Ghassan Charbel, 'Ayna kunta fi-l-Ḥarb?I 'atirafat Jiniralat as-Sira 'at-l-Lubnaniyya (Beirut: Riyad ar-Rayyis, 2011), p. 56.

[100]http://www.facebook.com/video/video.php?v=456035260497, rev. 24 March 2014.

[101]Isabelle Rivoal, 'Intimité, mise en scène et distance dans la relation politique au Liban', in Franck Mermier and Sabrina Mervin, eds., *Leaders et partisans au Liban* (Paris/Beirut: Karthala/Ifpo, 2012), pp. 137–163.

[102]http://www.facebook.com/video/video.php?v=456035260497, rev. 7 March 2013 (My translation).

alive, the heritage lives on, etc., etc.[103] At party rallies, members vow to the slain to 'wander in your footsteps' ('ā daʿasātak nakhna mshinā), and there is also a well-known song among followers that has the very same title.[104] Best-of compilations of his speeches are played via videos or DVDs to these assemblies, as if he himself were still speaking to the auditorium. One Internet user commented on Bashir Gemayel's death:

> Bashir Gemayel, we love and miss you! God saw there was more use for your skill and charisma in heaven! May he bless you! The Kataʾib and LF live on in strength in your honour. Your vision of a free and independent Lebanon is just around the corner.[105]

An LF publication puts it similarly:

> Bashir Gemayel suffered martyrdom, resurrection had begun: Every Lebanese became—in his principles, his ideas, his hopes—a second Bashir.[106]

Even during the Phalanges' most authoritarian phase, between 1936 and at least 1956, when the Supreme Leader Pierre Gemayel could appoint functionaries at will, although since 1942 only after consultation, he was the symbolization of the party and its 'ideals'.[107] Although he could be rightfully described as ruling the organization in an absolutist manner,[108] he was claimed to have been chosen by its members as their symbol,[109] to whom they are connected 'by the bonds of the heart, the mind, and the thought',[110] by 'fraternal affection',[111] since he was

> guardian of our embodied faith, [as] realized by unity ..., He will maintain, as he had [before] that courageously maintained, our ideal of purity, our loyalty in his simplicity, our force in his cohesion. He will be the first one responsible in facing our enemies and our friends .... To him the honours: [he] is our flag.[112]

Invocation also functions as an appropriation, resulting in a virtual competition regarding who might be the 'better Bashir' today. Some adherents of the FPM discuss this,[113] as the following quotation indicates:

> If Bashir was still alive he would be of ʿAoun's stance now... Lebanon changes by the day... we should all as Lebanese Muslims and Christians live together and build our country STRONG for 100 years from now as Bashir said... Bashir was never against the Palestinian cause he was against the PLO using and controlling our country, setting up road blocks, being armed in the streets etc.... ʿAoun wants a UNIFIED STRONG Lebanon while Geagea wants to destroy the country just to destroy the Shias.[114]

By evoking the leader's heritage in those invoking him, two seemingly opposed mechanisms are employed: he is included in all those 'wandering in his footsteps' and imitated from a distance. By doing so, both extraordinary qualities legitimating for holding power and the

---

[103]All from: Ibid.

[104]One of the many videos can be found at: http://www.youtube.com/watch?v=BRjHLrnzlnw, rev. 4 December 2013. All bigger Lebanese parties, especially those that participated in the war, have their own music compilations.

[105]http://www.youtube.com/watch?v=Jp0_NJaLhb4, rev. 20 December 2012.

[106]Quoted in Abou, *Bechir Gemayel ou l'Esprit*, p. 44.

[107]*Au Service au Liban. Connaissance des Kataeb. Leur Doctrine et leur Politique Nationales dans les Déclarations, Messages, articles et Lettres Officielles, depuis 1936*, ed. Pierre Gemayel (Beirut?: Les Phalanges Libanaises, 1948), p. 54.

[108]John P. Entelis, *Pluralism and Party Transformation in Lebanon. Al-Kataʾib, 1936–1970* (Leiden: E. J. Brill, 1974), pp. 86f.

[109]*Connaissance des Kataeb*, p. 54.

[110]Ibid., p. 131.

[111]Ibid., p. 54.

[112]Ibid., p. 57. The original text was a pledge for an early-years paramilitary manifestation.

[113]Whereas others do not appreciate the Bashir cult at all—the FPM are rather amalgamated.

[114]Comment below an FPM video on YouTube—capitals as in the original text, see http://www.youtube.com/watch?v=C_66H-ZlI3Cg, rev. 17 December 2013.

community are exemplified. Thus, on a symbolic level, a solution is offered for both the problems of 'democratic politics' as an intended 'dialogue' and building a nation according to the respective personal conceptions, by giving the community-to-be a symbolic representation through imitation performed by an individual. In doing so democratic characteristics based on an informal, charismatic, reciprocal relationship are implied.

Some limitations of contractility

So, what are the main limitations of this charismatic relationship and its contractility? A 'kitschy' effect can be seen as a central aspect of charisma as such: the personification of politics as a means to overcome and reduce complex, abstract structures of modern societies in favour of a personification that is easier to be understood.[115] Thus, charisma might lead to the elimination of contingency.[116] This is especially done by evoking notions of intimacy, such as Bashir Gemayel being an older brother to every member of the Phalangists' youth organization[117] instead of being chairman, the latter constituting an officially accountable position based on regulations. All those I met who had already left their parties indicated that the leadership in question tended to over-personalize politics. 'Over-personalization', therefore, seems to describe the highly subjective feeling of a misplaced personalism, i.e. where symbolization did not work out as expected. In parts of the *panegyrici* already mentioned, those portrayed seem to be celebrated a little too much and a little too often. This is a critical point, since it has a lot to do with *personal* judgment, for which no objective criteria could be offered.

This might, for example, be felt when expectations are not met any longer. Antoine Najm left the LF since he could not convince their chairman Samir Geagea to understand his call for decentralization also as a broader societal concept to restrict power by invoking natural law—which would have also meant to restrict Geagea inside his party.[118] Interestingly, Samir Geagea himself claimed his generation did not appreciate any longer the paramilitary antics inside the Phalanges when Pierre Gemayel ended discussions at times by indicating that it was him who founded the party and everyone would be free to leave if he did not agree with how he actually handled things.[119] And former FPM members felt alienated by 'Aoun's frequent refusal to enter meaningful discussions.[120] One FPM functionary put it like this:

> Unfortunately, General 'Aoun has a style of leadership that takes a bit from [...] the military. He is rather communicative; it is easy to communicate with him, to exchange standpoints with him, to exchange ideas. But unfortunately there are no institutions of the party who prepare the decision-making. [...] Actually it is here in the hands of General 'Aoun! He has his advisors, he has specialized cadres for proposing dossiers [...] but the final decision is in the hands of the general, it comes out of the general's office.[121]

---

[115]Werner Telesko, *Erlösermythen in Kunst und Politik. Zwischen christlicher Tradition und Moderne* (Vienna: Böhlau, 2004), p. 164.

[116]Christoph Schneider, 'Charisma: Sinnproduktion durch Reflexionsanästhesie', in Pavlína Rychterová, Stefan Seit, and Raphaela Veit, eds., *Das Charisma. Funktionen und symbolische Repräsentationen* (Berlin: Akademie-Verlag, 2008), pp. 129–153.

[117]*Mawsuw'at-l-Quwwat al-Lubnaniyya*, vol. 2, pp. 48–49.

[118]Interview with A. Najm, 20 July 2012 in Fanar.

[119]ash-Shartuni, *'Innahu huwwa*, pp. 118–119.

[120]Interview with a former functionary in Jbayl, 24 September 2012; 'Abi Samra and Sharara, *'Aqni'at-l-Mukhallis*, pp. 154, 160–171. Even well-intentioned functionaries lauded the general's ability to listen to advisors—adding with a grinning smile—and to decide finally all alone.

[121]Interview with a FPM functionary, 16 November 2012.

Thus, in all these cases the lack of more institutionalized channels of reciprocity failed to uphold the party discourses' very own premises of democratic *sha'bī*-representation.

But there are cases when there is certainly more at stake than personal taste. For example, a former LF soldier commented in the TV documentary 'Massacre' that an ice-cold wind blew into his face as soon as Bashir Gemayel entered the room.[122] The same applies to the depiction of Bashir Gemayel on a poster almost melting together the figures of him and Jesus Christ in a way that is reminiscent of a watermark.

The social contract in a formal, liberal version is bound to the immanence. This kind of sacralization related to the notion of martyrdom eliminates mechanisms of pluralist political styles. Whereas martyrdom in general in the Middle East means to have sacrificed oneself for a higher cause—this is also true for a non-believing background like that of the Communist Party—here it is to be understood religiously, although the political martyr is no outright saint. Through his martyrdom we see that the killed one was an advocate of truth. But martyrdom means to comply with the sacred; it does not establish a reciprocal relationship, *caused* by its reciprocity.[123] The cult of Bashir Gemayel fits into this category. He is praised as being a 'beautiful gift for Lebanon', as 'the best man that ever lived', as 'Lebanon's Messiah', 'Our head's crown', 'King of Lebanon', as 'Hero'[124] and 'Body and Soul of the Fatherland'.[125]

More mundanely, Samir Geagea comparing his LF to the 'majestic cedars of Lebanon' rooting there since 'biblical times'[126] or Michel 'Aoun simply claiming to 'be' the 'legitimate state'[127] is misleading. All these notions take their particularity to be unquestioned for the whole of Lebanon—a fact hardly supported by the respective political opponents. But settling into the limitedness of being 'only' particular, being reduced to no more than a particular party, is quite often a problem of the parties in question, at times greatly hampering their role as parties in society.[128] This difficulty is most bluntly expressed in Samir Geagea's categorical wartime verdict that 'the doubting of the LF's positions is a doubting of the whole society [of Lebanon and] of its people, its history, its Lord ...'[129]

The same difficulty would be true for one last point, which is hard to miss in Lebanon: sectarianism. All parties' narratives cannot help but reach out mostly to a specific group, only occasionally transgressing religious lines. This should not be that much of a problem—European parties experience the very same problem too, and I simply cannot see why

---

[122] Monika Borgmann, Lokman Slim, and Hermann Theissen, *Massaker* [Massacre]. TV documentary, Umam Productions, WDR, SF/DRS, 2004.

[123] In contrast to other authors writing on martyrdom, I do not draw a distinct line between the political and religious martyr. Voegelin observed in a seminal work that political orders are indeed drawing heavily on religious narratives until they turn themselves into an original sacred substance bringing about an inner-worldly salvation (utopianism). But that should not seduce us into overlooking that most 'political' martyrs are embedded in a religious reading that is not completely mundane but perceives them as taking *part* in the transcendent sacred. The same would hold true for most concepts of political martyrdom, cf. Eric Voegelin, 'The Political Religions', in Manfred Henningsen, ed., *Modernity Without Restraint: The Collected Works of Eric Voegelin*, Vol. 5 (Columbia, MO: Missouri University Press, 2000 [orig. 1951]), pp. 19–73.

[124] All comments posted on a single Facebook page under a video of Bashir Gemayel: http://www.facebook.com/video/video.php?v=456035260497, rev. 7 March 2013.

[125] Abou, *Bechir Gemayel ou l'Esprit*, p. 45.

[126] http://www.samirgeagea.com/articlesamirgeageatheleader.htm, rev. 5 April 2013.

[127] Abi Samra and Sharara, *'Aqni'at-l-Mukhallis*, p. 41.

[128] See especially al-Khazin, *al-'Aḥzab as-Siyasiyya*; Hazim Saghieh, *Ta'arib al-Kata'ib al-Lubnaniyya. al-Ḥizb, as-Sulta, al-Khauf* (Beirut: Dar al-Jadid, 1991).

[129] *Mawsuw'at-l-Quwwat al-Lubnaniyya: Min Bashir Gemayel 'ila Samir Geagea*, Vol. 17: *ad-Duktur Samir Geagea: Mawaqif wa Tasriḥat – 3* (Beirut: Dar al-'Ittiḥad ath-Thaqafi al-'Arabī, 2008), p. 31.

representing Catholics should be less democratic or less restricted than representing workers. Most importantly, no Lebanese political party currently portrays itself as being not Lebanese at all: even those that employ sectarian narratives most widely, the Hezbollah, the LF, or the Muslim Brothers, only formulate, to borrow from Fanar Haddad,[130] different versions of being Lebanese. This characterizes a society that is much better grasped by the notion of pillarization than by sectarianism that provides only a filter for social knowledge. The problem is rather not acknowledging that the respectively formulated common good is only a particular one, and does not exist objectively outside of a legitimate discussion.

Thus, Lebanese political parties surely are dysfunctional: not because they are 'undemocratic', 'meaningless', or 'instruments', but simply because they come out of a highly polarized society whose pillarization they truly reflect.

Disclosure statement

No potential conflict of interest was reported by the author.

---

[130]Fanar Haddad, *Sectarianism in Iraq: Antagonistic Visions of Unity* (London: Hurst & Co., 2011).

5   The party, the *Gama'a* and the *Tanzim*

The organizational dynamics of the Egyptian Muslim Brotherhood's post-2011 failure

Marie Vannetzel

ABSTRACT

In April 2011, the Egyptian Muslim Brothers (MB) founded the first political party in their 83-year-long history, known as the Freedom and Justice Party (FJP). Yet the party remained under the control of its parent organization—the *Gama'a* (literally the 'community')—and its internal apparatus, the *Tanzim*. While both had been shaped during decades of MB's semi-clandestine existence as a banned-yet-tolerated group, these did not adapt to the changing socio-political configuration and have resisted the transition to fully overt activity. Through an analysis of the FJP's uneasy creation and with a grounding of extensive empirical research, this article argues that the party's development was to a certain extent hampered by those pre-existing organizational structures. Organizational crystallization prevented the party from conforming to the emerging rules of the political field then under construction. Instead, the *Gama'a*'s undefined nature and opaque pattern of regulation were replicated within the FJP's structure. Thus, the article seeks to uncover a hitherto hidden aspect of in the MB's post-2011 failure, one which is rooted in organizational dynamics.

Introduction: the Muslim Brothers and the new party politics in post-2011 Egypt

The 2011 Arab Spring has given rise to an unprecedented flourishing of political parties in the region. In Egypt, the January 25th Revolution opened the way for the creation of more than 80 new parties. This spectacular development was spurred by the removal of Law 40 of 1977, which formerly enabled the Mubarak regime to exert strict control over political parties. Under this law, a committee, including the Ministers of Justice and of Interior, had the power to allow or refuse the registration of new parties, freeze existing ones, order their dissolution or close their newspapers. Emergency laws, in existence since 1981, also prevented any public gathering without authorization delivered by the Ministry of Interior, which confined parties to their headquarters and deprived them of social anchorage amongst the people.[1]

---

[1]Sarah Ben Néfissa, 'Les partis politiques égyptiens entre les contraintes du système politique et le renouvellement des élites', *Revue des Mondes Musulmans et de la Méditerranée*, 81(1) (1996), pp. 55–91.

On 28 March 2011, a new Law on Political Parties was introduced by the Supreme Council of Armed Forces, which ensured the transition after Mubarak's ousting. It abolished several restrictions and put the committee under the supervision of solely judges, thereby easing the registration of new parties. The lifting of repressive measures was supposed to favour parties' development in public life and to make the recruitment of members easier. However, organizational structure and social penetration still are crucially lacking within most of these nascent parties. Many of them remain largely unknown to citizens even now. Some have split, others have disappeared, and still others were replaced by new parties.[2] Out of the 67 parties which participated in the 2011 legislative elections, only 10 won more than 1% of seats in Parliament. In 2015, this was the case for 9 out of 44 parties running for office.

Strikingly enough, the party that succeeded in taking more than 43% of the seats in 2011 had disappeared from the Egyptian political landscape by 2015: the Freedom and Justice Party (FJP). Linked to the Muslim Brotherhood (MB), it was indeed forbidden and eradicated as a result of the violent repression which the MB endured from July 2013 onwards. The FJP had won the 2011 legislative elections, and its candidate, Mohamed Morsi, had been elected President of the Republic in June 2012. However, Parliament was dissolved just a few months after its formation, and Morsi was ousted by a joint popular uprising and military coup a year later. Since then, the MB and any affiliated group or structure have been repressed and decried as public enemies under the new military regime led by Field Marshall 'Abd al-Fattah al-Sisi.

While this specific and tragic destiny undoubtedly accounts for the disappearance of the party, I argue that before the repression occurred, the FJP was also faced with, and weakened by, significant internal difficulties. These constraints did not cause the party's disappearance, but rather explain its failure to develop in spite of the fact that it enjoyed several major advantages compared to other nascent parties. Contrary to most of the latter,[3] the FJP did not lack resources when it was created in April 2011. It was the first party to register under the new law, and had no challenge in gathering the required number of members, most of whom came from the MB's own ranks, according to the party's leaders.[4] Backed up by the Organization of the Muslim Brothers—which is called the *Gama'a*, i.e. 'the community'—the FJP benefited from the strong material, organizational and social resources that the *Gama'a* had accumulated during its 83-year-long existence.

First founded by Hasan al-Banna in 1928 as an Islamic charity association, the *Gama'a* swiftly expanded into a mass socio-political movement.[5] When the Free Officers and Nasser took power in 1952, the *Gama'a* was briefly spared the dissolution order which was meted

---

[2]Samer Soliman, 'Les nouvelles forces « civiles » égyptiennes face au défi électoral', *Confluences Méditerranée*, 82(3) (2012), pp. 161–169; Virginie Collombier, 'Politics without Parties. Political Change and Democracy Building in Egypt before and after the Revolution', *EUI Working Paper*, MWP, 2013/35.

[3]With the notable exception of the Salafist Nur Party linked to the association of the *Da'wa Salafiyya*, which won about 23% of seats in the 2011 Parliament, then 2% in 2015.

[4]The party announced as soon as 21 May that it had gathered 8821 founding members across Egypt's 27 governorates. Accordingly, 75% of them were MB members. See the Brothers' English website: http://www.ikhwanweb.com/article.php?id=28609; http://www.ikhwanweb.com/article.php?id=28808.

[5]Richard P. Mitchell, *The Society of the Muslim Brothers* (New York: Oxford University Press, 1969); Muhammad Shawqi Zaki, *al-Ikhwan al-muslimin wal-mujtama' al-misri* [The Muslim Brothers and Egyptian Society], 2nd ed. (Cairo: Maktabat al-Wahba, 1980); Brynjar Lia, *The Society of the Muslim Brothers in Egypt. The Rise of an Islamic Mass Movement, 1928–1942* (Reading, UK: Ithaca Press, 1998).

out to all political parties and associations. In 1954, a failed attempt to kill Nasser was attributed to the MB, and a harsh repression was enacted against it. Throughout the eras of Anwar Sadat (1970–1980) and Hosni Mubarak (1981–2011), the level of repression decreased and the *Gama'a* gradually rebuilt itself, but was never again granted legal status. It was said to be 'a forbidden yet tolerated' organization.[6] Officially excluded from the political field, the *Gama'a* had nonetheless managed to unofficially participate in legislative elections since the 1980s, running candidates on other political parties' lists or as independents. It scored up to 88 seats in the 2005 elections.[7] Therefore, the initial success of the FJP in the 2011 legislative elections built upon great resources, knowledge and know-how, which explained its superiority over other competitors.

However, I contend that, paradoxically, the FJP's development was to a certain extent hampered by those pre-existing resources and organizational structures. The creation of a political party proved difficult for the Egyptian Muslim Brothers, who had never before fully engaged in such a process.

This article will first build on a comparative analytical framework of party creation in a regime change context, distinguishing between the phase of 'primogenesis' and the phase of 'conforming process'.[8] It will clarify what makes the Egyptian Muslim Brothers' FJP a specific case: rather than ideology or repression, organizational specificities will be underlined. Second, I will show how the FJP's primogenesis was shaped by previous 'organizational crystallization'. Lastly, we will explore how this specific organizational dynamic undermined the 'conforming process' of the FJP and thwarted the transition from the *Gama'a*'s informal status of semi-clandestine organization to a fully overt political party. This failed transition seriously damaged both the *Gama'a* and the FJP's legitimacies, as both were unable to adapt to the changing socio-political configuration. Thus, the article demonstrates that the exploration of the FJP's uneasy creation enables us to disclose a hitherto hidden aspect of the MB's post-2011 failure, one which is rooted in organizational dynamics. It concludes more broadly that 'regime change' can have an unexpected negative impact on the modus operandi of political parties.

The article is based on a long-term qualitative study of the Egyptian Muslim Brothers' organizational pattern and mobilization practices between 2005 and 2010. I have conducted numerous interviews with MB leaders, members of parliament and activists, as well as with citizens and voters located in three suburbs of Greater Cairo. Additional fieldwork continued after 2011 among those networks and dissidents who broke from the *Gama'a*. These different insights build a comprehensive analysis of the MB's failed transition to a new pattern of organization and mobilization.

---

[6]Carrie R. Wickham, *Mobilizing Islam: Religion, Activism, and Political Change in Egypt* (New York: Columbia University Press, 2003); Hesham al-Awadi, *In Pursuit of Legitimacy: The Muslim Brothers and Mubarak, 1982-2000* (London: I.B. Tauris & Company, 2005).

[7]Huda Raghib 'Awad and Hasanayn Tawfiq, *al-Ikhwan al-muslimun wal-siyasa fi Misr (1984–1990)* [The Muslim Brothers and Politics in Egypt, 1984–1990] (Cairo: al-Mahrusa, 1996); Marie Vannetzel, *Les Frères musulmans égyptiens. Enquête sur un secret public* (Paris: Karthala, 2016).

[8]This framework is borrowed from: Myriam Aït-Aoudia and Alexandre Dézé, 'The Genesis of Political Parties. An Analysis of the Front National, the Movimento Sociale Italiano and the Islamic Salvation Front', *Revue française de science politique*, 61(4) (2011), pp. 631–657, English version online: www.cairn.info/revue-francaise-de-science-politique-2011-4-page-631.htm (accessed 26 January 2017).

The challenge of party creation

A comparative analytical framework: regime change and party creation

Studies of Middle Eastern politics have often put forward the shortcomings of party dynamics in authoritarian contexts. They have stressed inhibiting factors such as the 'colonial legacy',[9] the 'ruling hegemonic parties',[10] the 'divided structures of contestation',[11] the co-optation of opposition parties as 'support to authoritarianism',[12] the clientelistic pattern of politics[13] or the impact of electoral engineering.[14] While such studies insist that repression alone could not account for the weakness of party systems in those societies, they emphasize the various direct and indirect constraints that prevented the development of parties as proper channels of action and mobilization. However, the Arab Spring raised a new issue, which has barely been dealt with so far: Is the removal of these constraints enough to strengthen party politics? Regime change does not actually have self-evident results on the institutionalization of parties as major organizations of political life. Parties are confronted by the necessary reconversion of their practices and routines in order to fit with the emerging rules of the new political field and therefore be legitimate actors of the field.

This issue is all the more critical for those groups which previously were not political parties and which went on to create parties. The genesis of a new political party is rendered difficult by the necessity to reshape the group in such a way as to make it fit with the emerging rules of legitimacy in the political field under development. French political sociologists Myriam Aït-Aoudia and Alexandre Dézé have designed a comparative framework that posits that there is nothing deterministic in the creation of a party. Their framework distinguishes between two phases: (a) the 'primogenesis' of the pre-partisan group, on the one hand; and (b) the 'conforming process' to the 'party shape' that is legitimate in the given context, on the other hand.[15] The 'primogenesis' phase (a) depends on three factors: (i) the mobilization of the founders' previous networks and resources developed in various social worlds; (ii) the perception of a favourable context to engage into the political field; (iii) the 'dynamics of competition within "pre-party" circles and the outcome of the struggles on the definition of the [new] organization'.[16] In the second phase (b), the nascent party strives to 'make itself conform': 'in order to make themselves known and collectively recognised as a party, the actors must first and foremost build a conventional façade.' Aspects of this shaping process include (i) technologies of branding such as the name, the logo, the platform and the 'party narrative'; (ii) technologies of structural creation (design of the chart, creation of local offices etc.); and (iii) selection of socio-political profiles chosen to stand as forefront leaders of the party.

---

[9]Michele Penner Angrist, *Party Building in the Modern Middle East* (Seattle: University of Washington Press, 2006).

[10]Joseph Sassoon, *Anatomy of Authoritarianism in the Arab Republics* (Cambridge: Cambridge University Press, 2016).

[11]Ellen Lust-Okar, *Structuring Conflict in the Arab World: Incumbents, Opponents and Institutions* (Cambridge: Cambridge University Press, 2005).

[12]William Zartman, 'Opposition as Support of the State', in Adeed Dawisha and William Zartman, eds., *Beyond Coercion. The Durability of the Arab State* (London: Croom Helm, 1988), pp. 61–87; Holger Albrecht, 'How Can Opposition Support Authoritarianism? Lessons from Egypt', *Democratization*, 12(3) (2005), pp. 378–397.

[13]Maye Kassem, *Egyptian Politics. The Dynamics of Authoritarian Rule* (Boulder, CO: Lynne Rienner, 2004).

[14]Marta Posusney, 'Multi-party Elections in the Arab World: Institutional Engineering and Oppositional Strategies', *Studies in Comparative International Development*, 36(4) (2002), pp. 34–62; Kevin Koehler, 'Authoritarian Elections in Egypt: Formal Institutions and Informal Mechanisms of Rule', *Democratization*, 15(5) (2008), pp. 974–990.

[15]Aït-Aoudia and Dézé, 'The Genesis of Political Parties'.

[16]Ibid., p. 24.

This framework proves particularly useful to shed light on the specificities of the creation of the FJP to the extent that we can adjust it to the Egyptian context. Here, it is necessary to clarify, therefore, the usage of the concepts of 'field', 'world' and 'party' in this context. I build on sociologist Bernard Lahire's analysis of Bourdieu's 'theory of fields' and Becker's 'theory of social worlds'.[17] For Lahire, the differentiation of activities, in complex societies, generates a multiplicity of 'social worlds', only a few of which can be called a 'field'. A field is centrally organized around a struggle for a specific kind of power, involving a limited number of actors and abiding by specific rules. However, some fields are more autonomous than others, either because they are more specialized (specific rules, professionalized actors) or because they are more independent from other power struggles. Lahire calls 'secondary fields' lesser-specialized or dependent fields. In 2000s Egypt, the political field could be considered a 'secondary field' in so far as it was a space of power struggle with limited access and specific rules, but it was also highly dependent on top-ranking rulers' interests, and deeply entrenched in other 'social worlds'. Being a Member of Parliament, for example, required one to be embedded into local communities and thus able to do social services and to circulate resources. Actors engaged in the political field therefore had to comply to non-specific social rules as well. Political parties were, at once, highly dependent and co-opted, barely specialized and very localized groups, unable to cover the whole territory. In the post-2011 context, the limits of the political field, its rules, as well as the nature of its actors, were challenged.

It is within this context of redefinition of the political field that the MB, which formerly participated in this field without any status before the revolution, engaged in party creation. Drawing on the theoretical framework outlined, the following section analyses what makes the FJP's creation specific: namely, it was shaped by prior 'organizational crystallization' adapted to the previous position of the *Gama'a* as a 'forbidden yet tolerated' organization.

Searching for FJP's organizational specificities

Several studies have already underlined the wide diversity that can be found concerning Islamist parties, mostly due to the variety of the authoritarian contexts in which they developed.[18] As shown by the examples of the Jordanian Islamic Action Front, the Yemeni Islah Party, the Algerian Islamic Salvation Front (FIS), the Moroccan Justice and Development Party or the Tunisian Ennahda Party, a common ideological matrix—the Muslim Brothers' political conception of Islam as an encompassing rule meant to regulate every aspect of human and social life—offered contrasting experiences of party creation. But a thorough examination of the genesis process enables us to isolate the weight of the historical organizational trajectory from ideological justifications. It exposes how a similar ideology might cover different patterns of action, and refutes the widespread mono-causal explanation of Islamist parties' failures that states that ideology would prevail in the way these parties organize and would make them unable to properly adapt to political and social contexts.[19]

[17]Bernard Lahire, *Monde pluriel. Penser l'unité des sciences sociales* (Paris: Seuil, 2012).

[18]François Burgat, *Face to Face with Political Islam* (London: I.B. Tauris, 2003); Sameh Shehata, ed., *Islamist Politics in the Middle East: Movements and Change* (Abingdon: Routledge, 2012); Carrie R. Wikham, *The Muslim Brotherhood. Evolution of an Islamist Movement* (Princeton, NJ: Princeton University Press, 2013).

[19]Olivier Roy, *The Failure of Political Islam* (Cambridge, MA: Harvard University Press, 1994).

Table 1. Two cases of party creation: the Egyptian Freedom and Justice Party and the Algerian Islamic Salvation Front.

Phase	Components	Algerian FIS	Egyptian FJP
(a) Primogenesis	(i) Networks	Non-structured but overlapping social and religious networks of *da'wa*	Organizational crystallization
	(ii) Favourable context	October 1988 riots and transition to multi-party system	January 2011 uprising, fall of Mubarak, change of party and electoral legislation
	(iii) Internal competition	Intense competition, need to differentiate itself	Competition not taken seriouslyOverestimation of dominant position
(b) Conforming process	(i) Branding	Standardization process (imitating FLN)	Previous brand, Blurred identity with the *Gama'a*
	(ii) Structuration	Important efforts in territorial construction	Relied on pre-existing *tanzim* branches
	(iii) Leaders' profiles	MIA leaders put in background, selection of skilful agents, experience drawn from FLN	Under the control of *tanzim*, No specialization of skills

Note: FLN, National Liberation Front; MIA, Armed Islamic Movement.

Aït-Aoudia's study provides a detailed account of the Algerian FIS's genesis. Here, I do not aim to draw a full comparison between the two parties, but, rather, use the FIS as a counterpoint in order to enhance internal, organizational variables and help to identify the FJP's specificities. Table 1 assesses these contrasts, in line with the variables put forward by the party creation framework.

As Aït-Aoudia demonstrates, the primogenesis of the FIS was not 'an extension of a structured group' but was rather based on several movements and networks involved in proselytizing activities (*da'wa*).[20] Within the context of the opening of the political field, the creation of the Algerian FIS in February 1989 was motivated by concern regarding the internal competition in the field of Islamist activism, with the concomitant creation of other organizations by key protagonists. The form 'party' was chosen by FIS leaders so as to differentiate themselves from these competing projects and 'to move from a plurality of [*da'wa*] voices to a political structure'. FIS founders were eager to quickly shape and brand the new group as a formal political party and set up structures in all towns across the country. Nevertheless, the previous networks of *da'wa* were not enough to cover the whole territory, and the FIS had to invest greatly in territorial construction. To that end, they engaged in a kind of 'mimetism' vis-à-vis the FLN, imitating strategies of organization and appointing leaders who had previous experience in the party. Conversely, the members of the MIA—a prior armed group whose members played an important role in the FIS' creation—were not included on the official list of the party's founders in order to keep the party away from accusations of terrorism. Branding, structuring and selection of specialized profiles thus received much attention in the case of the Algerian FIS.

On the contrary, in Egypt the MB leaders neglected many of these aspects in shaping the FJP. The party was directly derived from a highly structured parent organization, the *Gama'a*. The FJP's primogenesis was therefore characterized by what I call a process of *organizational*

---

[20] Aït-Aoudia and Dézé, 'The Genesis of Political Parties', §9; see also, Myriam Aït-Aoudia, 'La naissance du Front islamique du salut: une politisation conflictuelle 1988–1989', *Critique internationale*, 30 (2006), pp. 129–144.

crystallization. It was created by a group that already had its own 'brand', electoral experience, territorial and hierarchical apparatus and its own leaders—in short, a group which did not need a party to exist. This organizational crystallization induced the MB leadership to neglect the conforming process of the new party, which had disrupting effects on the group's legitimacy.

The FJP's primogenesis: the weight of organizational crystallization

Previous networks: the strength of Tanzim

Surely, the *Gama'a*'s process of organizational crystallization had been a non-linear and conflict-ridden one. Between 1928 and 1948, the group emerged as a legally registered association, though it far exceeded the defined scope for charity action. After Nasser's repression and the disbandment caused by it, a new organization was illegally re-organized from the 1970s onwards, building on the connection between old MB leaders released from prison, returned religious preachers and businessmen who had been exiled in the Gulf, Islamic student movements and white-collar middle-class constituencies. Several generations and social groups were slowly aggregated into a structured organization, which managed to expand and crystallize around a clandestine apparatus headed by a Supreme Guide and composed of thousands of local cells, neighbourhood sections, regional units and national decisional organs.[21]

This apparatus was internally called the '*tanzim*' and considered by many members as the main strength of their group. As one of them, a 50-year-old school teacher in a working-class area of Cairo, who headed a small local-level unit in the apparatus, once told me in 2009:

> There is a very important point, which is that nobody, neither the regime nor international powers, can deny the Muslim Brothers' presence. They are concretely present on the grounds. There is an effective *tanzim*. You cannot deny this, you cannot say 'there is no sun'.

Comparing the *Gama'a* to political parties, he then added: 'I mean that, take any organisation, if you go on the grounds and look for it, you might not find it, whereas us, we are rooted into the fabric of society, this is tangible.' Members thus perceived the *tanzim* as the main guarantee of their social existence, compensating for the lack of legal existence. They also valued it as the proper frame to ensure the group's cohesion as well as members' commitment under conditions of semi-clandestinity:

> Muslim Brothers cannot communicate much about the *tanzim*. For security reasons, I even don't know everything about it, I don't know the details of the hierarchy. And this is also because it does not matter much to us, being at a leading position or not. I am in charge of a function, but tomorrow I can be asked to drop it and be in charge of something else. It's not like in political parties, we are not like them, we are committed (*multazimin*) to a shared idea. It does not matter who is the president, as in parties, he is not the one who is above and takes the decision. We commit ourselves to the principle of *shura* (consultation), we agree on who fit for which role, but nobody is above nobody. I have to play my role because I am committed to *shura*, but I am not *sahib al-qarar* (the chief).[22]

---

[21]The smallest *tanzim* unit is called a *usra* (i.e. 'family', 5–6 members); 10 *usar* form a *shu'ba* (i.e. 'section', 50–60 members); *shu'ab* are gathered into *manatiq* (regions), then *muhafazat* (governorates), each level having administrative offices. These structures are placed under the authority of the *maglis al-shura* (Consultative council, legislative body of the tanzim) and the *maktab al-irshad* (Guidance office, executive body), headed by the Supreme Guide (*al-murshid al-'amm*).
[22]Author's interview, December 2009.

This emphasis on principles of *iltizam* (commitment) and *shura* (consultation), both echoing Islamic notions, was recurrent in members' discourses. In line with this sense of selfless dedication encapsulated in *iltizam* and *shura*, members also insisted that they were not supposed to ask or apply for a leading position, according to the Islamic principle that 'the one who asks for rule does not rule' (*talib al-wilaya la yuwwala*).

However, throughout the 1990s and 2000s, hot debates erupted over the meaning of these principles and over the issue of reforming the *tanzim*. The question divided between '*tanzimiyyin*' ('organizationists'), who controlled the apparatus and whose priority was to secure its preservation; and '*islahiyyin*' ('reformists'), who pressed for more transparency inside of the *tanzim* and criticized the fact that disagreements were stifled in the name of *iltizam* and *shura*. They also advocated for a more rationalized division of tasks and special-ization of skills.[23] While many members took no clear stance on the issue, the majority was imbued with the *tanzimiyyin*'s vision: discussing decisions was viewed as damaging *shura* and causing troubles within the ranks, then endangering the *tanzim* itself.[24] In 1995 and 1996, the debate over the creation of a party led to a split within the ranks of the *Gama'a*, though only a small group eventually left. This group tried to establish a political party, the *Wasat* ('the Centre', representing the idea of moderate Islamism), but the former Committee on Parties rejected its authorization request. The *Wasat* founders, most of whom were edu-cated professionals and held positions in doctors' or engineers' syndicates, supported the idea that politics required professionalization, which could not be achieved within the frame of the *tanzim*.[25] In the 2000s, a new generation of young, highly qualified activists, trained in Information Technology, also raised voices about the need to reform *tanzim* rules, which they considered a cause of political stagnation. In November 2010, during the last, heavily controlled, legislative elections of the Mubarak era, Khalil,[26] a 27-year-old engineer working in a multinational car construction firm, explained to me:

> The problem of the *Gama'a* is that it aims to grow quantitatively rather than qualitatively. It needs to recognize and promote specialized skills and good governance (*'amaliyya idaria*), in order to develop a clear and efficient strategy. It needs to communicate and be more transparent. They [i.e. the *tanzimiyyin*] believe that secret is the key for survival, but we don't need a secret *tanzim* anymore, why aren't you more open? In 80 years, it should have brought more results than it did. But they don't know how to play politics, not just participate, but *playing*. The local *tanzim* leaders, who vote for decisions like boycotting elections or not, don't know anything about politics. They are not competent. Trained cadres, not local leaders, should be responsible for this kind of decisions and be allowed to apply for political positions.[27]

Young dissident activists like Khalil were not numerous but proved very influential as they used new technologies, such as weblogs and Facebook, in order to make the debate visible. Some of them were also involved in internal thematic organs of the *Gama'a*, such as the Political or Media Office, which gave them a position of cadres, despite not having any hierarchical authority over the apparatus. However, their efforts were met by the *tanzimiyyin*'s obstinate refusal. This growing debate reached a new level with the fall of the Mubarak

---

[23]Husam Tammam, *Tahawwulat al-ikhwan al-muslimin: tafakkuk al-aydilujiya wa nihayat al-tanzim* [The Transformations of the Muslim Brothers: Ideological Dismantling and End of the Organization] (Cairo: Madbuli, 2005).

[24]Hazem Kandil, *Inside the Brotherhood* (Cambridge: Polity Press, 2014).

[25]Mona al-Ghobashy, 'The Metamorphosis of the Egyptian Muslim Brothers', *International Journal of Middle East Studies*, 37(3) (2005), pp. 373–395; Clément Steuer, *Le Wasat sous Moubarak. L'émergence contrariée d'un groupe d'entrepreneurs politiques en Égypte*, Collection des thèses de la fondation Varenne/LGDJ, 2012.

[26]All interviewees' names have been changed to preserve anonymity.

[27]Author's interview, November 2010.

regime and the subsequent removal of coercion: conflicting views were expressed as to how to adapt to the new context. Two main issues were raised as to whether the *Gama'a* should be transformed and whether a party should be created.

Adapting to a new context? The undefined Gama'a and its refusal to legalize

What is striking in the case of the Egyptian MB is not that it did not dissolve the *Gama'a* when the FJP was created. This, if we look at other Islamist parties, is quite commonplace. More original was the fact that the *Gama'a* resisted any kind of legalization after the lifting of coercion: while it was not compelled to maintain a clandestine nature, the group refused to enter any ordinary legal category. Instead, the MB asked for the removal of their ban order. Several lawsuits were filed against the *Gama'a* which demanded the reasoning behind why this organization remained illegal, given that nothing prevented its registration. Only in March 2013 did the group officially register as an association, due to great pressure by the Supreme Administrative Court which threatened to order its dissolution. But the *Gama'a* did not actually *become* a legal association: rather, a legal association was created beside the original, unchanged, and thus undefined *Gama'a*. Evidence for this may be found in the fact that the declared president of the association was not the Supreme Guide of the *Gama'a*, Mohamed Badi', but a former Guide, Mahdi 'Akif, who had resigned in 2009.

This resistance was linked to the historical ambition of the *Gama'a* to be recognized as a unique ad hoc organization. Already under Hasan al-Banna's leadership, the *Gama'a* had fallen into a legal vacuum and was characterized by its multifaceted nature. Its founder defined it as 'a collective idea including in it all categories of reform', being at once 'a Salafiyya message, a Sunni way, a Sufi truth, a political organization, a sport group, a cultural-educational union, an economic company and a social idea'.[28] When the *Gama'a* re-emerged in the 1970s and was denied any legal status, it developed through a web of various Islamic formal and informal institutions: mosques, schools, local charity associations, clinics, publishing houses, media outlets etc. This pluralistic nature fostered the *Gama'a*'s own vision as an undefined and therefore unique entity. Paradoxically this very lack of definition has been part of the *Gama'a*'s identity since its foundation and even more so since its re-emergence.

However, the lack of definition became increasingly less acceptable, due to the greater transparency and abidance to the law which became a necessity following Mubarak's fall from power. Other political actors questioned the undefined nature of the *Gama'a* as did media outlets and segments of the population, as well as an increasing number of MB members (beyond the small circle of early dissidents). On 26 March 2011, a meeting known as the 'Brotherhood Youth Conference: New Visions from Inside' was held in Cairo, building on the initiative of some activists. They claimed that they were not defecting from the *Gama'a* but rather attempting to reform it. The event gathered about 400 members, coming from several regions. Participants attempted to redefine what the nature and role of the *Gama'a* in the new configuration should be, and called for it to focus solely on religious and social activities. Politics, they argued, should now be left to fully independent political parties, far

---

[28]Excerpt from Hasan al-Banna's 'Epistle of the Fifth Congress', cited and translated in English by Richard P. Mitchell, *The Society of the Muslim Brothers* (New York: Oxford University Press, 1993 [1969]), p. 14.

away from the *Gama'a*—a stance that strongly contradicted the view of the leadership, who disapproved of the event.[29]

Conflicting visions of party creation and competition

Similarly to the full preservation of the undefined *Gama'a*, the *tanzimiyyin* leaders regarded the creation of the FJP as an obvious necessity. The Supreme Guide quickly announced, as soon as 21 February (nine days after Mubarak's fall), the group's intention to create a party, which was officially established on 30 April and registered on 6 June. This quick move was designed in order for the group to take a lead in the emerging formal political field[30]. It also sent signals to the interim government led by the Supreme Council of Armed Forces (SCAF) that they would endorse it against ongoing street demonstrations, and favor instead electoral politics. Indeed, the *Gama'a* was the only political force represented in the committee formed in late February by the SCAF in order to elaborate the transitional framework. MB leaders, similarly to other actors, anticipated the change of party and electoral legislations. The new Law on Political Parties was passed on 28 March, and later, the single-member voting system was changed into a mixed parallel voting system including party-list proportional representation—i.e. two thirds of the seats were reserved to party candidates. MB leaders thus tactically needed a party.

However, as a self-manifest tactical option, the creation of the FJP was dealt with as a formality by the MB leadership. According to some young cadres, who at the time were not close to the dissident group of *islahiyyin* (but who then developed a critical stance), the leadership did not engage in any process of reflection and discussion about the shaping of one, or several, parties. One of them, Wissam, who worked in Morsi's team in 2012, explained:

> Let me tell you how the party's founders were chosen. Each local section in the *Gama'a* chose four or five persons among its members and said: 'here they are, the party's founders.' They registered them and that was it. They didn't ask: 'Listen guys, we are going to create a party, who wants to be in?' They didn't choose founders according to their political experience or skills. They took the ones who would do whatever they are told to. This is why I didn't want to be part of it, because it was not properly thought out. After all, why should it be one party, and not two or three or four? My own brother, who was like me quite conservative, had the idea of creating a party with some MB friends, but he dropped it quickly because the leadership launched sharp attacks against him, they threatened to exclude him.[31]

In March 2011, the MB leaders indeed made a statement forbidding any MB member to create or join another party than the FJP. While some members, like in the quoted example, resigned themselves to the decision or simply did not join any party, young *islahiyyin* vehemently contested the lack of collective discussion on the issue. They were supported by a few high-ranking leaders, like the former vice guide of the *Gama'a*, Mohamed Habib, or ex-member of the Guidance office, 'Abd al-Mun'im Abu al-Fotouh, who clashed with the

---

[29] Author's interviews with two organizers of the event, December 2013.
[30] The hypothesis can be made that the FJP's announcement was also a strategy not to leave the playing field wide open to a rival Islamist party. Indeed, the *Wasat* Party had officially been legalized two days before by a Court that overturned the former ban. The MB were equally pressed by the political emergence of Salafists. As early as 18 February, the main Salafi movement, *al-Da'wa al-Salafiyya*, organized an important public meeting in which leaders announced that they had revised their traditional stance and that they had decided to engage into formal politics, through the participation in electoral processes and the creation of political parties.
[31] Author's interview, September 2014.

Figure 1. Logo of the Gama'a, logo of the FJP and logo used by MB parliamentarians in 2005–2010.

tanzimiyyin. Several dissidents then left the *Gama'a*—or were excluded by it—to create other parties such as al-Nahda Party (Mohamed Habib), al-Tayyar al-Masri (young activists) or Misr al-Qawia (Abu al-Fotouh).

The *tanzimiyyin* leadership did not take these disputes seriously. Indeed, they were confident with the strength of the *tanzim*. The latter surpassed any other former or newly created party, which obviously lacked channels within society—with the exception of the Salafi Nur Party. Yet, MB leaders considered these new rivals as inexperienced players in the political field, and did not judge it necessary to invest much in upgrading their own capacities to play politics.

Consequently—and contrary to what has been noted in the Algerian FIS case—the previous structuration of the *tanzim* and accumulation of resources diverted investments away from a proper party shaping and conforming process: as the following section shows, the characteristics and structures of the *Gama'a* were simply transposed to the party, through minor adaptions.

A neglected 'conforming process': transposing the *Gama'a* into the party

The FJP had its own TV channel (Misr 25), daily newspaper (*Al-huriyya wal-'adala*) and propaganda material (posters, flyers etc.) that made it more visible than any other party in the public space. However, the FJP's own brand was never clearly differentiated from the *Gama'a*'s, a confusion which subsequently harmed the former's credibility.

The ambiguous branding of the FJP

According to the campaign manager of the FJP, the name of the party was chosen in tribute to the January 25th Revolution, whose main motto was 'Bread, Freedom, and Social Justice', as well as in reference to the centrality of these values in Islam.[32] These values were symbolized by the newly created logo, representing a balance (sign of justice) stylized as a star-shaped (freedom) growing flower. As shown in Figure 1, an analogy can be noted with the *Gama'a*'s historical logo, as well as with the logo used by the MB Members of Parliament in 2005 and 2010. These MPs used a slogan that was then chosen to be inscribed in the FJP's logo: '*Nehammal al-khayr li-misr*', i.e. 'We bring goodness to Egypt'.

---

[32]Amal-Fatiha Abbassi, 'Les Frères musulmans au sortir de la semi-clandestinité : le parti de la Liberté et de la Justice dans les élections législatives', *Égypte/Monde arabe*, 10 (2013). http://ema.revues.org/3124, accessed 7 February 2017.

The new party's programme also showed similarities with the previous ones. The FJP platform drew considerably on the controversial 2007 draft party platform that the MB had released at the time in order to gauge how their positions would be received at large. Although most controversial elements were withdrawn from the FJP platform,[33] its content was roughly the same with regards to political, economic, social and religious reforms. New ideas were hardly introduced in the FJP 2011 platform.

The official founding statement of the party, or what can be called the 'party narrative', further demonstrates the blurring of the new FJP with the old *Gama'a*. On its official website, published in both Arabic and English,[34] the party is presented both as a part of the *Gama'a*, i.e. as a component of a specific organization, and as a group that rose out of the Egyptian people taken as a whole:

> *English version*: 'We are the Freedom and Justice Party, a civil party with an Islamic frame of reference, *founded by the Muslim Brotherhood for all Egyptians*, of different creeds and races and social positions, without discrimination.'

> *Arabic version*: 'The Supreme Guide of the Gama'a announced the foundation by the *Gama'a* of a political party which believes in the thought of the MB and which builds the *Gama'a*'s vision in the party politics field. The FJP was born officially on June 6th 2011 from the womb of the January 25th Revolution, which was provoked by the great Egyptian people, and the party seeks *to build the demands of the Revolution and to achieve its goals through the construction of a sound human being…*'

This double origin brought about a double objective for the party: achieving the demands of the Revolution as well as a more fundamental mission, which consisted in the 'construction of a sound human being'. On the English website, this mission is detailed in a chapter called 'Vision and methodology of the FJP'. It states that 'the first component of the program of our party is to support the purification of the souls' and the 'cleansing of the hearts'. In the Arabic version, the text goes as follows: 'The party believes that the individual citizen is the first goal of development' and 'the cornerstone and the instrument of change', so 'reforming the individual is the way society is reformed'. The party believes in 'the complete shaping of the individual, on the spiritual, cultural, intellectual and physical levels, by which he preserves his identity and belonging'.

Obviously, this mission far exceeded the scope of a political party: it was actually the *Gama'a*'s own mission, which had been defined since its first creation by Hasan al-Banna. In the *Gama'a*'s own narrative, very similar terms are used to describe this mission. The *Gama'a*'s famous *minhag* calls for the same bottom-up strategy as described in the FJP's mission: 'forming the Muslim individual, then the Muslim family, then the Muslim society, then the Islamic state and nation'.

Although the FJP was said to be the 'political wing of the *Gama'a*' whereas 'the *Gama'a* focused on religious and community outreach projects',[35] the distinction, both between the entities and between activities, was anything but clear. Both logos would appear on the propaganda material used by the MB during the legislative elections; posters would mention 'the FJP, founded by the Muslim Brothers for all Egyptians'; the historical slogan of the

---

[33]For a comparison of those texts, see Mariz Tadros, *The Muslim Brotherhood in Contemporary Egypt: Democracy Redefined or Confined?* (Abingdon: Routledge, 2012).

[34]The English website is fjponline.com and the Arabic one (currently closed) hurryh.com.

[35]This was stated numerous times by MB leaders and FJP founders in interviews to the press or on their own websites. See for example, http://www.ikhwanweb.com/article.php?id=28808.

Gama'a—'Islam is the solution' (*al-islam huwa al-hall*)—would often be used, on flyers or in oral comments, jointly with the official slogan ('We bring goodness to Egypt'). Altogether, these technologies of branding presented the FJP as a part of the organization and of the mission of the *Gama'a*. The transposition of the latter's features into the party was further achieved through the structuration process, which was controlled by the *tanzim*.

The control of the Tanzim over party structuration

The *tanzim* exerted control over the FJP through both the technologies of structure construction and the selection of the party's agents.[36] This was made clear in the first official act of formation of the party, which took place on 30 April: a press conference was held in front of the *Gama'a*'s new headquarters on the hill of Muqattam in Cairo, after the 109-member general consultative assembly (*maglis al-shura al-'amm*)—the legislative body of the *Gama'a*—had gathered in its first plenary meeting since 1995. While affirming the independence of the party, the assembly declared that it had appointed Mohamed Morsi as president of the FJP, 'Esam al-'Aryan as vice-president for political affairs and Sa'ad al-Katatni as secretary-general. The three of them were members of the Guidance Office, the higher executive body of the *Gama'a*, and, although they announced that they would formally resign from it, this was a clear signal of the *tanzim*'s grip on the newly born party.

The *majlis al-shura* also devised the main contours of the party's bylaws and organizational chart. Although the latter differs from the *Gama'a*'s own chart (it includes several organs with no equivalent inside the *tanzim*), it is entirely backed by the *Gama'a*'s apparatus. According to several activists who were critical of the way the party was structured, the leaders of the party's offices in governorates and districts were chosen from among the *tanzim* supervisors at the same level. General internal elections were then held between October 2012 and February 2013, after Morsi was elected president of the Egyptian Republic, and resigned from the party. Numerous conflicts erupted during those elections. The most visible and critical one opposed the candidates running for the party's presidency, Sa'ad al-Katatni (who finally won) and 'Esam al-'Aryan. These conflicts highlighted the patterns of socio-political selection inside the party.

Indeed, the promotion of Morsi and Katatni as presidents of the FJP rightly illustrates these patterns. Both leaders followed a similar trajectory inside the *tanzim*, up to the Guidance office (in 2004 for Morsi, 2008 for Katatni). They shared two kinds of resources: on the one hand, their experience as Members of Parliament and head of the parliamentary bloc during Mubarak's era (from 2000 to 2005 for Morsi, 2005–2010 for Katatni) gave them public outreach; on the other hand, their special links to the *tanzimiyyin* ensured them support within the leadership of the *Gama'a*. The fact that they were chosen as heads of the party highlighted the tension between the necessity to open up the party to public personalities and the *tanzimiyyin*'s eagerness to keep it under tight control.

The place of Members of Parliament inside the party is worth commenting on as well. A special organ was dedicated to them in the leadership of the party (Office of the Parliamentarians) and they were represented (10% of them) in the Higher Council of the party. This constituted a promotion for parliamentarians, compared to what prevailed before:

---

[36]A full analysis would require access to the party's and to the *Gama'a*'s archives, which is not possible considering the repressive conditions and the MB's reluctance in disclosing internal documents. However, this section relies on interviews with activists, debates covered by the press, and analysis of the FJP's official bylaws.

in the 2000s, their role was hardly institutionalized inside of the *Gama'a* and very few of them held organizational positions within the *tanzim*. They were at best lower-ranking leaders. Therefore, the FJP's creation was an opportunity to climb the ladder. However, the *tanzim* managed to contain their influence: in the 2011 legislative elections, the candidates of the FJP were appointed by the *majlis al-shura* of the *Gama'a*, and about 20 former MPs were left aside, while some leaders of the *tanzim* were included in the selection to become MPs.

The side-lining of some experimented parliamentarians hints at a determining feature in the FJP creation process: although it was supposed to be the 'political wing of the *Gama'a*', the party regulation actually obeyed the same promotion rules as in the *tanzim*, giving priority to MB loyalty over political specialization.

Promoting 'virtue', marginalizing political skills

Tariq, a young rank-and-file cadre who was in charge of student mobilization in the 2000s and then became more critical over the course of 2011–2013, comments:

> I remember when we used to organize student elections, during Mubarak's time, we were sometimes told [by the *tanzim*] not to run this person as our candidate, but to pick up that one instead. They used to say 'look, he is better, his morals are good, he comes from a MB family, he listens to us', even if this person was even not interested in being candidate! You know the story, *talib al-wilaya la yuwwala*. But the same logics applied for the party. During the FJP elections, MB members were told that 'Esam al-'Aryan makes too many problems. Regional *tanzim* leaders told us that Khayrat al-Shater,[37] the head of the *tanzimiyyin* who is admired by everybody inside the *Gama'a*, would prefer Katatni to be elected. So most members voted for Katatni to please Shater. They don't tell you 'Aryan is not good', but they say that he always disagrees and raises controversies. Another example is Mohamed Beltagi, he was an experienced and active parliamentarian. But he lost in the party internal elections in Cairo, because he was accused of being media-hungry, of speaking for himself whereas he was not a leader in the *Gama'a*, etc.[38]

According to Tariq and other activists who witnessed the process, the principles of regulation promoted inside the *Gama'a*—*iltizam*, *shura*, selfless dedication—were replicated inside the party. What members refer to as 'MB qualities' (*al-mizaya al-ikhwaniyya*) were valued more than political skills to access positions in the party. These 'MB qualities' resulted from a long socialization process within the ranks of the *Gama'a*. This process consisted in the incorporation—even physical—of a way of life, a behaviour conformed to the requirements of a 'virtuous model' defined by the Cultivation Office of the *Gama'a* (*lagnat al-tarbiyya*). Integration into the *Gama'a* depended on the individual's ideological and bodily conformity with this virtuous model. New recruits gradually learned to fit the mould. And as they did so, they could move up towards higher levels of membership in the *Gama'a*.[39] This pattern was well-adapted to the security pressures and illegality constraints that prevailed before, as it ensured secrecy and cohesion. Entering and progressing through the ranks was at once a highly codified *and* a very diluted process: both made it difficult to know exactly who was a MB and who was not. Activists themselves often found it impossible to identify exactly when they had joined the organization. A 'pledge of allegiance' (which had been established

---

[37]Khayrat al-Shater was considered the real strongman in the *tanzim*. A multi-millionaire businessman, he had been jailed several times during Mubarak's era, and enjoyed a special aura among members—even among young *islahiyyin* until 2011. He was first chosen as the MB's candidate to run for the presidency in 2012 but was prevented from doing so by a Court order.

[38]Author's interview, September 2014.

[39]H. Kandil, *Inside the Brotherhood*, chapter 1.

by Hasan al-Banna) consecrated their full integration, but it often happened years after they had actually entered the organization.

Interestingly enough, the FJP bylaws tended to replicate this pattern. A 'pledge of allegiance' was required upon formal entry. Moral criteria were also institutionalized as the basis for party members' evaluation. They would prevail over recruitment (after a probationary period) as well as over internal promotion, through the decision of the FJP's own Cultivation office (*lagnat al-tathqif*). This regulation, based on moral promotion, stands in sharp contrast with new norms of activism governing other political parties. Dissident MB member Abu al-Fotouh's Misr al-Qawia, for example, only required free online registration by simply filling out a form, and it was organized around the specialization of skills and qualifications.

This pattern ended up devaluing specialized political skills—including the ability to debate, raise contradictory arguments and discuss strategies—against morals inside the party itself. As Khalil, Wissam and Tariq put it, each one in his own words, political skills were regarded with suspicion as a source of polemics, and, therefore, of indiscipline; whereas politically incompetent members, who did not raise any critiques or discussions, were seen as loyal and moral fellows. 'Let's talk frankly, what is the *Gama'a*'s *majlis al-shura* made of?' asked Wissam, adding that:

> among the 100 leaders who sit in it, about 80 do not understand anything related to politics, they just listen to the handful of powerful people inside of the *tanzim* and they vote like them. Debates and discussions are poorly looked upon into the *Gama'a*'s ranks. And this was the same inside of the party. The individual, for the MB, should not be like that, polemical.[40]

Conclusion

While the creation of the FJP has often been regarded as an artificial process, and thus as an insignificant issue, this detailed examination of the party creation process has in fact highlighted major features of the Muslim Brothers' failed trajectory in the course of the 2011–2013 period in Egypt. Indeed, not only has the article shown how the *Gama'a* and the *tanzim* held the upper hand in the newly born party, but it has also brought out the determining weight of crystallized patterns of organization and regulation. These patterns prevented the party from obtaining autonomy, as well as impeding the transition of the *Gama'a* to a fully overt nature. Unable to break with the past, the *Gama'a* resisted legalization to retain its undefined identity, and reproduced regulation schemes based on opacity, self-dedication, unquestioned loyalty and promotion of 'virtuous qualities' over specialized skills. These schemes were to a certain extent replicated inside the party itself. As a consequence, both entities endured swift delegitimization, for these organizational features proved unsuitable for the demands of transparency and proficiency that were being expressed (from inside and outside) in the post-2011 context. The reproduction of these organizational patterns raised suspicion about the *Gama'a*'s hidden agendas. Just as the FJP was perceived as a smokescreen, president Mohamed Morsi was accused of being a mere puppet in the hands of a secret *Gama'a*, which kept operating outside the law and under the rule of powerful, unknown *tanzimiyyin*. Organizational crystallization also hindered politically skilled leaders from emerging as decision-makers in the party. Such marginalization caused important

---

[40] Author's interview, September 2014.

internal rifts inside the group and it explains considerable errors of judgement, such as, for example, the decision to run for the presidency: while the FJP had first announced that it would not run its own candidate, it then changed its strategy and supported its former head, to retaliate against the dissident Abu al-Fotouh's candidacy. This was broadly perceived to have been lacking consistency and was interpreted as evidence of the MB's thirst for power. In conclusion, studying the FJP's creation process helps us understand how balances within the *Gama'a* were disrupted within the changing political configuration.

On a more theoretical level, this study also brings about insightful results. First, as the FJP case shows, the end of coercion can have a disrupting impact on the internal and external balances on which previous parties or groups rested. Second, organizational resources are not necessarily enough, or even helpful, to adapt to the new political field emerging during a regime change process. Pre-existing groups, in particular, may have to cope with a phenomenon of organizational crystallization. Massive organizational resources can therefore hamper the ability of the group to take into account the changing configuration and increasing competition. Third, from a methodological point of view, the study of party creation should be considered as a relevant analytical tool, one which is not limited to 'measuring' the level of autonomy or institutionalization of the nascent party. It sheds light on the wider changes affecting the group or the networks from which it was born. Finally, it enables us to concretely grasp how rules of political legitimacy evolve in those contested contexts.

Disclosure statement

No potential conflict of interest was reported by the author.

6 Party and governance in the Arab republics

Joseph Sassoon

ABSTRACT

By focusing on political memoirs as an important source, the article deals with the ruling party and governance in the Arab republics, whether they had a one-party system such as Iraq and Syria, or a multi-party system such as Egypt and Tunisia. However, one country among the republics, Libya, annulled political parties and parliament and created its own unique system of governance. Through memoirs of party members, parliamentary opponents, and ministers, the article analyses the substantial role of the ruling parties in perpetuating the regimes. While the triangular relationship between the leadership, the party, and the bureaucracy differed from one republic to another, the overall structure of governance did not vary widely, except in the case of Libya.

Introduction

In the eight Arab Republics (Algeria, Egypt, Iraq, Libya, Sudan, Syria, Tunisia, and Yemen) the regimes relied on the autocracy of their hegemonic parties to sustain their rule. In two countries, Syria and Iraq, there were single-party systems, while in Egypt, Tunisia, and Algeria it was called a multi-party system but in reality, definitions of single or multi are superfluous because the ruling party in all these republics behaved in a more or less similar fashion. In fact, after independence, Algeria and Tunisia began with a single party and then moved to what was portrayed as multi-party rule.[1] In most republics, there was a structure of two interlocking pyramids: the state and the party, ruling with substantial overlap between the two, allowing the state to control and monitor the party. This is very similar to the classic communist model.

Although the dictatorial regimes in single-party countries occasionally included other groups or factions, this never constituted a true multi-party system, which was apparently not an impediment to any of the regimes that hosted regional conferences for Arab parties.[2]

---

[1] For a theoretical discussion of political parties and single-party systems see Samuel P. Huntington, *Political Order in Changing Societies* (New Haven, CT: Yale University Press, 2006); Clement H. Moore, 'The Single Party as a Source of Legitimacy', in Samuel P. Huntington and Clement H. Moore, eds., *Authoritarian Politics in Modern Society: The Dynamics of Established One-Party Systems* (New York: Basic Books, 1970), pp. 48–72.

[2] Jennifer Gandhi, *Political Institutions under Dictatorship* (New York: Cambridge University Press, 2008), pp. 36–39. The regimes under the Ba'th rule in Iraq and Syria on a number of occasions 'invited' other factions and parties, such as the Communist Party, to be part of a 'national front'.

Damascus twice hosted such a conference under the auspices of Bashar al-Asad, and no irony was intended in the document issued by the second conference declaring 'democracy and political pluralism are the exemplary means for the conduct of relations between the ruler and the ruled, and in building the state's institutions'.[3]

In Libya, about two years after the coup d'état that brought him to power, Mu'ammar al-Qaddafi announced the formation of the Arab Socialist Union as a single-party system styled after its Egyptian counterpart. Two years later this ill-equipped party was abandoned when popular committees were created to encourage the masses to participate in the system.[4] The leadership wanted to create a society without a parliament or governing party, based on Qaddafi's philosophy, as laid out in his *Green Book*, that 'the party is the contemporary dictatorship. It is the modern dictatorial instrument of governing. The party is the rule of a part over the whole'.[5] Asked how he wanted history to remember him, Qaddafi replied: 'For having implemented direct democracy in my country. For having enabled my people to rule themselves, without government, without members of parliament, without representatives'.[6] However, in the other republics that did not heed Qaddafi's advice, the leaders of the dominant parties were able to mobilize large sections of the population and demand their loyalty, which in turn allowed them to rule for decades.

The article will discuss how these parties were structured; how and whom they recruited; their political activities; and their connections with other organs of the state such as the security services. It will also examine governance, the role of senior officials and ministers, and their relations with the ruling parties. Drawing on memoirs of party and parliamentary members, opposition politicians, and senior government officials, it becomes clear that the ruling party played a critical role in the durability of these regimes, and was the vital link that allowed the state to exercise its power. In spite of the drawbacks of memoirs, they are still an excellent source for our understanding of the political history of the Arab world. They provide an interesting source of information from different points of views and they shed light on the relationship between the parties and the executive branch. Indeed, they uncover many intriguing stories that secondary sources such as newspapers and party publications never reveal. Given the fact that apart from the Iraqi Ba'th archives, researchers do not have access to any ruling party's papers, memoirs of political personalities (supporters and opponents of the regimes) add new dimensions to our understanding of these parties.

Structure of political parties and their ideologies

In these republics, the mass-mobilizing parties emerged from 'the impact of imperial powers' policies on traditional elites' socio-political standing'.[7] The patron–client relationship that

[3]Rihab Makhal, 'Tarikh al-Mu'tamarat al-Qawmiyya' [History of the Regional Conferences], in Muhammad Jamal Barut, ed., *al-Ahzab wa al-Harakat wa al-Tanzimat al-Qawmiyy fi al-Watan al-'Arabi* [Nationalist Parties, Movements, and Organizations in the Arab World] (Beirut: Center for Arab Unity Studies, 2012), p. 917. The general conference for Arab parties began to meet on a yearly basis in 1996. This large study of about 1100 pages spans all the parties in the Arab world, and has interesting articles about some of the smaller ones.
[4]Ronald Bruce St. John, 'Libya's Authoritarian Tradition', in Noureddine Jebnoun, Mehrdad Kia, and Mimi Kirk, eds., *Modern Middle East Authoritarianism: Roots, Ramifications, and Crisis* (New York: Routledge, 2014), pp. 127–130.
[5]Mu'ammar al-Qaddafi, *The Green Book* (Tripoli: Public Establishment for Publishing, n.d.), p. 11.
[6]Muammar Gaddafi with Edmond Jouve, *My Vision* (London: John Blake, 2005), pp. 87–88.
[7]Michele Penner Angrist, *Party Building in the Modern Middle East* (Seattle: University of Washington Press, 2006), p. 32.

developed allowed collaboration between different groups of society, and empowered the state to exercise control over not only the educational and legal systems, but also the religious establishment. These authoritarian regimes could not transform society by simple bureaucratic methods, and thus 'people have to be mobilized, different groups integrated, opposition contained'.[8] The ruling party was the instrument that provided 'a political setting for mediating elite disputes and preventing elite defections to the opposition'.[9] Indeed, with the exception of Libya, the party system became a critical tool used by the leadership of these states to sustain their longevity. Even in countries such as Algeria, where the army was the dominant force, the party was pivotal in controlling the country. After Chadhli Bendjedid became president of Algeria in 1979, he realized the need to strengthen the ruling party in order to penetrate and control the army, so he appointed one of his loyal aides as the party's secretary-general.[10]

The origins of the ruling parties are diverse: some were more ideological such as the Ba'th party in Syria or Iraq and were created to compete with an opposing ideology, that of Communism. Other parties such as the Front de Libération Nationale (FLN) arose out of an armed struggle, in the FLN's case to liberate Algiers from France. Some, such as the Egyptian National Union, were created for the sole purpose of galvanizing supporters and enabling the regime to rule more efficiently. Furthermore, ruling parties underwent many changes and transformations. In Egypt, al-Hizb al-Watani al-Dimuqrati, known in English as the National Democratic Party (NDP), evolved in 1976 on the heels of al-Ittihad al-Ishtiraki (the Socialist Union), and before that it was called al-Ittihad al-Qawmi (the National Union). Egypt's three presidents prior to the revolution of 2011 (Gamal 'Abd al-Nasser, Anwar al-Sadat, and Hosni Mubarak) were integral elements of the ruling party's inner circles.[11] Similarly, in Tunisia in 1964, the Neo-Destour was officially renamed Parti Socialiste Destourien (PSD) (Constitutional Socialist Party), and in 1989 its name was changed to Rassemblement Constitutionnel Démocratique (RCD) (Constitutional Democratic Rally) to underline Tunisia's so-called multi-party system. Other parties such as the FLN in Algeria were utterly transformed—in this case, from its origins as a group fighting French colonialism. But in essence it remained more a network of different groups within the power structure than a fully fledged political party.[12]

Although the structure of the ruling parties differed from one republic to another, the one important common denominator was centralization, which inevitably led to the top of the pyramid: the president. In Iraq and Syria, the president also functioned as the party secretariat (*amin sir*) in charge of the regional command (*al-qiyada al-qutriyya*), which, in

---

[8]Roger Owen, *State, Power and Politics in the Making of the Modern Middle East*, 3rd ed. (New York: Routledge, 2008), p. 27.

[9]Jason Brownlee, *Authoritarianism in an Age of Democratization* (Cambridge: Cambridge University Press, 2007), p. 42.

[10]Riyad Saydawi, *Sira'at al-Nukhab al-Siyasiyya wa al-'Askariyya fi al-Jazai'r: al-Hizb, al-Jaysh, al-Dawla* [Political and Military Clashes of the Elites in Algeria: The Party, the Army, the State] (Beirut: Arab Institute, 1999), p. 49. Chadhli was a senior officer in the Algerian army and stayed on as president until he was persuaded by the military to resign in January 1992.

[11]Rabab el-Mahdi, 'The Democracy Movement: Cycles of Protest', in Rabab el-Mahdi and Philip Marfleet, eds., *Egypt: The Moment of Change* (New York: Zed Books, 2009), p. 88. Interestingly the term 'party' was not used in the first two decades after the 1952 Revolution in order to avoid division and obscure the lack of a national purpose. See Maye Kassem, *Egyptian Politics: The Dynamics of Authoritarian Rule* (Boulder, CO: Lynne Rienner, 2004), p. 51.

[12]Michael J. Willis, *Politics and Power in the Maghreb: Algeria, Tunisia and Morocco from Independence to the Arab Spring* (New York: Columbia University Press, 2012), pp. 122–124.

turn, was the executive body in charge of party operations in every town and village.[13] In Syria in June 2003, the regional command issued a directive reiterating 'the party leader provides direction, planning, supervision, and control of the general policy'.[14] Already in 1971, a slogan of *qa'id al-masira* (the march leader) was announced for the party leader and began to be heavily promoted by the regional command of the Syrian Ba'th Party among its party cadres.[15] Remarkably, the pyramid structure in the multi-party countries was very comparable; the RCD in Tunisia had President Zine al-'Abidine Ben 'Ali at the top of the pyramid, just as the Syrian Ba'th had Asad.[16] In Iraq, Syria, and Tunisia, the bottom of the pyramid was the *khaliyya* (cell), while in Egypt it was the unit, followed by the division or centre, then the province, and at the top were the party secretariat and the political bureau.[17] In Egypt, the president of the republic was the head of the party and there was no distinction between the presidency and the party in terms of policy.

The structure of the ruling parties differed in terms of discipline and governance. Within the Ba'th parties (in Syria and Iraq), there was far more emphasis on discipline, and any opposition to the leadership of the party was suppressed—in certain cases very violently. Membership in the ideological parties was, as will be shown, more rigid and structured, in comparison to the non-ideological ones such as the Egyptian ruling party.

In Iraq, Syria, and Tunisia, the ruling party reached into every aspect of life. As the formal ideology of parties such as the Ba'th diminished (discussed later), the party's main function was to be the eyes and ears of these regimes. A diary of a party member in Iraq indicates that the activities of the party's cells and divisions spanned a variety of tasks: security; organizing seminars and conferences to spread the word of the Ba'th; cultural activities; and political education. Every week, the cells around the country listed cultural, political, organizational, military, criticism and self-criticism, and miscellaneous topics on their agendas.[18]

One difference between the two Ba'th parties in Iraq and Syria in comparison to the other ruling parties in the other republics is the concept of self-criticism, a practice borrowed from the Communist Party whereby members had a duty to criticize their own activities and role. A Syrian Ba'th Party report emphasized the importance of criticism and self-criticism as 'one of the basics of the internal system of the party', which helped to guarantee proper coordination and discipline in dealing with members.[19] In Tunisia, Béatrice Hibou argues that the

---

[13]For details about the structure in Iraq, see Joseph Sassoon, *Saddam Hussein's Ba'th Party: Inside an Authoritarian Regime* (New York: Cambridge University Press, 2012), pp. 34–38; for Syria, see Souhaïl Belhadj, *La Syrie de Bashar al-Asad: Anatomie d'un Régime Autoritaire* [The Syria of Bashar al-Asad: Anatomy of an Authoritarian Regime] (Paris: Belin, 2013), pp. 139–144; Raymond Hinnebusch, *Syria: Revolution from Above* (New York: Routledge, 2002), pp. 76–83. Apart from the structure, the book has statistics on the occupations of members as of 1980 and 1984.

[14]Directive 408–409, issued on 15 June 2003, is quoted in Belhadj, *La Syrie de Bashar al-Asad*, p. 141.

[15]Munir al-Hamash, 'Hizb al-Ba'th al-'Arabi al-Ishtiraki fi Suriya (1953–2005)' [The Arab Socialist Ba'th Party in Syria (1953–2005)], in Barut, ed., *al-Ahzab wa al-Harakat*, p. 140.

[16]Steffen Erdle, *Ben Ali's "New Tunisia" (1987–2009): A Case Study of Authoritarian Modernization in the Arab World* (Berlin: Verlag, 2010), annex 4a, 4b, pp. 504–505. See also Zuhair al-Muzzafir, *Min al-Hizb al-Wahid ila Hizb al-Aghlabiyya* [From the Single Party to the Majority Party] (Tunisia: Sanbakit, 2004), p. 104.

[17]Al-Hizb al Watani al-Dimuqrati, *Ru'ya li-Mustaqbal Misr: Watha'iq al-Mu'tamar al-'Amm al-Thamin lil-Hizb al-Watani al-Dimuqrati wa Tashkilat al-Hizb* [A Vision of the Future of Egypt: Documents from the Eighth General Conference of the National Democratic Party and the Structures of the Party], 15–17, September 2002 (Cairo: al-Jumhuriyya Publishing, 2002), p. 23.

[18]A diary of Bayji branch given to the author which details, in longhand, the weekly agenda and comments of the participants (ranging from 7–12 in number).

[19]Hizb al-Ba'th al-'Arabi al-Ishtiraki, *Hawla al-Dimuqratiyya al-Markaziyya* [About the Centralized Democracy] (Damascus: Cultural Bureau and Party Preparatory Publications, n.d. (1970s)), p. 7.

main function of RCD was not security, but 'the minute network of surveillance of the country constitutes one of central modalities'. While this is a subtle difference compared to the two Ba'th Parties, Hibou confirms that apart from the police, 'the bodies of the RCD are indisputably the most significant and most systematic means of surveillance.'[20] In fact, the party 'functioned as a mechanism of social control at all levels of society', and neighbourhood watch committees were created by the party to monitor Islamists' activities.[21]

In Egypt, although the political activities, recruitment, and promoting of the NDP programmes and policies were the main functions of the different organizations of the party,[22] in reality members were also asked, from time to time, to keep an eye on someone or to report activities in campuses and offices. It is difficult, in the case of Egypt, to determine the exact demarcation between the party and the security services, but senior ministers, particularly the minister of interior, were usually members of the political bureau, the executive body of the NDP. According to Robert Springborg, in the elections of 1986, Minister of Interior Zaki Badr addressed numerous party meetings 'railing against the opposition and lauding his audience for their activities in cementing alliance between the party and the popular bases'.[23] Hasan Abu Basha, who occupied the post of minister of interior and was for many years in charge of Egypt's security forces, confirms the deep relations between the ministry and all political parties, but argues that the role of the minister was 'to supervise all political forces, ensure that they follow the legal path, and abide by the rules that govern the society.'[24]

Irrespective of country, recruitment was a core function of all the ruling parties. Some parties that originally had a more ideological base used their teachings and principles to attract new cadres. For instance, the Iraqi Ba'th Party had a special school called *madrasat al-i'dad al-hizbi* (party preparatory school), to groom those destined for higher positions, and to instruct them in the intellectual and ideological aspects of party philosophy.[25] Recruitment of youth, the educated, and women was a high priority for most parties. In countries such as Egypt and Tunisia, joining the party was not onerous: the candidate had simply to declare that he or she was not a member of another party and that they believed in the principles of the ruling party. In Syria and Iraq, there was more monitoring, and forms to complete, as the Ba'th was very security conscious, and apart from the lowest level of party membership, known as *mu'ayyid* (sympathizer), promotion was more rigorous.[26] By 1992 the Iraqi Ba'th had a clear slogan: 'Let us capture the youth, so we can capture the future.'[27] Iraqi documents from the 1990s show that in some major branches the percentage of those aged below 35 reached over 50%, while that of women members topped 40%.[28] In

[20]Béatrice Hibou, *The Force of Obedience: The Political Economy of Repression in Tunisia*, trans. Andrew Brown (Cambridge: Polity, 2011), pp. 86–87.

[21]Noureddine Jebnoun, 'Ben Ali's Tunisia: The Authoritarian Path of a Dystopian State', in Jebnoun et al., eds., *Modern Middle East Authoritarianism*, p. 110.

[22]Al-Hizb al Watani al-Dimuqrati, *Ru'ya li-Mustaqbal Misr*, p. 23.

[23]Robert Springborg, *Mubarak's Egypt: Fragmentation of the Political Order* (Boulder, CO: Westview Press, 1989), p. 155.

[24]Hasan Abu Basha, *Mudhakkirat Hasan Abu Basha fi al-Amn wa al-Siyasa: Yanayir 1977*, Uktubir 1981, Ramadan 1987 [Memoirs of Hasan Abu Basha in security and politics: January 1977, October 1981, Ramadan 1987] (Cairo: al-Hilal Publishing, 1990), p. 151.

[25]For a comprehensive discussion of *madrasat al-i'dad al-hizbi*, see Joseph Sassoon, 'The Iraqi Ba'th Party Preparatory School and the "Cultural" Courses of the Branches', *Middle Eastern Studies*, 50(1) (2014), pp. 27–42.

[26]For the requirements to join the Egyptian NDP, see al-Hizb al-Watani al-Dimuqrati, *Ru'ya li-Mustaqbal Misr*, p. 47; for the Iraqi Ba'th, see Sassoon, *Saddam Hussein's Ba'th Party*, Chapter 2.

[27]Sassoon, *Saddam Hussein's Ba'th Party*, pp. 54–55.

[28]See for example Salah al-Din branch in *Ba'th Regional Command Collection* (BRCC), 174-3-2, 1992; and a report from one section in Baghdad to Party Headquarters, 11 November 2002, BRCC, 004-5-6.

Syria, the proportion of women among party activists ranged from 29 to 31%, and Syrian data indicated that by 2004 the number of young members had reached almost 67%.[29]

It would be wrong to assume that the Ba'thification process in Syria diminished with the rise to power of Bashar al-Asad after his father's death. A documentary investigating the issue of flooding related to the building of the Euphrates dam clearly shows the deep penetration of the Ba'th even in small villages and towns. Living in a valley near the Euphrates River, one tribal head and his family were all connected to the party. The headmaster in the local school, himself a senior party member, was in charge of ensuring that the students joined the different youth groups of the party. In his words, it was critical that 'the principles of the Ba'th are planted in every child, so the child would love freedom, socialism, and Arab unity [the party's motto]'.[30] Almost identically to Iraq, emphasis was laid on what was termed *tala'i' al-Ba'th wa jil al-mustaqbal* (the avant-garde of the Ba'th and the future generation).[31] According to one scholar, membership in this organization was compulsory for all children and although education was free, parents had to purchase the uniforms for their children.[32] Interestingly, all the students in the village had to wear military uniforms, an idea borrowed from the Soviet Union and Eastern Europe, and continued in North Korea.

In Egypt, the eighth conference of the NDP in 2002 called for expanding the role of women in society by increasing the membership of women, and of youth in general, in order to modernize the country.[33] In Tunisia, party reports showed that 30% of members were women, and the RCD was proud to announce that many academics and professors from different universities joined the party after 7 November 1987 (when Ben 'Ali, then minister of interior, seized power from Habib Bourguiba, the founding father of the Republic after its independence from France), having previously boycotted the party. One report indicated that 2772 university professors had joined the RCD by 2003, and underlined that 29% of party members had tertiary education.[34]

There is no doubt that many young and educated people joined these parties because of their political beliefs, but the majority joined simply for economic reasons, knowing that promotions and government jobs were more widely available to party members. Whether in Tunisia, Syria, or Iraq, it was almost impossible for a non-member of the ruling party to join the military, the police, or the security forces. Furthermore, party members predominantly filled senior positions in government, the judiciary, and academic institutions. Essentially, this became a fundamental part of the rewards system that, in turn, guaranteed a significant increase in membership, and, more critically, a high quality of cadre that the leadership could rely on. Thus the party was no longer about ideology, but more about a co-optation that allowed these regimes to indirectly control the population at large, in particular the young and educated, of whom the leadership was naturally wary.

---

[29]Belhadj, *La Syrie de Bashar al-Asad*, p. 149.

[30]Omar Amiralay, dir., *Tawafan fi Bilad al-Ba'th* [Flood in the Country of the Ba'th], a film produced in Syria and France in 2003. The producer admits that he decided to make the film after his first movie supported the Ba'th modernization plans that led to the building of the dam and the flooding of small villages. The film was chosen as one of the best 100 Arabic movies in the 2013 Dubai Film Festival.

[31]For a discussion on children and youth under the Iraqi Ba'th Party, see Sassoon, *Saddam Hussein's Ba'th Party*, pp. 268–273.

[32]Sally K. Gallagher, *Making Do in Damascus: Navigating a Generation of Change in Family and Work* (New York: Syracuse University Press, 2012), p. 66.

[33]Al-Hizb al-Watani al-Dimuqrati, *Ru'ya li-Mustaqbal Misr*, pp. 111–119.

[34]Al-Muzzafir, *Min al-Hizb al-Wahid*, p. 79.

As Hinnebusch points out, careerism was an important motivation in recruitment to the ruling parties in Egypt and Syria, although his research conducted in the early 1980s shows that in Syria many young men and women were attracted to careers through their association with the Ba'th because of their low social status.[35] Intriguingly, a recent report about the Communist Party in China showed similar trends: while there was no real zeal for the party's ideology, many university students were rushing to join it because 'public-sector employers usually prefer party members and often require membership for better positions'.[36] No wonder then that membership swelled dramatically; in Tunisia, based on the statistics of the RCD, Hibou claims that there were almost 2 million members out of a population of 10 million, a high number indeed compared to many other countries.[37] In Iraq, for instance, internal documents of the Ba'th indicated a total membership by 2002 of about 4 million out of a population of roughly 25 million.[38] Belhadj, quoting Syrian reports, posits that there were 2.4 million members in the Syrian Ba'th by 2005 (out of a population of roughly 18 million) but only 547,000 were active.[39] A major caveat in all this data is that the vast majority was in the lower levels of the pyramid and joined the party either under duress or to enjoy the benefits of belonging to a ruling party.

Ideology played a more important part in the 1970s and 1980s compared to the following three decades. Some ruling parties, in particular the Ba'th, had strong ideological beginnings, and although it changed its policy over time, its fundamentals and motto (Arab Unity, Freedom, and Socialism) remained intact, at least on paper. A good example of lacklustre ideology is recounted by one of Egypt's ministers. In 1976, he recounts, when Sadat decided to transform the Arab Socialist Union, the original focus was to be more on socialism, and hence the new party was called Hizb Misr al-Ishtiraki (Egypt Socialist Party). But within a short period Sadat changed his views and did not want a party defined as socialist, and thus the new NDP was created. Amazingly, all the senior ministers and most of those in the first party emigrated to the new party headed by the president, and no one thought it bizarre to switch a party and its ideology so swiftly.[40] Some members of ruling parties, whether due to opportunistic considerations or to a genuine belief in their party's ideology, wrote extensively about the reasons they joined the ruling parties. One such description is by Dr 'Abd al-Mun'im Sa'id, an Egyptian academic, who presents four reasons for joining the NDP: (1) more freedom than those who belong to other parties, given that the NDP was the right platform for discussions and exchange of ideas; (2) the fact the NDP was very strict in collecting fees from its members (120 Egyptian pounds, equivalent to US$20 in the mid-2000s), which according to Sa'id reduced opportunism in the party, and furthermore, the numerical rise of the youth within party ranks; (3) the NDP had a clear policy toward Israel, the USA, and the West, which was important as Egypt was in a region where sectarianism and fundamentalism were on the rise; and (4) the NDP, after long internal travail, had come to the

---

[35]Raymond A. Hinnebusch, 'Party Activists in Syria and Egypt: Political Participation in Authoritarian Modernizing States', *International Political Science Review*, 4(1) (1983), pp. 84–93. This study is based on a small survey sample of youth recruits and was conducted among recruits to the Syrian Ba'th Party and the Egyptian Wafd Party.

[36]'Students and the Party: Rushing to Join', *Economist*, 22 February 2014, p. 38.

[37]Hibou, *The Force of Obedience*, p. 86 and n. 24, p. 309. A Tunisian study confirms this number and claimed that in 2001 there were 2.3 million. See al-Muzzafir, *Min al-Hizb al-Wahid*, p. 102.

[38]Belhadj, *La Syrie de Bashar al-Asad*, p. 397, n. 44.

[39]Sassoon, *Saddam Hussein's Ba'th Party*, appendix II, p. 286.

[40]'Abd al-Wahhab al-Burlusi, *Kuntu Waziran ma'a 'Abd al-Nasser* [I Was a Minister with 'Abd al-Nasser] (Cairo: Arab Mustaqbal Publishing, 1992), pp. 114–115.

conclusion that the only way to rid Egypt of its poverty was to focus on human development and Egypt's resources.[41] Unfortunately, Dr Sa'id does not present a thorough analysis of these four 'push' factors. Indeed, a review of ideological discussions and writings of some party members in those republics is far from impressive. Few of the party conferences delved in detail into theoretical and ideological issues, although many of the important topics were actually raised. For instance, the fourth annual conference of the NDP, which took place in September 2006, emphasized that the 'National Democratic Party does not monopolize constitutional amendments and welcomes dialogue with all parties'. The head of the Committee for Citizenry and Democracy Politics had on its agenda themes such as equilibrium between the different powers of the state; a re-examination of the relationship between the executive and judicial authorities; more independence for the judiciary; and increasing local governance in order to reduce the centralization of power.[42] Needless to say, all those significant questions remained as ideas without any serious discussion, and definitely without implementation.

In Tunisia, some of the RCD's philosophy and ideas remained strictly on paper, such as democracy and equality among citizens. In other areas, however, there was indeed significant progress such as modernization, increased literacy, and more rights for women.[43] Overall, the RCD became 'largely devoid of ideology, but it retained the system of patronage'.[44] In Iraq, an analysis of the Ba'th Party's preparatory school's curricula clearly shows how ideology lost its allure by the late 1980s and was replaced by the personality cult of President Saddam Hussein; instead of having the recruits focusing on the ideology of the founder, Michel 'Aflaq, and writings about socialism, the teaching shifted to the writings and speeches of 'the great leader Saddam Hussein'.[45] In Syria, Ba'th ideology and party writings were vague and had many meanings and interpretations. One scholar argues that this was intentionally done to 'incorporate disparate groups into a nation-state, minimizing conflict and promoting consensus'.[46] For instance, a party report discussed in detail *al-dimuqratiyya al-markaziyya* (centralized democracy), but a thorough reading of this publication shows it is mainly about party discipline and 'creating a deep foundation for the popular structure and party activities'.[47] In fact, the regional command was worried about the vagueness of discussion and uninspiring style of the political activities, attributing it mostly to the 'weakness of the intellectual effort, and the continuation of nebulous and incomplete ideology, which in turn is leading the apparatus to hesitate and reduce the confidence of the party cadre'.[48] Similarly to Iraq, the personality cult of President Hafiz al-Asad in Syria dominated its ideology and, with the passage of time, overshadowed the fundamental ingredients of the party's philosophy.

---

[41] 'Abd al-Mun'im Sa'id, *Islah al-Sasa: al-Hizb al-Watani wa al-Ikhwan wa al-Libraliyyun* [Reform of Governance: The National Party and the Brothers and Liberals] (Cairo: Nahdat Misr Publications, 2010), pp. 93–96.

[42] Al-Hizb al-Watani al-Dimuqrati, *al-Mu'tamar al-Sanawi al-Rabi'* [The National Democratic Party, the Fourth Annual Conference], 19–21 September 2006, minutes of the meetings of the conference (Cairo, 2006), pp. 118–119. The head of the committee was Dr Mufid Shihab.

[43] For an example of a detailed discussion of the ideas and policies of the RCD, see Tariq al-Qayzani, *al-Hizb al-Dimuqrati al-Taqaddumi* [The Progressive Democratic Party] (Tunisia: Dar Muhammad for Publishing, 2011).

[44] Jebnoun, 'Ben Ali's Tunisia', p. 110.

[45] Sassoon, 'The Iraqi Ba'th Party Preparatory School'.

[46] Lisa Wedeen, *Ambiguities of Domination: Politics, Rhetoric, and Symbols in Contemporary Syria* (Chicago, IL: University of Chicago Press, 1999), p. 40.

[47] Hizb al-Ba'th, *Hawla al-Dimuqratiyya al-Markaziyya*, p. 13.

[48] *Nidal al-Ba'th: Watha'iq Hizb al-Ba'th al-'Arabi al-Ishtiraki* [The Struggle of the Ba'th: Documents of the Arab Socialist Ba'th Party], vol. IV: *Regional Command 1955–1961* (Beirut: al-Tali'a Publishing, 1964), p. 207.

Weak or even lack of ideology was one of the reasons for the waning of ties between the upper and lower echelons of these parties. As one ex-member of the Central Committee of the PSD lamented after five years as a senior party member:

> Among the members of the Central Committee in charge of the political bureau, those at the top of the pyramid, see no alienation between their thinking and the thinking of the rank and file of the party ... When one of them declares and announces their protests about marriage, abortion, pregnancy, and inheritance, I asked myself: does this senior person have the same culture and civilization of the [Tunisian] people?[49]

This member's seniority did not help him when he heard, to his utter disbelief, an announcement during a large party meeting that he had withdrawn his candidacy for the Central Committee.[50] Throughout the Arab republics, the pyramid structure of power allowed a small group of people to make decisions, which were communicated to the central committee or politburo of the ruling parties. These were disseminated down the line all the way to the lowest echelons, rarely with any discussion, and mostly without any explanation. The absence of ideology combined with the lack of unity of purpose (apart from staying in power and reaping the associated rewards) must have contributed to the inability of these ruling parties to keep the population under control by 2011. The paralysis of the Syrian Ba'th Party in the 2012 elections can be partly explained by the violence spreading in the country, but also by its inability to counter opposition and regain popular support for the regime. This weak connection between the leadership and the party cadre was already highlighted in the late 1970s, at the time of an internal crisis in the Syrian Ba'th Party, and it was recommended to 'review the relationship between the party and the leadership in a way that guarantees a truthful leadership of the party'.[51] Four decades later, it became obvious that this recommendation was never properly implemented.

Governance

The authoritarian republics developed a large management apparatus, and at the apex of the hierarchical pyramid was a small number of trusted and loyal individuals on whom the leadership relied. In some cases, the leaders did not want even their ruling party to become too dominant and therefore competitive with the centre of power. Springborg believes that Mubarak did not push the NDP forward because of his fear that 'it will develop a will of its own or serve as a platform on which talented, aspiring political leaders could demonstrate their abilities'.[52] Hence, the reliance on this bureaucratic apparatus, which was rewarded for loyalty and was relatively easier to control and manipulate than other arms of the state. The Tunisian politician Mzali discussed the criteria for choosing his staff. While ostensibly focusing on creativity and integrity, he reiterated: 'I would like to give full attention to a noble quality

---

[49]Al-Munji al-Ka'bi, *Mudakhalat 'Udu bil-Lajna al-Markaziyya* [Interjections of a Member of the Central Committee] (Tunis: al-Kitab Publishing, 1986), p. 57.

[50]Ibid., p. 6.

[51]Hizb al-Ba'th al-Arabi al-Ishtiraki, *al-Haraka al-Tashihiyya: Min al-Mu'tamar al-Qawmi al-'Ashir al-Istithna'i ila al-Mu'tamar al-Qawmi al-Thalith 'Ashir* [The Corrective Movement: From the Extraordinary National Tenth Conference to the Thirteenth National Conference] (Damascus: Cultural Bureau and Party Preparatory, 1983), p. 15. The Corrective Movement took place in November 1970 when Hafiz al-Asad seized power. For more details on those events, see: Nikolaos Van Dam, *The Struggle for Power in Syria: Politics and Society under Asad and the Ba'th Party*, revised 4th ed. (London: I.B. Tauris, 2011), pp. 65-74.

[52]Springborg, *Mubarak's Egypt*, p. 155.

that goes beyond simple devotion, and is one of the dearest and most powerful spiritual qualities, and that is loyalty.'[53] Indeed, loyalty is the most essential factor for being close to the leadership, and in many places, such as Iraq, loyalty was far more critical than tribal affiliation or even family connections. Another senior Tunisian politician describes how loyalties were defined: *La lil-wila'at illa li-Bourguiba* (No allegiance but to Bourguiba).[54] In other words, allegiance and devotion to a president and his authority were above everything else. Under Ben 'Ali, the state bureaucracy in Tunisia preserved three features developed by the Bourguibian regime: centralization; strong and overlapping ties with the RCD; and a leading role in public life.[55]

To better understand how those on the inside saw matters, it is worthwhile perusing some memoirs that assess their authors' role in government and recount their relationship with the country's leaders. In Egypt, ministers were appointed according to the wishes of the president.[56] 'Abd al-Wahhab al-Burlusi explains how Nasser, during a meeting of the Arab Socialist Union, called him and offered him the post of minister of health. After he accepted, the Ministry of Higher Education became vacant, and without consulting al-Burlusi, another presidential decision rescinded the original offer of minister of health so that he could become minister of higher education. For both appointments very little deliberation took place, not least with the prospective candidate.[57] Another senior Egyptian politician, Khalid Muhyi al-Din, who occupied many important roles after the 1952 Revolution that toppled the monarchy, bemoans the fact that it had already become clear in 1953, first with Muhammad Neguib, the senior general who led the revolution, and then with Nasser, who dislodged Neguib and kept him under house arrest, that both men were intent on creating a small committee, later called Majlis Qiyadat al-Thawra (Revolutionary Command Council), that would concentrate power in its hands. Muhyi al-Din also blames the Muslim Brothers for petitioning against a parliamentary system and allowing political parties to operate freely.[58] He recounts the inner conflicts within the Egyptian leadership in the early 1950s, and how Nasser, after displacing Neguib, continually reiterated to his senior colleagues the two choices available to them: 'Either absolute democracy, or a policy of discipline and revolution. Either utter freedom and giving up our role, or allowing the Revolutionary Council to resolutely exercise all its powers.'[59] Reading Muhyi al-Din's memoirs leaves us with no doubt that Nasser was intent on becoming authoritarian in his governance, and that he laid the foundations for repression and denying civil liberties.

Al-Burlusi, however, judges Nasser otherwise; in his two years as a minister in the mid-1960s, he believed that Nasser was a good listener and open to other ministers' ideas and suggestions. 'Nasser was not a dictator as some people think. He was polite, strict, clear and honest. He understood what was discussed and then made his decisions. Sometimes he

---

[53]Mohamed Mzali, *Hadith al-Fi'l* [The talk of action] (Tunis: Tunisian Society for Publications, 1985), p. 347.

[54]Al-Ka'bi, *Mudakhalat 'Udu bil-Lajna al-Markaziyya*, p. 39.

[55]Erdle, *Ben Ali's "New Tunisia"*, pp. 149–150.

[56]An interesting analysis with many examples of the different ministries in Egypt can be found in Springborg, *Mubarak's Egypt*, chapter 5: 'The System of Political Control', pp. 134–181.

[57]Al-Burlusi, *Kuntu Waziran ma'a 'Abd al-Nasser*, pp. 72, 78.

[58]Khalid Muhyi al-Din, *Wa al-'An Atakallam* [Now I Speak] (Cairo: Ahram Center for Translations and Publications, 1992), pp. 212–213. Muhyi al-Din was a member of the Revolutionary Command Council and later became head of the leftist Nasserist faction.

[59]Ibid., p. 302.

would revise his thinking and explain his ideas.' The problem, in al-Burlusi's opinion, was that other ministers always consented to his views, thus creating an atmosphere of dictatorship.[60] Tharwat 'Ukasha has a totally different view of Nasser: during the cabinet meetings, Nasser would ask for ideas and suggestions on how to improve matters, but 'Ukasha felt that in reality there were no deep debates about the crux of issues. He also describes the conflicts within the government apparatus, which began expanding during this period and created an overlap of responsibilities.[61] As minister of culture and information, he strongly believed that these two ministries should be split and that there is a central distinction between information and culture. In spite of his efforts and a number of conversations with Nasser, 'Ukasha reached the conclusion that the differences between the two men were wide, and he tendered his resignation. While in London for medical treatment, he found out that two senior assistants in his ministry had been arrested. Furious, he returned to Cairo to learn that the reason for the discontent with him and his senior staff was the accusation that these two men were passing on jokes about Nasser to his brother, who lived in London.[62]

Needless to say, the faults in governing the country did not lie with just one man, and the ministers definitely carry some culpability for failure. In a sardonic portrayal of ministers in Egypt, a book about 'Amru Musa informs us:

> The ministerial job in Egypt carries expansive influence in all the corridors of power within the state. It is a golden key to enrich one's self, and to utterly enjoy the honour and popularity [of the position]. Protocol dictates that a minister must be extremely elegant and stylish, beginning with his shoes all the way to the chair he sits on. The uniform of his secretary, the ministry building, the make of the car driven by his chauffeur [all are important].[63]

Discussing 'Amru Musa's career, the book highlights an intriguing point about those in senior positions in the Foreign Ministry, claiming that since the end of the 1970s 'the secret code in the Egyptian diplomacy is that Israel managed with dexterity and canniness to topple many of the most gifted men in Egyptian politics', including three foreign ministers: Muhammad Ibrahim Kamil, Butrus Butrus Gali, and 'Amru Musa, because of their opposition at one point or due to close ties with Israel, or for what the Israelis characterized as their intransigence during the negotiations between the two sides.[64]

Egyptian ministers were mostly drawn from a relatively small circle of well-educated men and women, retired senior military and police officers, and numerous people who spent their lives in the government bureaucracy or in running governorates. These men and women were, throughout their careers, mostly connected to the top echelons of the regime. In a fascinating and very pro-regime book that could even be seen simply as propaganda, a journalist interviews and details the lives and careers of 33 men and 2 women working close to President Mubarak. Only one out of this group was appointed from the outside, a scientist who spent her life in research and science, while the rest were from the inner circle and spent

---

[60]Fathi Radwan, *Fathi Radwan Yarwi li-Dhia' al-Din Bibars Asrar Hukumat Yuliyu* [Fathi Radwan Recounts to Dhia' al-Din Bibars the Secrets of the July Government] (Cairo: al-Ma'rifa Publishing, 1976), pp. 225–226.

[61]Tharwat 'Ukasha, *Mudhakkirati fi al-Siyasa wa al-Thaqafa* [My Memoirs in Politics and Culture], vol. II (Cairo: al-Hilal Publishing House, 1990), p. 132.

[62]Ibid., pp. 139–140.

[63]Shihab Nasir, *'Amru Musa: al-Malaffat al-Sirriyya* ['Amru Musa: The Secret Files] (Cairo: Center for Arabic Civilization, 2001). Musa was a foreign minister in Egypt from 1991, secretary of the Arab League for the next 10 years, and a presidential candidate in the 2011 elections that were won by Muhammad Morsi from the Muslim Brotherhood.

[64]Ibid., pp. 26–27.

their careers climbing the ladder to get near the president.[65] Interestingly, the journalist was told by Dr Venice Kamil Jawdat, who was appointed as minister for scientific research, that she never joined any political party, but she quickly added that the 'NDP is the most moderate party; it is a respectable party with fine ideas attempting to develop Egypt forward, and if I was offered a party to join, I would choose the National Democratic Party.'[66] Many observers have rightly concluded that the formal structure of the government and the state did not change to any great extent during the almost six decades following the 1952 Revolution.[67]

Running the two vital organs of the state in these regimes, the military and the security forces, was critical, but suffice to say here that in countries such as Egypt, the management of the Ministry of War, throughout its numerous military conflicts (in Yemen, and against Israel), was nothing short of cataclysmic. One startling example is the decision making during the period preceding the Six-Day War in June 1967, when Shams Badran was minister of war. Badran, one of the Free Officers who participated in the 1952 Revolution, was later tried for his incompetence in preparing the armed forces for the 1967 War. The problem was not just inefficient management; corruption, nepotism, and lack of real interest in the burning issues all contributed to the calamity that shook the country after a few days of war.[68]

A few words are in order about governance in Libya, given its fundamental differences from other authoritarian regimes. In the mid-1970s, Qaddafi's philosophy, as expressed in the *Green Book*, was based on the creation of a *jamahiriyya* (state of the masses) to replace the 'normal' state in other countries. As a result, revolutionary committees were formed to supervise the running of this new state; they were charged with enforcing Qaddafi's ideology and to 'circumvent the hierarchy of decision-making processes of almost all state institutions (with the exception of the oil sector and the armed forces)'.[69] As Roger Owen points out, a large bureaucracy with an expanding army and security forces continued to operate in this new system, where the people were supposed to rule and not the state.[70]

Conclusion

The function of the ruling party in the Arab republics, whether in single-party or multi-party systems, was to ensure the durability of these authoritarian regimes. When elections took place in countries such as Egypt and Tunisia, history showed that these hegemonic parties managed to control the elections and to assure their own dominance. Opposition parties in these countries were weak and fragmented, but accepted the system of parliament, and of 'managed' elections, because, as Jennifer Gandhi put it:

---

[65]Nura Rashid, *Rijal hawla al-Rai's: Hiwar ma'a Shakhsiyyat Hamma* [Men around the President: Dialogue with Important Personalities in Egypt], vol. I (Cairo: Egyptian Institution for the Book, 1997). Another minister who was relatively outside the circle is Faruq Husni, who was appointed minister of culture. Prior to his appointment, he spent most of his career in the art world, except for a short stint as head of the technical bureau in the Ministry of Culture and later the head of the Egyptian Academy for Art in Rome. See pp. 111–125.

[66]Ibid., p. 267.

[67]See for example Kassem, *Egyptian Politics*, p. 43.

[68]Hamada Husni, *Shams Badran: al-Rajul alladhi Hakama Misr* [Shams Badran: The Man who Ruled Egypt] (Beirut: Beirut Library, 2008).

[69]Hanspeter Mattes, 'Formal and Informal Authority in Libya since 1969', in Dirk Vandewalle, ed., *Libya since 1969: Qaddafi's Revolution Revisited* (New York: Palgrave Macmillan, 2008), p. 67. For a more detailed historical analysis of the *Green Book* and the revolution, see Dirk Vandewalle, *A History of Modern Libya* (New York: Cambridge University Press, 2006).

[70]Owen, *State, Power and Politics*, p. 55.

For the potential opposition, assemblies and parties provide an institutionalized channel through which they can affect decision-making even if in limited policy realms. For incumbents, these institutions are a way in which opposition demands can be contained and answered without appearing weak.[71]

Indeed, as Magaloni showed in the case of Mexico, elections can be used by these regimes as a way 'to regularize payments to their supporters and implement punishment to their enemies, among both the elite and the masses, so as to induce them to remain loyal to the regime and to have a vested interest in its survival'.[72] Unfortunately, the masses in these republics not only accepted this structure, but also had to play a role in sustaining it. A good example was Algeria, where the tentacles of the FLN helped to secure for 'Abd al-'Aziz Bouteflika, the incumbent president, about 85% and 90% of the votes in the 2004 and 2009 elections, respectively. It is impossible to conclude how much of this high percentage is due to vote fraud or to large mobilization of the population.

In the single-party systems such as Syria and Iraq, co-optation through the Ba'th Party was essential for their durability, and they did not need or care to show the world that they had an electoral system. Democracy and freedom, in their philosophy, were to be exercised as members of the Ba'th, and the party was open to all.

It has been shown here that the common denominators among the ruling parties, whether in single- or multi-party systems, are numerous. For example, the structure of centralization, not only of the party, but also of the governance mechanism, was common to all. The overlapping of the ruling party with the other arms of the state, particularly the security services, was robust in many of these countries. For the leadership, the challenge was, in David Art's words, that 'Dictators must craft coercive institutions that can deal with threats without undermining support for the regime. They must also not allow these institutions to become alternative power centers.'[73] And that is exactly what happened in these republics for more than three decades: their leaders managed to create a centralized and overlapping system that allowed institutions such as the ruling party to thrive and expand, but not to an extent that could threaten them.

Acknowledgements

My deep gratitude goes to Dr Eskandar Sadeghi-Boroujerdi, Siavush Randjbar-Daemi, Lauren Banko, and the anonymous reviewer for their suggestions and help. An expanded version of this article appeared in Joseph Sassoon, *Anatomy of Authoritarianism in the Arab Republics* (Cambridge: Cambridge University Press, 2016).

Disclosure statement

No potential conflict of interest was reported by the author.

---

[71]Gandhi, *Political Institutions under Dictatorship*, p. xviii.
[72]Beatriz Magaloni, *Voting for Autocracy: Hegemonic Party Survival and its Demise in Mexico* (New York: Cambridge University Press, 2006), p. 19.
[73]David Art, 'What Do We Know about Authoritarianism after Ten Years?', *Comparative Politics*, 44(3) (2012), pp. 351–373, quote on p. 362.

7 The origins of Communist Unity

Anti-colonialism and revolution in Iran's tri-continental moment

Eskandar Sadeghi-Boroujerdi

ABSTRACT

This article analyses the historical emergence of the Organization of Communist Unity, which coalesced out of the National Front of Iran and its Organizations abroad. In the aftermath of the MI6/CIA-orchestrated 1953 *coup d'état*, a new generation of political activists left Iran for Europe and the United States to pursue their higher education. While politically active in the Organizations of the National Front Abroad, they gradually turned to revolutionary Marxism against the backdrop of the torrential waves of decolonization and resistance to imperial military interventions undulating across the Global South. This same constellation of activists was not only fiercely anti-imperialist, but also opposed any form of dependence on the U.S.S.R. or the People's Republic of China. They would move from Europe and the United States to establish themselves in several locations across the Arab world, and pursue political activism and their advocacy of guerrilla warfare, as part of their ambition to launch a national liberation struggle against the Pahlavi regime. By examining Communist Unity's predecessors and their manifold transnational ideological, political and logistical networks with like-minded revolutionary movements inside the Middle East, this article brings to the fore hitherto under-explored South–South connections, and situates Iran's revolutionary opposition within the global moment of '1968'.

Introduction

Despite the lingering vestiges of several intermittent traumas of modern Iranian history, few have rivalled the profound impact of the MI6/CIA-orchestrated *coup d'état* which ousted the nationalist premier, Muhammad Musaddiq, on 19 August 1953. In this article, I examine how during the 1960s and 1970s in the aftermath of the coup, the discursive and practical framing of resistance to the late Pahlavi regime began to shift and transform in decisive ways. This is achieved through an exploration of the history of the transnational Organizations of the National Front of Iran Abroad (Middle East Branch) (henceforth, ONFME) and the Organization of Communist Unity (*Sazman-i vahdat-i kumunisti*, henceforth OCU), which evolved out of the former, as well as the domestic and international contexts in which they both emerged.

The trajectory of these two intricately related groups illustrates how the language of armed resistance and revolutionary insurrection challenged and sought to dislodge prevailing ideological and political practices centred on civil protest and electoral contestation and how liberal nationalism gave way to revolutionary Marxism amongst active and vocal elements of the dissenting opposition. The latter shift was a theoretical and practical transformation that would be enacted by a new generation, many of whom had experienced the coup in their teenage years and for whom the memory of both the nationalist-popular government's euphoric ascendancy and its tragic demise continued to live on.[1]

Like the Cuban, Fidel Castro, or the Palestinian, George Habash,[2] these men's formative political experiences began as nationalists and anti-imperialists.[3] However, unlike the aforementioned, several leading members of ONFME and OCU came to embrace revolutionary socialism in the imperial metropolises of Europe and the United States. It was thus largely in the metropole where they first came to conclude that American imperialism, the world capitalist system and the oppression and exploitation they were held to perpetuate, were inextricably intertwined. ONFME and OCU's partisans were born of a foundational trauma for which they contended foreign imperialists and home-grown reactionaries were responsible, giving rise to the search for a radical explanation and political praxis in the face of what they took to be Iran's authoritarian political impasse.

I will first provide a detailed account of the OCU's origins in the Organizations of the National Front of Iran Abroad and the formation of the ONFME—a series of political constellations that cannot be understood apart from the numerous problems and antagonisms which afflicted the Second and Third National Fronts and their supporters, both inside and outside of Iran during the 1960s: in short, the domestic and organizational factors contributing to ONFME and OCU's emergence and development.

However, a further contention of this article is that the transformation of the activists comprising ONFME and OCU, who during the late 1950s and first half of the 1960s moved from the politics of liberal nationalism to fierce advocacy of democratic socialism, anti-imperialism and proletarian internationalism, must also be framed within the wider context of the politics of tri-continentalism and South–South solidarity. This was a solidarity that harboured important logistical, political and imaginative dimensions. Though one could cite myriad events and political struggles both before and after 1953,[4] such solidarity saw its chief programmatic expression first in the Afro-Asian Conference convened in Bandung,

---

[1]Bihruz Muʿazzami, 'Az tajrubah-yi Musaddiq va tashkil-i hukumat-i milli chih natayiji ra mitavan barayi ayandah itikhaz kard?', in *Tajrubah-yi Musaddiq dar chishm andaz-i ayandah-yi Iran*, ed. Hushang Kishavarz Sadr and Hamid Akbari (Bethesda: Ibex, 2005), 357–365. Bizhan Iftikhari and Hamid Ahmadi, Interview with Bizhan Iftikhari, *Research Association for Iranian Oral History (RAIOA)*, Vienna, 2013, Part 1. Kambiz Rusta and Hamid Ahmadi, Interview with Kambiz Rusta, *RAIOA*, Berlin, 1995, Parts 1 and 2.

[2]Walid W. Kazziha, *Revolutionary Transformation in the Arab World: Habash and His Comrades from Nationalism to Marxism* (London: Charles Knight & Company, 1975), chapters 3 and 4.

[3]Iran's experience of colonialism was distinct, insofar as unlike either India, Egypt or Algeria, it was never formally colonized or subject to direct rule from the imperial centre. It was, however, divided de facto into mutual spheres of influence by Russia and Britain in 1907, and once more by the Soviet Union and Britain following the Allies' invasion in 1941. Moreover, the Anglo-Persian (later Iranian) Oil Company during the first half of the twentieth century often behaved as a colonial enclave within south-western Iran, possessing its own police force, as well as effectively introducing various disciplinary mechanisms and spatial processes of class segmentation and racial segregation. See, Touraj Atabaki, 'Far from Home, But at Home: Indian Migrant Workers in the Iranian Oil Industry', *Studies in History* 31, no. 1 (2015): 104; Kaveh Ehsani, 'Oil, State and Society in Iran in the Aftermath of the First World War', in *The First World War and Its Aftermath: The Shaping of the Middle East*, ed. T.G. Fraser (London: Gingko Library, 2015), 203.

[4]For a history of the 'Third World' as a political identity and agency, see Vijay Prashad, *The Darker Nations: A People's History of the Third World* (London and New York: The New Press, 2007).

Indonesia in April 1955,[5] followed by the inaugural conference of the Non-Aligned Movement in Belgrade, Yugoslavia in September 1961, and the founding of the Organization of Solidarity with the People of Asia, Africa and Latin America at the Tricontinental Conference in Havana, Cuba in January 1966.[6] A new generation of Iranian activists coming of age in the 1960s consciously embraced these historic events of tri-continental solidarity, while also introjecting them into the meaning and significance of the Musaddiq era and the coup simply referred to as '28 Murdad' (19 August 1953), to construct a popular revolutionary politics in Iran which unmistakably located itself *within* the fold of the Global South. In the words of Kambiz Rusta, a leading student activist in the National Front Abroad, 'we believed that the evolution of the political line (*khatt*) of Musaddiq was that of Ben Bella, then Castro, the path of revolution.'[7]

Even if it would be somewhat crude to identify the birth of the 'post-colonial subject' with a specific date,[8] the articulation of tri-continentalism undoubtedly nurtured the emergence of new political subjectivities, agencies and identifications, including in Pahlavi Iran and the Iranian diaspora. Thus, whilst the domestic context and organizational travails of the National Front of Iran (henceforth, NFI) are indispensable to understanding the ONFME and OCU's emergence, they are far from sufficient. An examination of Iran's revolutionary opposition through the wider lens of the global 'Tri-continental moment' and its transnational networks inside the Arab world is pivotal to an adequate understanding of its political and ideological development preceding the Iranian Revolution of 1979. However, this Iranian case study also contributes to the ever-growing literature on the historic period of decolonization following WWII and the 'Tri-continental moment', further complicating the picture vis-à-vis the latter's global reception and resonance as well as its disparate and uneven repercussions.

In the words of Arif Dirlik, the 'global sixties' and their denouement in 1968:

> were directly inspired by the crisis of colonialism, and the implications for capitalism of de-colonization, but also by the seeming crisis of 'actually existing socialism', until then the only challenger to capitalism. The crisis gave renewed hope to Third World struggles for liberation, autonomy, and new modes of development that would avoid the pitfalls of capitalism as well as of Stalinist Communism.[9]

The ONFME and OCU are an aperture through which we might view this global moment and thereby eschew the prevailing 'methodological nationalism' defining many accounts of Iran's revolutionary opposition, understood solely through the perspective of domestic causes and events.[10]

By examining the ideational and logistical networks of the ONFME and OCU, which crisscrossed the metropole and West Asia and North Africa, while also being imaginatively

---

[5]Christopher J. Lee, *Making a World After Empire: The Bandung Moment and its Political Afterlives* (Athens: Ohio University Press, 2010), Introduction; Jeffrey James Byrne, *Mecca of Revolution: Algeria, Decolonization, and the Third World Order* (Oxford and New York: Oxford University Press, 2016), Introduction.

[6]Thea Pitman and Andy Stafford, 'Introduction: Transatlanticism and Tricontinentalism', *Journal of Transatlantic Studies* 7, no. 3 (2009): 197.

[7]Rusta and Ahmadi, Interview with Kambiz Rusta, *RAIOA*, Part 4.

[8]Robert J.C. Young, *Postcolonialism: A Historical Introduction* (London and New York: Wiley-Blackwell, 2016), Loc 6187.

[9]Arif Dirlik, 'The Third World in 1968', in *The Third World in the Global 1960s*, ed. Samantha Christiansen and Zachary A. Scarlett (New York and Oxford: Berghahn Books, 2015), Loc 200.

[10]For a pertinent critique of such 'internalism', see Alexander Anievas and Kerem Nisancioglu, *How the West Came to Rule: The Geopolitical Origins of Capitalism* (London: Pluto Press, 2015); Kamran Matin, *Recasting Iranian Modernity: International Relations and Social Change* (London and New York: Routledge, 2013), Introduction and Conclusion.

connected to anti-colonial and national liberation struggles in Egypt,[11] Algeria, the Congo, Vietnam and Palestine, we are able to ascertain a more global vantage point on Iran's revolutionary opposition during this period.[12] In this way, we might begin to understand Iran's revolutionary and transnational dissidents as participating in what Alex Lubin has called 'geographies of liberation', namely, those 'dialectical spaces produced in the collision between nationalism and colonialism, on the one hand, and subaltern decolonial and liberation politics, on the other'.[13]

I have sought to avoid a teleological reading of OCU, *as if* its final form was already nascent in the Organizations of the National Front of Iran Abroad. To do so would be a patent misrepresentation, not to mention bad history. Rather, what we observe are fluid political engagements by a relatively small constellation of activists in the metropole, predominantly Continental Europe and the United States, subsequently followed by a period focussed in Beirut, but also Baghdad, Syria, Libya and Turkey. Upon entry into the Middle East, this network of activists took different names commensurate with distinct phases and purposes, including the Organizations of the National Front of Iran Abroad (Middle East Branch), the Star Group (*Guruh-i sitarah*), the Communist Alliance Group (*Guruh-i ittihad-i kumunisti*, henceforth CAG) and lastly the OCU following the 1979 revolution (see Figure 1). Despite appearances to the contrary, these transformations were more of a gradual slow-burn than a series of epiphanic metamorphoses. 'Shift', in the course of the narrative presented herein, acts more as a heuristic and clarificatory device than a determinate temporal marker in the flow of historical time. I have tried to give a basic account of such ideological and political shifts and their relationship to domestic, regional and international developments.

Despite some continuity of personnel, it is also crucial to acknowledge that the organizations which make up the historical genealogy of OCU significantly changed over time and its final form was far from determined at the outset. What we see is a complex transnational network of activists undergoing a series of discernible transformations, first in relation to questions of internal organization in the Organizations of the National Front of Iran Abroad, but more importantly, in relation to a global moment, namely, that of decolonization and the proliferation of national liberation movements. Not as a passive and orderly process, but framed as part and parcel of formerly colonized nations' struggle for collective liberation, and the emergence of the 'Third World' as a substantive geopolitical category striking an independent path in the face of great power bi-polarity.

This article avails itself of relevant Persian-language newspapers, primarily two different series of *Bakhtar-i imruz*, inspired by the memory, example and famed newspaper of the same name published by Dr Husayn Fatimi, Musaddiq's outspoken Foreign Minister who was executed by the Pahlavi regime in 1954. They were published by the Organizations of the National Front Abroad during the 1960s and 1970s in New York and Beirut/Iraq, respectively. This has been complemented by the political and ideological literature of the CAG, encompassing various pamphlets published during the 1970s, as well as subsequently

---

[11]Gamal 'Abd al-Nasser's triumph in the face of the British, French and Israeli invasion during the Suez Crisis also made its mark on the evolving political consciousness of this generation of Iranians, including Ali Khansari, a leading activist of the National Front Abroad and the OCU. 'Dar guzasht-i 'Ali Khansari; buzurg zist va buzurg raft', *Inqilab-i islami*, 18 Farvadin 1393, https://www.enghelabe-eslami.com/component/content/article/36-didgagha/khane-ahzab/8135-2014-04-07-09-21-08.html (accessed 6 June 2017).

[12]Sebastian Conrad, *What is Global History?* (Princeton, NJ: Princeton University Press, 2016), Introduction.

[13]Alex Lubin, *Geographies of Liberation: The Making of an Afro-Arab Political Imaginary* (Chapel Hill: University of North Carolina Press, 2014), 7.

published memoirs, oral history accounts and correspondence of members of the Star Group and OCU. Because of the well-known secretiveness of the organization and the unwillingness of erstwhile members, with a few exceptions, to go on the record, alternative histories of its inner workings and personnel are extremely limited. There were charged and partisan exchanges between the OCU's forebears, namely, the Star Group, and the Organization of the Iranian People's Fada'i Guerrillas (OIPFG), when the two groups' planned merger unravelled, particularly on the question of who was to blame for the process's failure. These exchanges have continued to colour extant historiography of the so-called 'homogenization process' (described later), even if it is not the chief focus of this article. Nonetheless, I have tried to draw upon other accounts where tenable, including those by former members of the OIPFG.

The NFI: historical bloc or haphazard coalition?

The lineages of ONFME and OCU are to be found in the history of the NFI, first and foremost the National Front Abroad and the chapters established by its activists and sympathizers in Europe and the United States. The Organizations of the National Front of Iran Abroad (*Sazman-ha-yi jibhah-yi milli-yi Iran kharij az kishvar*, ONFA), out of which the OCU emerged in 1979, sought to continue the legacy of the original NFI. The latter was an essentially tenuous umbrella of political personalities and disparate groupings, which had first been established in 1949, and had pioneered the nationalization of the Anglo-Iranian Oil Company in 1951 and the Musaddiq government's defence of the principle of oil nationalization.[14] Many years later Musaddiq would contend that the Organizations were bound by the NFI's charter approved at the first and only congress of the Second National Front in January 1963. But since no explicit mention was made of them in the new charter of the Third National Front of 1965, they were thereafter free to pursue political activism and agitation consonant with their own needs and local conditions, bestowing these diaspora-based organizations with a significant degree of autonomy.[15]

While the majority of the individuals who would go on to form ONFME and later OCU were initially liberal nationalist and anti-imperialist in orientation, a number of them, like other prominent Marxists of subsequent decades[16] and student activists in the Second National Front of Iran, had begun their political lives in the Youth Organization of the Tudah Party before the 1953 *coup d'état*.[17] They were profoundly invested in the moral and political authority of Musaddiq who remained under house arrest until his death in March 1967,[18] and had become antagonistic to the Tudah Party, whose highest echelons had shown

---

[14]Homa Katouzian, *Musaddiq and the Struggle for Power in Iran* (London: I.B. Tauris, 1990), 71–3.

[15]This was affirmed in Musaddiq's letter to the European Organizations of the National Front of Iran, 3 February 1965 [14 Bahman 1343]. Sayyid 'Ali Shayigan and Ahmad Shayigan, *Sayyid 'Ali Shayigan: zindigi namah-yi siyasi, nivishtahha va sukhanraniha*, vol. 2 (Tihran: Agah, 1385), 168.

[16]Hasan Ziya-Zarifi and Bizhan Jazani of the Jazani-Zarifi Group are one such example. Peyman Vahabzadeh, *A Guerrilla Odyssey: Modernization, Secularism, Democracy, and the Fadai Period of National Liberation in Iran, 1971–1979* (New York: Syracuse University Press, 2010), Loc 346.

[17]This included activists such as Muhammad Ali Khansari, Khusraw Parsa, Kambiz Rusta and Bizhan Mussahibnia, all of whom became disillusioned as high school students with the Tudah Party over the leadership's intractable hostility towards the Musaddiq government. Also see 'Yad-i rafiq shahid Manuchihr Hamidi garami bad', *Raha 'i*, no. 80 (28 Khurdad 1360), 21.

[18]Jazani's assessment of Musaddiq by contrast is sober, measured and at times critical. Bizhan Jazani, *Tarh-i jami 'ih shinasi va mabani-yi istaratizhi-yi junbish-i inqilabi-yi khalq-i Iran, bakhsh-i duvvum* (tarikh-e si salih-yi siyasi-yi Iran) (Tehran: Maziyar, 1357 [1978]), 51–2.

considerable disagreement and/or antipathy towards the nationalist premier in the period preceding the coup.[19] It should be emphasized that there was a significant degree of political fluidity prevailing among students at the time insofar as several individuals who went on to advocate for armed struggle as members of either the OIPFG, Organization of the People's Mujahidin or Organizations of the National Front in the Middle East (ONFME), had been active in the Second National Front founded in the summer of 1960. By the mid-1960s, a great many of these young activists had become disillusioned with the conduct of the leaders of the Second National Front, as well as their general political outlook during the Amini government (1961–1962) and the aftermath of its fall. The key difference was that despite their overlapping experiences surrounding the demise of the Amini government and the authoritarian consolidation of the Shah's regime, which entered a new phase with the inception of the 'White Revolution' in 1963,[20] the founders of OCU had been radicalized outside of the country, in Europe and the United States, and predominantly active in the Organizations of the National Front of Iran Abroad and the Confederation of Iranian Students (National Union).[21] The latter purported to be the political and corporate representative of Iranian students abroad, as well as inside Iran during the 1960s and 1970s.[22]

The formation of the National Front Abroad began in 1961, and according to CAG/OCU's retrospective analysis,[23] was beset by contradictions from the outset. These issues could be traced back to the NFI, which never became nor was even intended to become a unified party with a single coherent ideology and political programme. The forces comprising the National Front coalesced around the issue of the nationalization of Iran's most important natural resource, namely oil, which in turn became a symbol of Iran's national sovereignty and independence against the threat posed by British imperialism.[24] The capaciousness and galvanizing thrust of the demand for unalloyed national self-determination and the power to fully control the nation's most vital natural resource cut across a wide cross-section of socio-political classes, cleavages and groupings. This was the very reason it had been conceived as a *front* in contradistinction to a tightly knit and hierarchical party organization. Between 1951 and 1952 it could even be considered akin to what Antonio Gramsci famously referred to as a 'historical bloc', entailing the mediation of a variety of different class interests

---

[19]Kambiz Rusta, a member of the Star Group (and who saw himself as intimately associated with the ONFME), explicitly mentions the formative role of the coup and his stern criticisms of the Tudah Party leadership (despite his well-known familial links to the party), and how it shaped his activism in the student diaspora during the early 1960s. Rusta and Ahmadi, Interview with Kambiz Rusta, *RAIOA*, Berlin, 1995, Part 2.

    The Tudah leadership was also criticized by Bizhan Jazani, who contends the party's policy was based on a flawed analysis and underestimation of the still perfidious role of British neo-colonialism inside Iran. Jazani, *Tarh-i jami'ih shinasi*, 54.

    Also see, Maziar Behrooz, 'The 1953 Coup in Iran and the Legacy of the Tudeh', in *Mohammad Mosaddeq and the 1953 Coup in Iran*, ed. Mark J. Gasiorowski and Malcolm Byrne (Syracuse, NY: Syracuse University Press, 2004), Loc 2472.

[20]Ervand Abrahamian, *Iran between Two Revolutions* (Princeton, NJ: Princeton University Press, 1982), chapter 9.

[21]Hasan Masali, *Nigarishi bih guzashtah va ayandah: panjah sal-i mubarizah dar rah-i azadi*, vol. 1 (Wiesbaden, 1392 [2013]), 135.

[22]Afshin Matin-asgari, *Encyclopaedia Iranica*, s.v. 'Confederation of Iranian Students, National Union', vol. VI, Fasc. 2, 122–125, https://www.iranicaonline.org/articles/confederation-of-iranian-students (accessed 7 June 2017).

[23]In this instance, I will be using the CAG and OCU interchangeably. But for the sake of historical accuracy it should be noted that the pamphlet *Chih nabayad kard?* was in fact authored by Khusraw Parsa as a CAG position paper during the final assembly of a sizable number of activists of the Organizations of the National Front of Iran Abroad in Giessen, West Germany in January 1978. It would be published after some revisions in the same year by the CAG and following the publication of several other pamphlets such as *Dar barah-yi purusah-yi tajanus*, *Istalinism*, etc. also drawn upon in the course of this article. The OCU would later republish several of these pamphlets under their name.

[24]For an account of British neo-colonialism and American imperialism in Iran, see Ervand Abrahamian, *The Coup: 1953, the CIA, and the Roots of Modern U.S.-Iranian Relations* (New York: The New Press, 2013), Introduction.

propagated throughout society, 'bringing about not only a unison of economic and political aims, but also intellectual and moral unity…on a "universal" plane'.[25]

This is not to say that the leaders of the National Front conceived of it in such terms, but rather that the principles of national sovereignty, self-determination, democratic constitutionalism and the coalition of social forces which rallied behind them, temporarily engendered a considerable degree of a moral and political unity around Musaddiq and his programme in its stand-off with Great Britain. For a brief time, this platform was able to forge a hegemonic consensus as well as constitute and mobilize a collective nationalist anti-imperialist political subject in the government's defence throughout much of Iran's urban populace.[26] In this vein, the Marxist-Leninist, Bizhan Jazani, argued in a retrospective analysis regarding his own involvement in the movement that:

> our collaboration in public activism under the banner of the National Front was to realize an historic issue, namely, that of the collaboration of the progressive forces of society. This collaboration allowed us to have a healthy and sound understanding of the national anti-imperialist struggle, and to become intimately acquainted with the forces of the National Front.[27]

This popular anti-imperialist hegemony was harnessed to great effect by Musaddiq during his time as prime minister, and bestowed an air of moral authority that he and other members of his inner circle would continue to wield among their partisans long after their removal from power. The nationalist PM was, however, both sceptical and hesitant about mobilizing the fervour his persona and platform provoked in his supporters and devotees, and never seriously considered providing it with an organizational form of substance. This decision was arguably to his great detriment and contributed to the movement's ultimate defeat and failure to bring about a lasting social transformation. Moreover, as the example of the Second National Front shows us, despite Musaddiq's great moral standing it did not always translate into political authority or ensure his epigones would abide by his prescriptions for the movement's policies and trajectory.

CAG/OCU's analysis of the Second National Front of Iran helps us understand not only the group's own thinking about the Front's often dysfunctional modus operandi, but how the Front's vicissitudes were interpreted by younger activists at home and abroad more generally. The OCU delineated three key groups comprising the Second National Front and its Organizations abroad in the first half of the 1960s.

The *first* group had a historic association with and investment in the original Front, which went back to its initial formation in 1949, the Musaddiq government and the coup. These groups included those affiliated with the Iran Party (*Hizb-i Iran*) led de facto by Allahyar Salih, and populated by other notable figures such as Karim Sanjabi, Ahmad Zirakzadah and Shapur Bakhtiyar. It consisted of salaried professionals and technocrats, including many engineers and lawyers, who sought to participate and achieve piecemeal reforms through the electoral process. Muhammad Nakhshab, a one-time member of the Iran Party, later split to form his

---

[25]Gramsci quoted in Adam David Morton, *Unravelling Gramsci: Hegemony and Passive Revolution in the Global Political Economy* (London: Pluto, 2007), Loc 2497.

[26]For more on the constitution of collective subjects in contentious politics, see John Chalcraft, *Popular Politics in the Making of the Modern Middle East* (Cambridge and New York: Cambridge University Press, 2016), Loc 762.

[27]In this instance, Jazani is apparently referring to his involvement in the Second National Front. Bizhan Jazani, 'Namah bih yak dust', in *Bih zaban-i qanun: Bizhan Jazani va Hassan Ziya Zarifi dar dadgah-i nizami*, ed. Nasir Muhajir and Mihrdad Baba 'Ali (Créteil and Berkeley: Nuqtah, 1394), 333.

own party, the Iranian People's Party (*Hizb-i mardum-i Iran*), with its own unique blend of Islamic pieties and socialism. Next was the Socialist League of Iran (*Jami'ih-yi sawsiyalist-ha-yi Iran*) headed by Khalil Maliki, which enjoyed a strong bond with the National Front and Musaddiq personally. This dated back to the period when Maliki had remained steadfast in his support for the Musaddiq government as leader of the Toiler's Party of the Iranian Nation, Third Force (*Hizb-i zahmatkishan-i millat-i Iran, Niru-yi sivvum*). This was complicated by the secession of two prominent figures from Third Force. Muhammad Ali Khunji and Mas'ud Hijazi broke with Maliki, became highly critical of his stewardship and decried him as a traitor for having met with the Shah.[28] The Party of the Iranian Nation (*Hizb-i millat-i Iran*) led by Dariyush Furuhar were staunch nationalists, anti-British, anti-communist and harboured well-known Pan-Iranist leanings. CAG/OCU gloss over the role of Ghulam Husayn Sadiqi during this period; a widely respected nationalist politician and academician,[29] he had been Musaddiq's Interior Minister during the nationalist government, and played a notable role in supporting the Second National Front's formation.[30] This was most likely because of his advocacy of principled dialogue and the need to reach an accommodation with the ruling regime.[31]

According to CAG/OCU, the *second* grouping which had attached themselves to the Organizations of the Front Abroad were supporters of the Tudah Party, who surreptitiously strove to steer the Front in their own favoured direction. But the *third* and largest group of supporters making up the National Front of Iran Abroad (*Jibhah-yi milli-yi Iran kharij az kishvar*) were new to political activism and were individuals, for the most part students, who had only recently been politicized.[32] This last constituency followed events in Iran from afar, but they were nevertheless crucial to the National Front's political fortunes going forward. Moreover, this collection of individuals cannot be understood in isolation either from events inside Iran or from the waves of anti-imperialist radicalism colouring a huge swathe of protests in cities throughout the metropole during the late 1960s and early 1970s.[33] In this way, both *geographical* (south–north/south–south) and *generational* (pre- and post-1945) differences within the National Front and its sympathizers made themselves manifest, and converged to reinforce the ideological and political rupture that was in the offing. Such a variegated constituency would have been difficult to maintain under the best of circumstances, let alone those where conditions of severe political repression prevailed inside the country, and the Pahlavi state's security services, namely SAVAK (*Sazman-i ittila'at va amniyat-i kishvar*), sought to infiltrate dissident and student organizations across Europe.[34]

---

[28]Katouzian, *Musaddiq and the Struggle*, 227–8.

[29]Ahmad Ashraf, 'Sadighi: Ethics, Politics and Social Sciences', *International Institute of Social History* (Amsterdam, 2011), 15.

[30]H.E. Chehabi, *Iranian Politics and Religious Modernism: The Liberation Movement of Iran under the Shah and Khomeini* (London: I.B. Tauris, 1990), 130.

[31]A more charitable reading holds that the scant mention of Sadiqi is because he was above the factional fray of the National Front and thus widely respected.

[32]Sazman-i vahdat-e kumunisti-yi Iran, *Chih nabayad kard? Naqdi bar guzashtah rahnamudi barayi ayandah* (December 1978), v.

[33]A comparable dynamic whereby the radicalization of Third World intellectuals took shape in the metropole is demonstrated to great effect by Michael Goebel, albeit with a focus on Paris during the 1920s and 1930s: Michael Goebel, *Anti-Imperial Metropolis: Interwar Paris and the Seeds of Third World Nationalism* (Cambridge: Cambridge University Press, 2015). Also see, Quinn Slobodian, *Foreign Front: Third World Politics in Sixties West Germany* (Durham, NC: Duke University Press, 2012), chapter 4.

[34]Masali, *Nigarishi bih guzashtah va ayandah*, 1, 290; Afshin Matin-asgari, *Iranian Student Opposition to the Shah* (Cost Mesa, CA: Mazda, 2002), 154.

The dispute over party (*Hizb*) admission in the Second and Third National Fronts

While it is beyond the remit of this article to explore the genesis of the Second and Third National Fronts and their relationship to the Organizations of the National Front of Iran Abroad, I will now try to address the crux of the disagreements which led up to the formation of the ONFME.

After a prolonged period of political repression following the 1953 coup, it was not until 1960 (1339) that the Front's leading activists, many of whom had been members of the underground Movement for National Resistance (*Nihzat-i muqavimat-i milli*), felt there was a political opening and opportunity in which the Front might resume open political activity with enlivened momentum. As alluded to above, disagreements over ideology and strategy, but above all organization persisted and characterized the internal dynamics of the Second National Front from its inception. The most important bone of contention was how the National Front ought to be ordered and the role and status of political parties in any such formation. While some insisted that all parties should effectively dissolve themselves, and enter the Second National Front on an individual basis, others, including Musaddiq under house arrest at his family compound at Ahmadabad, argued forcefully to the contrary. Khunji had dissolved his small breakaway organization, which some dispute ever in fact existed,[35] the Socialist Party (*Hizb-i sawsiyalist*), and entered the National Front, while essentially assuming control of its ideological and organizational apparatus as well as the role of its pre-eminent theoretician.[36] In the words of Homa Katouzian, Khunji, Hijazi and Bakhtiyar came to form a 'triumvirate', which sought to exclude Maliki on the shaky grounds that he might detract from the organization's cohesion, with Bakhtiyar going as far as to accuse him of being a serial splitter (*inshi'abchi*)—a not-so-subtle allusion to Maliki's break with the Tudah Party following the Azerbaijan Crisis of 1946.[37]

In any event, this insistence that parties dissolve and in lieu subject themselves to the triumvirate, rather than unite the Front, led Mahdi Bazargan, the cleric Mahmud Taliqani and Yadullah Sahabi to break away and found the Liberation Movement of Iran (*Nihzat-i azadi-yi Iran*) in 1961.[38] The debate over whether parties *qua* political parties would be allowed to join the NFI, however, was far from settled. Musaddiq had consistently held that the National Front should be made up of political parties and that the executive council of the NFI must be composed of these parties' representatives.[39] This principle was spelt out in a message to the first congress of the National Front in January 1963, a document Musaddiq would explicitly reference in subsequent admonitions.[40]

The key point to take away when analysing the National Front of Iran Abroad (*Jibhah-yi milli-yi Iran kharij az kishvar*) was that the fissures afflicting the Second National Front were

---

[35]Contrary to Katouzian, Jazani does take the formation of the Socialist Party by Khunji and Hijazi to be genuine, though he says it only had tens of members. Jazani, *Tarh-i jami'ih shinasi*, 85–6.

[36]Khunji is reputed to have circulated a paper in which he called for the self-dissolution of all parties in the National Front. Chehabi, *Iranian Politics and Religious Modernism*, 147.

[37]Katouzian, *Musaddiq and the Struggle*, 228.

[38]*Chih nabayad kard?*, 11; Chehabi, *Iranian Politics and Religious Modernism*, 155.

[39]Hamid Shawkat, *Parvaz dar zulmat: zindigani-yi siyasi-yi Shapur Bakhtiar* (Cologne: Baztab, 2014), 299.

[40]Katouzian, *Musaddiq and the Struggle*, 244.

largely reproduced outside of the country as well.[41] As in the case of the Second National Front, the crux of the dispute abroad was over the status of political parties in the Organizations of the National Front of Iran Abroad.[42] In March 1964, in reaction to the news that the Organizations of the National Front in Europe had disbanded its associated parties, Musaddiq wrote a scolding rebuttal emphasizing

> The National Front should be regarded as the central organization of all those parties which believe in a common principle, namely the freedom and independence of the country. If parties and groups are not to join the Front, the Front will become exactly what it is now…and [they] are incapable of taking one step in defending [the rights of the people].[43]

The ramifications of this unambiguous salvo were immediately felt. As documented by Katouzian, the NFI's central council in Tehran sought to diffuse matters by disingenuously claiming it had only taken issue with the Tudah Party's accession to the National Front. This claim was quickly brushed aside by Musaddiq as a red herring, insisting that his statement on the necessity of parties had been strictly reserved for those forces which had been committed to the oil nationalization from the outset. He questioned in direct terms why Maliki's Socialist League had not been admitted to the NFI's 1963 congress.[44]

Within the Organizations of the National Front in Europe there is also evidence that grassroots activists were exceedingly displeased with the conduct of tribal leader, Khusraw Qashqaʾi, and his Tudah associates who oversaw the publication of *Bakhtar-i imruz* (2nd series) in Munich, Germany.[45] Qashqaʾi stood accused not only of misrepresenting the views of National Front activists and sympathizers based in Europe, but of imposing his views by fiat and force of will alone.[46] These conflicts came to a head at the first congress of the Organizations of the National Front in Europe held in Wiesbaden, Germany in early August 1962, where Qashqaʾi refused to place the newspaper under the congress's control and subsequently abandoned the meeting.[47] In the place of *Bakhtar-i imruz* (2nd series), a new publication called *Iran-i azad* would be published as the official organ of the Organizations of the National Front in Europe. Its first issue appeared in November 1962 with Ali Shariʿati as editor, the man who would in the following decade rise to fame as one of the chief ideologues of the Iranian Revolution of 1979.[48]

---

[41]Shayigan and Shayigan, *Sayyid ʿAli Shayigan*, 2, 127.

[42]Because of Musaddiq's forceful and clear position on the issue, Shayigan in the United States also supported the necessity of a Front composed of political parties. Shayigan and Shayigan, *Sayyid ʿAli Shayigan*, 2, 128.

[43]Katouzian, *Musaddiq and the Struggle*, 245.

[44]Ibid., 247.

[45]Qashqaʾi's commitment to the National Front during the Musaddiq government appeared to derive more from animosity towards the Shah than any veritable commitment to constitutional government. Moreover, according to Abbas Milani, following the intervention of Ardashir Zahidi during the late 1960s in a bid to improve relations between the exiled brothers and the Shah, the Shah provided the Qashqaʾis and their mother with a monthly stipend of 6000 West German marks. Abbas Milani, *Eminent Persians: The Men and Women Who Made Modern Iran, 1941–1979* (New York: Syracuse University Press and Persian World Press, 2008), 262–3.

[46]See letter of 15 June 1962 from Parviz Amin, a student activist of the National Front in Europe, to Shayigan, and the 7 August 1962 letter of the Organizations of the National Front of Iran in Austria and France to the Executive Committee of the National Front in America, in Shayigan and Shayigan, *Sayyid ʿAli Shayigan*, 2, 129–30.

[47]Matin-asgari, *Iranian Student Opposition to the Shah*, 54.
   A letter from the Organizations of the National Front in Austria and France appears to confirm this incident. Letter from the Organizations of the National Front of Iran in Austria and France to the Executive Committee of the National Front in America, 7 August 1962, in Shayigan and Shayigan, *Sayyid ʿAli Shayigan*, 2, 129–30.

[48]Matin-asgari, *Iranian Student Opposition to the Shah*, 54.

Back in Iran, the conduct of Bakhtiyar and Khunji was criticized in several quarters. It was claimed that Bakhtiyar feared being overshadowed by Maliki, if he and his Socialist League took up a prominent role within the National Front, while Khunji's deeply antagonistic relationship with Maliki detracted from the Front's very *raison d'être*.[49] Musaddiq's dressing down of the Second National Front's executive committee eventually left them with little choice but to resign, paving the way for the establishment of the Third National Front, whose draft constitution was approved by Musaddiq in early 1965, and which codified the central role of political parties and civil society organizations such as unions, religious and student societies, and local associations.[50] Though the Socialist League were now permitted entry into the Third National Front, the Iran Party refused to cooperate due to a spate of arrests, several on the personal orders of the Shah himself. This latest initiative was thus deprived of any serious prospect of becoming a viable movement beyond the release of two public statements,[51] and was dissolved within a month of its founding.

The National Front Abroad: fragmentation and the embrace of revolutionary politics

Such disarray could not but affect the Organizations of the National Front of Iran Abroad. In a bid to resolve ongoing disagreements, the Organizations of the National Front Abroad in Europe called for an extraordinary congress which was convened in Kiel, West Germany in 1966. A more moderate faction including figures such as the post-revolutionary president, Abulhasan Bani Sadr, and Minister of Foreign Affairs, Sadiq Qutbzadah, continued to express support for the defunct Third National Front. Meanwhile the leftist faction within the Organizations, which included individuals such as Hasan Masali, Manuchihr Hamidi, and Kambiz Rusta, defended membership of the Front on an individual basis. This most likely was because they held that the condition of party membership would prove advantageous to the established parties and their leaderships, and effectively bring about their marginalization within the Organizations of the National Front Abroad. This factional grouping had, however, been radicalized beyond recognition, and forcefully supported armed struggle against the Pahlavi regime and sought to bring about a revolution through the formation of professional cadres predicated on Marxist ideology.[52] In contrast to those in the National Front who had dithered over the question of party organization, this faction called amongst themselves for the strict observation of party discipline.

Clusters of activists had taken to studying Marxist texts and considering the prospects of armed struggle in light of Iran's own socio-historical development and this gradually came to be reflected in the content of the NFI's newspaper in Europe, *Iran-i azad*.[53] This marked

[49]Hijazi's response to Katouzian and explanation of the events which led to the rift with Maliki was later published in the former's memoirs; see Mas'ud Hijazi, *Ruyidadha va davari: 1329–1339* (Tihran: Intisharat-i nilufar, 1375), 683.
[50]Katouzian, *Musaddiq and the Struggle*, 250.
[51]*Chih nabayad kard?*, 14.
[52]Ibid., 16. Rusta and Ahmadi, Interview with Kambiz Rusta, *RAIOA*, Part 4.
    Bizhan Iftikhari, a student activist in the Organizations of the National Front Abroad and one of the representatives of the Star Group in Europe, also recounts the gradual transition towards advocacy of socialism in the Organizations of the National Front while he was a student in Graz, Austria. Iftikhari and Ahmadi, Interview with Bizhan Iftikhari, *RAIOA*, Part 2.
[53]Issues of *Iran-i azad* were flush with pictures and articles of Ernesto 'Che' Guevara and Ho Chi Minh by the late 1960s. See, *Iran-i azad*, no. 64 (September/October 1969). They also published statements by Guevara in booklet form, e.g. Payam-i Ernesto 'Che' Guevara, *Iran-i Azad* (October 1967).

political and cognitive shift was experienced by a fairly loose group of younger activists, and in such a way that those who were the key proponents of this position remained unidentified and below the proverbial parapet. During the congress, the so-called 'conservative' or moderate faction found themselves in the minority and a series of new measures and regulations were approved resulting in many members abandoning the meeting, where nonetheless a new executive committee (*hay'at-i ijra'iyyah*) was elected. Those who accepted the new stricter organizational regulations were welcome to remain in the National Front Abroad, while those who refused were exhorted to withdraw from its committees. According to one account, as a direct result of this drastic change of positions at the executive level, the membership of the National Front in Europe decreased from 700 to 400, amounting to what some decried as a 'legal' purge.[54]

The National Front's presence in the United States was distinct insofar as the role of Dr Ali Shayigan, a senior member of the National Front, esteemed law professor, parliamentarian and confidant of Musaddiq, remained a constant and enduring source of gravity for younger activists based stateside.[55] Following the coup, he had been imprisoned, but soon after his release was exiled to Europe and then the United States.[56] The Organizations of the National Front in America included a slew of politically engaged university students who would go on to play important roles on the revolutionary road to 1978–1979 and in its aftermath. These included Ali Muhammad Fatimi, Mustafa Chamran, Ibrahim Yazdi, Khusraw Parsa and Yusif Tavassuli.[57] In 1962 there were an estimated 7000 Iranian citizens in the United States, rising to 21,000 in 1964 and 40,000 by 1969.[58] Shayigan stewarded the body for the first two years of its existence, i.e. 1961–1963,[59] but continued to have an influential role thereafter delivering rousing speeches to Iranian students across the United States.[60] His presence allowed the committees of the National Front in America to dissent from the line set down by the executive committee, which continued to be dominated by those of a more conservative orientation.

While CAG/OCU alleged that many of these individuals were largely unresponsive to the demands of grassroots activists, they also acknowledged that not all of those who disagreed with the institutionalization of political parties were motivated by the desire to retain their personal prerogatives and control of the organizations and their capacities. Some of those individuals who were sceptical apropos the admission of political parties argued that those parties eligible to join the Organizations of the National Front were themselves unstable, disorganized coalitions, and insisted they would only further exacerbate the Front's organizational shambles.[61]

Nevertheless, the Organizations of the National Front in America were invariably more critical and radical in tone than had been the leadership of the Second National Front.[62] It was believed that preponderating differences were reconciled during the National Front in

[54]*Chih nabayad kard?*, 17.
[55]Mu'azzami, 'Az tajrubah-yi Musaddiq', 359.
[56]Shayigan and Shayigan, *Sayyid 'Ali Shayigan*, 2, 115.
[57]Ibid., 118.
[58]Hassan Mohammadi-Nejad, 'Elite-Counterelite Conflict and the Development of a Revolution: The Case of the Iranian National Front' (PhD thesis, Southern Illinois University, 1970), 143.
[59]Shayigan's letter to Musaddiq, 5 September 1964, in Shayigan and Shayigan, *Sayyid 'Ali Shayigan*, 2, 165–6.
[60]'Duktur Shayigan dar kalifurniya', *Bakhtar-i imruz* 3, 1 Ordibehesht 1344 [21 April 1965].
[61]*Chih nabayad kard?*, 19.
[62]Shayigan and Shayigan, *Sayyid 'Ali Shayigan*, 2, 119; Mohammadi-Nejad, 'Elite-Counterelite Conflict', 225–6.

America's Second Congress in 1963,[63] but within a matter of months a left-wing tendency constituting a segment of the membership and minority in the executive committee seceded and formed a new organization called the National Front of Iran in Exile (*Jibhah-yi milli-yi Iran dar tab'id*). The organization quickly grew and included activists who had been impacted by the Sino-Soviet split and subsequent denunciation of perceived Soviet détente with the Pahlavi regime. It was this group which oversaw the publication of the third series of *Bakhtar-i imruz*, published in New York by the Organizations of the National Front of Iran, America Branch, between 1966 and 1969.[64] The editors added 'exploitation' (*istithmar*) to the old National Front slogan of 'the struggle against despotism and colonialism' (*mubarizah ba istibdad va isti'mar*) and reprinted a quote attributed to Ernesto 'Che' Guevara in bold in several issues: 'it is the inviolable right of the masses to respond to the violence of imperialism with revolutionary violence.'[65] These activists had ceased to believe in the possibility of civil resistance or in the prospects of reforming the Shah's regime. A strong anti-colonial sentiment in solidarity with those individuals,[66] organizations and countries fighting European and American imperialism was already unmistakable. As early as 1963 with the assent of Shayigan in the United States, activists of the National Front Abroad first began to send willing and committed individuals to revolutionary hotspots such as Algeria, Palestine/Jordan and Egypt under the name of the Organization for Students' Revolutionary Preparations (*Sazman-i tadarukat-i inqilabi-yi danishjuyan*).[67]

In April 1966, the National Front in Exile and National Front in America held a joint congress in New York City and decided to unify, though this time the executive committee and council were dominated by the left. Shayigan was the keynote speaker.[68] The new organization was renamed the Organizations of the National Front of Iran Abroad, America Branch (*Sazman-ha-yi jibhah-yi milli-yi Iran kharij az kishvar, bakhsh-i Amrika*), and they suggested that the European Organization take the same name, albeit in the capacity of the European Branch.[69] While there was prima facie organizational unity between the European and American branches it was never realized in substance, underwritten by the fact that an inter-continental Executive Committee was never established.

Bakhtar-i imruz (3rd series) continued to be published in New York and became increasingly open in its advocacy of armed struggle against the Pahlavi state. Meanwhile, in 1967 the Israeli state, with whom the Shah's regime had known, albeit low-level diplomatic ties, launched a war against Egypt, Syria, Jordan and Iraq, occupying parts of the first three Arab countries and the entirety of historic Palestine. This watershed event also led Arab nationalist governments to publicly support Palestinian guerrilla activities, where they had formerly sought to curb them and suppress their coverage. This vindicated the position that had long been held by the Palestinian movement Fateh (*harakat al-tahrir al-watani al-filastini*). Since its establishment in the late 1950s, Fateh had argued that Palestinians needed to take the lead role in their collective liberation instead of relying on the benevolence of the Arab

---

[63]A counterpart convention was held by members of the National Front in Munich, Germany at around the same time. Ibid., 145.
[64]*Chih nabayad kard?*, 18.
[65]Shayigan and Shayigan, *Sayyid 'Ali Shayigan*, 2, 178; *Bakhtar-i imruz* 3, Farvardin/Ordibehesht 1348 [April/May 1969].
[66]'Dar Congo: Lumumba, hanuz mi jangad', *Bakhtar-i imruz* 3, 1 Ordibihisht 1344 [21 April 1965].
[67]Shayigan and Shayigan, *Sayyid 'Ali Shayigan*, 2, 178; Masali, *Nigarishi bih guzashtah va ayandah*, 1, 307.
[68]Mohammadi-Nejad, 'Elite-Counterelite Conflict', 148.
[69]Shayigan and Shayigan, *Sayyid 'Ali Shayigan*, 2, 177.

nationalist regimes in Egypt, Syria and Iraq. Fateh announced its first military operation inside Occupied Palestine on 1 January 1965. Although it initially faced hostility, notably from Nasser's Egypt, it rapidly consolidated its position after the 1967 war, emerging as the largest faction in the Palestinian Liberation Organization (PLO).[70] Its focus on armed struggle was quickly adopted by other major Palestinian groups after 1967, and the Palestinian *fidayin* (freedom fighters) soon became iconic figures of resistance across the globe.[71]

It was in this context that in April/May 1969 *Bakhtar-i imruz* reproduced and praised in the highest terms a fatwa issued from Najaf by the exiled Ayatullah Ruhollah Khumayni, which was interpreted as the cleric's endorsement of 'armed struggle against Zionism and imperialism' in the Middle East. Khumayni, with special reference to the Palestinian armed struggle, had approved the dispensation of religious alms in support of fellow Muslims engaged in the armed defence of 'Muslim lands' (*bilad-i muslimin*).[72] The publishers of *Bakhtar-i imruz* contended that the fatwa 'will be considered an important step in transforming the approach to the struggle inside Iran…it will open new pathways of struggle'.[73] In the same vein, they serialized a Persian translation of Guevara's *Reminiscences of the Cuban Revolutionary War* as part of their effort to dislodge what they held to be the longstanding ideological hegemony of civil contestation through peaceful marches and the ballot box.[74] Such exercises amounted to a normative and political challenge to the way resistance towards the Pahlavi regime ought to be conceived and practised and thereby sought to initiate something of a paradigmatic shift: a shift that was intimately bound up with the wider international context in the lead up to and aftermath of 1968. While it is questionable they were successful in this endeavour,[75] it remains important to note that it was integral to a deeper transformation experienced within the post-Tudah Iranian left and a slew of like-minded international movements elsewhere in the Global South. As in the case of Khumayni's fatwa, the PLO was never far from these young Iranian activists' minds.[76]

Founding the National Front in the Middle East

According to the account provided by CAG/OCU, the Organizations of the National Front Abroad continued to drift along, albeit with little success or effect into the next decade. In 1970, due to accumulated frustration with the latter's ongoing lack of theoretical rigour, strategic vision and organizational competency, a group of activists within the Organizations of the National Front Abroad decided to form a new branch of the National Front in the Middle East,[77] its official title being the Organizations of the National Front of Iran Abroad, Middle East Branch (ONFME).[78] The latter essentially acted as the public face of their activism and as cover, first for their clandestine Marxist organization, the Star Group (*Guruh-i sitarah*), which from 1973 to 1976 partook in a process to merge with the Fada'i Guerrillas. With the

[70]Rosemary Sayigh, *The Palestinians: From Peasants to Revolutionaries* (London: Zed Books, 2013), 155.
[71]Charles Tripp, *The Power and the People: Paths of Resistance in the Middle East* (Cambridge: Cambridge University Press, 2013), 30.
[72]'Fatva-yi Ayatullah Khumayni', *Bakhtar-i imruz* 3, Farvardin/Ordibehesht 1348 [April/May 1969].
[73]Ibid.
[74]Ernesto 'Che' Guevara, 'Havadith-i jangha-yi inqilabi', *Bakhtar-i imruz* 3 (April/May 1969).
[75]Khumayni's scepticism of armed struggle need not be rehearsed here.
[76]Rusta and Ahmadi, Interview with Kambiz Rusta, *RAIOA*, Part 4.
[77]Guruh-i ittihad-i kumunisti, *Nukati dar barah-yi purusah-yi tajanus*, Bahar 1356 [Spring 1978], 28.
[78]Ibid., 7. Shayigan and Shayigan, *Sayyid 'Ali Shayigan*, 2, 179.

merger's failure in 1977, several members of the Star Group founded the Communist Alliance Group (*Guruh-i ittihad-i kumunisti*), which following the revolution became the Organization of Communist Unity (*Sazman-i vahdat-i kumunisti*).[79]

By late 1969 or early 1970, the decision was made unilaterally and without broader consultation to move to the Middle East,[80] as the small band of cadres made their way to the region and took Beirut, Damascus and Baghdad as their main locations of activity.[81] Hasan Masali and K.K. (Ahmad) were the first to go to the Middle East, visiting Baghdad to participate in the Iraqi Students Congress as representatives of the Confederation of Iranian Students, National Union. It was there that they contacted Fateh's Walid Ahmad Nimr al-Nasir, better known as Abu Ali Iyad, who was already familiar with Iranian militants such as Ali Akbar Safa'i Farahani, a founding member of the Fada'i Guerrillas. Safa'i Farahani had left Iran to train and fight alongside the Palestinian resistance and would later be executed by the Shah's regime following his capture in the aftermath of the assault against the Siahkal gendarmerie on 8 February 1971.[82] The ONFME's initial cadres amounted to fewer than 10 dedicated activists, while in subsequent years they were able to attract a couple of hundred student supporters in Europe and the United States.[83] In the early 1970s, Jazani too was able to discern a palpable ideological and political transformation in the new generation of activists still cleaving to the legacy of Musaddiq and the National Front, and its consonance with the revolutionary *zeitgeist*: 'the struggling forces of the National Front have lost their faith in the leadership and parties. They have turned to Marxism, having ceased to regard "nationalism" as responding to the problems of Iran's national liberation movement.'[84]

This process of disillusionment with the leadership and politics of the National Front was spelled out in CAG/OCU's pamphlet *What Should Not Be Done?* (*Chih nabayad kard?*), an allusion to Lenin's own famous pamphlet. This work is important not only because of the information it contains about Communist Unity's 'pre-history', but also because it is one of very few pamphlets coming out of the revolutionary left around this time which can be read as an exercise in self-criticism and as part of an ongoing process of searching introspection, in lieu of the usual accounts chronicling a succession of unparalleled acts of bravery and heroism:

> Awareness of the shortcomings of the past, and especially the lack of a clear programme, led to the emergence of new movements. This included the formation of a group, close to the small communist currents which had come into being in Europe and America in 1970, and their initiation of special activities in the Middle East.[85]

The first individuals to leave Europe for the Middle East were Hasan Masali and K.K. (Ahmad). They were later joined from the United States by Khusraw Parsa (a distant relative of Ali Shayigan), Bizhan Mussahibnia, K.F. (Tahir) and B.M. (Mahmud Irani).[86] Manuchihr Hamidi first supported the initiative from Munich and acted as a crucial liaison. He then briefly went

---

[79]Masali, *Nigarishi bih guzashtah va ayandah*, 317.
[80]*Chih nabayad kard?*, 18.
[81]Masali, *Nigarishi bih guzashtah va ayandah*, 318.
[82]Correspondence with Mahmud Irani, 11 June 2017.
[83]Masali claims that ONFME had around 400 supporters in Europe and the United States during the 1970s. Masali, *Nigarishi bih guzashtah va ayandah*, 241.
[84]Jazani, 'Namah bih yak dust', 334.
[85]*Nukati dar barah-yi purusah-yi tajanus*, 22.
[86]Correspondence with Mahmud Irani (*nom de guerre*), 4 June 2017.

to Iraq for training, before surreptitiously crossing the Iraqi border into Iran as part of the 'homogenization process' (*purusah-yi tajanus*), namely, the merger of their small group and the OIPFG.[87] Beginning in 1973, both groups agreed in principle that their ideological differences could be resolved through a period of theoretical discussion, criticism and exchange (see next section).[88] Virtually all of those just mentioned had been active in Iranian diaspora student politics revolving around the work of the Confederation of Iranian Students and the Organizations of the National Front Abroad. Like-minded activists in these diaspora organizations, such as Kambiz Rusta, Muhammad Ali Khansari and Bizhan Iftikhari, also later became members of the 'Star Group', but they were not permanently based in the Middle East. Rusta and others did visit the region for meetings and consultations. He also undertook a short period of guerrilla training.[89] Though these activists acted primarily as the Star Group's representatives and advocates in Europe and the United States, one key objective was to dispatch cadres from the metropole to training camps in the Middle East, and from there to Iran so they could participate in armed struggle.[90] Ahmad Shayigan, son of Ali Shayigan, was based in New York, though he later moved to Europe where he was active in the Confederation of Iranian Students, before leaving for Libya in the mid-1970s.

But at the outset of the 1970s, these activists felt a genuine need to establish contact with like-minded groups inside Iran. In the summer of 1970 they began by broaching relations with Mas'ud Ahmadzadah in the north-eastern city of Mashhad. They achieved this through one of their own number, who happened to be a cousin of Ahmadzadah. The latter was of course the co-founder of one of the clandestine groups that would eventually unite to form the Marxist-Leninist People's Fada'i Guerrillas.[91] They later also established relations with the Organization of the Iranian People's Mujahidin, before the release of its first communique, which, incidentally, would also be issued from Beirut on 9 February 1972.[92]

This assortment of individuals had already broached contact with Fateh's representative in Germany in the final years of the 1960s, but went on to establish more systematic ties with the Palestinian group and its representatives in Beirut, which showed great willingness to support the young Iranian revolutionaries. Individuals comprising the National Front in the Middle East came from Europe, the United States and even Iran to undergo military training, while affiliated activists continued their work in European and American cities:[93] publicizing the fate of political prisoners, exposing further the improprieties and violations of the Shah and his regime, and holding protest rallies besmirching the international reputation and public relations of the latter.

Regular cooperation between the Mujahidin and the National Front in the Middle East continued, even after the Mujahidin's now infamous 'change of ideological positions' (*taghyir-i mavaza'*) in 1975, when members who protested its abandonment of Islam and adoption of Marxism-Leninism were brutally killed.[94] Alongside the Mujahidin and Fada'i Guerrillas, ONFME initiated and contributed to the operation and content of three Persian-language

---

[87]The OIPFG added 'Iran' to their name in 1974–1975.

[88]*Nukati dar barah-yi purusah-yi tajanus*, 10; Hasan Masali, *Sayr-i tahavul-i junbish-i chap-i Iran va 'avamil-i buhran-i mudavim-i an* (Los Angeles, CA: Dihkhuda, 2001), 127.

[89]Rusta and Ahmadi, Interview with Kambiz Rusta, *RAIOA*, Part 4.

[90]Ibid., Part 4.

[91]Masali, *Nigarishi bih guzashtah va ayandah*, 357.

[92]H.E. Chehabi, 'The Anti-Shah Opposition in Lebanon', in *Distant Relations: Iran and Lebanon in the Last 500 Years* (London: I.B. Tauris, 2006), 186.

[93]Iftikhari and Ahmadi, Interview with Bizhan Iftikhari, *RAIOA*, Part 3.

[94]Ervand Abrahamian, *Radical Islam: The Iranian Mojahedin* (London: I.B. Tauris, 1989), chapter 6.

anti-regime radio stations expedited and broadcast from within Iraq with the support of the Ba'thsit regime. These were Sida-yi Inqilabiyun (Revolutionaries' Voice) (1972–1973), Radio Mihan Parastan (Patriots) (1973–1975), which was later broadcast from Libya until the revolution,[95] and Radio Surush (1974–1975), which was shut down following the conclusion of the Algiers Accord between the Iranian and Iraqi governments in 1975.[96] ONFME were also the driving force behind the fourth series of the newspaper, *Bakhtar-i imruz*, as well as a newspaper in Arabic by the name of *Iran al-thawra*,[97] of which there were no more than a couple of issues.[98] According to one former member of OCU only a single issue of *Bakhtar-i imruz* was printed in Beirut, while the rest were printed in Iraq, despite representations to the contrary. Each issue had a circulation of approximately 500.[99] The activists understandably harboured a desire to distance themselves and their activities from the Iraqi Ba'thist regime and not appear beholden to the latter.[100] But the publication of *Bakhtar-i imruz* sought once again to connect their political praxis to the historic legacy of Musaddiq's executed Foreign Minister, Husayn Fatimi, and an anti-imperialist imagination, which had continued to evolve and change.[101] Following the Algiers Accord, a number of ONFME activists moved to Libya where they were provided with cars, houses and other facilities with which to carry on their political activities and anti-regime agitation.[102]

As mentioned previously, the debates within the Organizations of the National Front during this period had closely tracked those within Iran itself and were symptomatic of the NFI's precipitous decline inside Iran and the seismic shift taking place within much of the Global South. Manifold national liberation and anti-colonial struggles found themselves enveloped by the discourse and practice of armed struggle as the leading modality of resistance to American imperialism and the authoritarian regimes the United States was held responsible for arming and providing with political and diplomatic cover. In the eyes of these small clusters of young activists based primarily in Beirut, Baghdad and Damascus, the Soviet and Chinese models too were thoroughly discredited, and to their great chagrin, seen as pursuing détente with the profoundly maligned Shah.[103] Because of the fractiousness plaguing the National Front both inside and outside the country, and the Pahlavi regime's authoritarian consolidation accompanied by successive waves of repression,[104] the veteran opposition of 1953 had been severely demoralized. The young activists who formed the National Front in the Middle East and the Star Group had become convinced of the pertinence of Marxist-Leninist organizational principles, namely the need for a vanguard of professional cadres and its accompanying revolutionary ideology. In a retrospective assessment of their own development CAG/OCU insightfully remarked that:

---

[95]Correspondence with Mahmud Irani, 2 April 2017.

[96]Tabrizi states that a condition of launching the radio stations in Iraq was that the Iraqi government not interfere in the content of the broadcasts, though as he later makes clear, as bilateral negotiations between Iran and Iraq progressed, the Iraqis prohibited anti-Pahlavi regime propaganda on Radio Mihan Parastan. Haydar Tabrizi, *Ravabit-i burun marzi-yi sazman-i chirik-ha-yi fada 'i-yi khalq-i Iran ta Bahman 1357* (Cologne: Baqir Murtazavi, 1395), 28; Mahmud Du'a'i, *Gushah 'i az khatirat-i Hujjat al-Islam wa al-muslamin Sayyid Mahmud Du'a'i* (Tehran: 'Aruj, 1387), 90.

[97]*Nukati dar barah-yi purusah-yi tajanus*, 11.

[98]Interview with Jalil (*nom de guerre*), 26 June 2017.

[99]Ibid.

[100]Ibid.

[101]This is confirmed by one of their better-known members, Hasan Masali. Masali, *Sayr-i tahavul-i junbish-i chap-i Iran*, 124.

[102]Interview with Jalil, 26 June 2017.

[103]On the issue of Soviet détente, see Roham Alvandi, 'The Shah's Détente with Khrushchev: Iran's 1962 Missile Base Pledge to the Soviet Union', *Cold War History* 14, no. 3 (2014): 423–44.

[104]*Mawj-i nawvin-i mubarizah, Bakhtar-i imruz* 4, no. 7, Day 1349 [December 1970–January 1971].

The activists of our group (*guruh*) came out of currents that had developed separately from one another and without reciprocal influence, and were not in an organic relationship together. This group's adherence to Marxism-Leninism was not created through an acute class struggle tied to the struggles of the working class. In this respect, our knowledge and understanding of Marxism-Leninism were replete with points of weakness.[105]

These activists, having agreed on the *tactical* necessity of urban guerrilla warfare, began to translate and disseminate seminal texts by Castro, Guevara, Carlos Marighella and the Uruguayan Tupamaros National Liberation Movement, with an even greater sense of urgency.[106] CAG/OCU indeed claim that Mas'ud Ahmadzadah had read their translations of Marighella's famous text on urban guerrilla warfare before the two groups had established formal contacts and the People's Fada'i Guerrillas' armed assault on the gendarmerie at Siahkal.[107] The advocacy of armed struggle had not been a radical break, however, as can be seen in the late issues of the third series of *Bakhtar-i imruz* published in New York. It had very much been on the agenda, and came to occupy tactical primacy over civil modalities of political struggle and organization, regarded as untenable under the present conditions. On this point, at least, the individuals who made up ONFME and the Star Group had reached conclusions comparable to those found in Amir Parviz Puyan's (d. 1971) *The Necessity of Armed Struggle and the Repudiation of the Theory of Survival* (spring 1970), and Ahmadzadah's (d. 1972) *Armed Struggle: Both Strategy and Tactics* (summer 1970).[108] Both pamphlets, influenced by the writings of Guevara and Régis Debray, contended that civil contestation was impossible under the prevalent repressive and stultifying political atmosphere, and armed struggle was necessary not only to demonstrate the vulnerability of the Pahlavi state, but to awaken the people and thus ignite a larger struggle for national liberation.[109]

According to Bizhan Iftikhari, a member of the Star Group, his views and those of his comrades were not only closely aligned with Ahmadzadah and Puyan, but the group also helped disseminate the two aforementioned pamphlets and shared similar exemplars in the anti-colonial struggles of Latin America, Cuba and Vietnam.[110] They also rejected not only the tutelage of the Soviet Union, but, unlike their Maoist compatriots in the Revolutionary Organization of the Tudah Party of Iran, the People's Republic of China as well.[111] Like other fellow Iranian revolutionaries at this time, the members of the National Front in the Middle East held that the tactical pursuit of urban-based armed struggle would provoke mass resistance and the eventual formation of a popular liberation army.[112]

CAG/OCU insist that when they first moved to the Middle East, they were still committed to reviving the National Front Abroad, albeit on a new footing. They hoped to witness the emergence of new political formations with a coherent and rigorous ideological and

---

[105]By their own acknowledgement their relationship and ties to organized labour inside Iran during this time were negligible to non-existent. *Nukati dar barah-yi purusah-yi tajanus*, 28.

[106]Masali, *Nigarishi bih guzashtah va ayandah*, 308.

[107]Marighella's text was published in Persian as a separate pamphlet and not in *Bakhtar-i imruz*. Correspondence with Mahmud Irani, 2 April 2017. Also see, *Nukati dar barah-yi purusah-yi tajanus*, 12.

[108]The advocacy of armed struggle remained consistent throughout the 1970s as can be seen from the final issue of *Bakhtar-i imruz*: 'Dar defa' az mubarizah-yi musalahanah', *Bakhtar-i imruz* 4, no. 77, Day 1355 [December 1975–January 1976].

[109]Masali, *Nigarishi bih guzashtah va ayandah*, 357; Vahabzadeh, *A Guerrilla Odyssey*, chapter 4; Michael Löwy, *The Marxism of Che Guevara: Philosophy, Economics, Revolutionary Warfare*, 2nd ed. (Lanham, MD: Rowman & Littlefield, 1973), chapter 11.

[110]Iftikhari and Ahmadi, Interview with Bizhan Iftikhari, *RAIOA*, Part 3; Rusta and Ahmadi, Interview with Kambiz Rusta, *RAIOA*, Part 3.

[111]Ibid., Part 3.

[112]This position would be publicly articulated in *Bakhtar-i imruz*: 'Jang-i chiriki-yi shahri ta tashkil-i artash-i khalq', *Bakhtar-i imruz* 4, no. 3 (10–21 November 1970). Also see *Nukati dar barah-yi purusah-yi tajanus*, 43.

theoretical approach, which could then be fostered and further expanded. At the beginning of the 1970s the activists of the ONFME continued to cling to the vague possibility that a slew of independent militant organizations would continue to collaborate and work together under the auspices of the NFI, and thereby transform the latter into a genuine popular front as they believed already existed in Vietnam. They were still, in their own words, partaking in organizational 'fetishism', instead of making a clean break with the loose coalition in which they had received their early political education.[113]

Nonetheless, a more vanguardist organizational model quickly emerged as the ONFME began the deployment of small cadres to conflict zones in the Arab world, which saw radical armed movements and status quo powers pitted against one another, and where they could acquire military and strategic training in the conduct of guerrilla warfare.[114] According to Ahmad Shayigan, when the decision was first taken to send members of the Organizations of the National Front in Europe and the United States to the fertile enclaves of the Palestinian revolution,[115] most likely PLO camps in Jordan prior to 'Black September' 1970, for military training, his father and elderly statesman in exile gave his approbation, but 'this kind of struggle was a far cry from what he knew'.[116] At this time, the National Front in the Middle East not only operated under the imprimatur of the Organizations of the National Front Abroad, but was also a powerful voice in the Confederation of Iranian Students, where its representatives and supporters vigorously lobbied in favour of the Fada'i Guerrillas inside Iran, receiving messages of support from them in turn.[117] The extent of their influence was palpable when despite a Maoist majority in the Confederation's Secretariat in 1971, Manuchihr Hamidi, a founding member of the National Front in the Middle East/Star Group, was elected to the secretariat, and held the key position of head of Organization and Defence. During this time, he was especially active in calling for an international boycott of the lavish and highly controversial 2500 year celebrations of the establishment of the 'Imperial State of Iran'.[118]

In what might appear to be a reprise of the stultifying wrangling of past gatherings of the National Front and its Organizations, the 1972 congress of the Organizations of the National Front Abroad and 1973 plenum again ran into divisive arguments over the character of 'Front' versus 'group activity'. Some saw no contradiction between a Front sustained by professional political organizations, while others continued to resist such an eventuality. The deadlock over the nature and modus operandi of the National Front Abroad and the very character of the struggle it ought to conduct, and the division between a core of committed activists who advocated revolutionary insurrection as opposed to more casual activists, proved too much to surmount.

Despite the election of executive committees for the European, American and Middle Eastern branches, these organizations except for the radical cadre in the Middle East fell into dereliction. Thus, they concluded:

---

[113]Ibid., 43.

[114]'9 sal-i mubarizah 'alayhah impiriyalism va dast nashandaganish: zindigi namah-yi mukhtasar-i rafiq Murtaza Sayyid Isma'il (Abu Shahin)', *Raha 'i*, no. 31 (29 April 1980 [9 Urdibihisht 1359]).

[115]See, Karma Nabulsi and Abdel Razzaq Takriti, 'The Palestinian Revolution', 2016. https://learnpalestine.politics.ox.ac.uk (accessed 5 June 2017).

[116]Shayigan and Shayigan, *Sayyid 'Ali Shayigan*, 2, 179.

[117]Matin-asgari, *Iranian Student Opposition to the Shah*, 140.

[118]Ibid., 126; Hamid Shawkat, *Junbish-i danishju'i: kunfidarasiyun-i jahani-yi muhassilin va danishjuyan-i Irani (ittihad-i milli)*, vol. 1 (Los Angeles, CA: Shirkat-i kitab, 2010), 237.

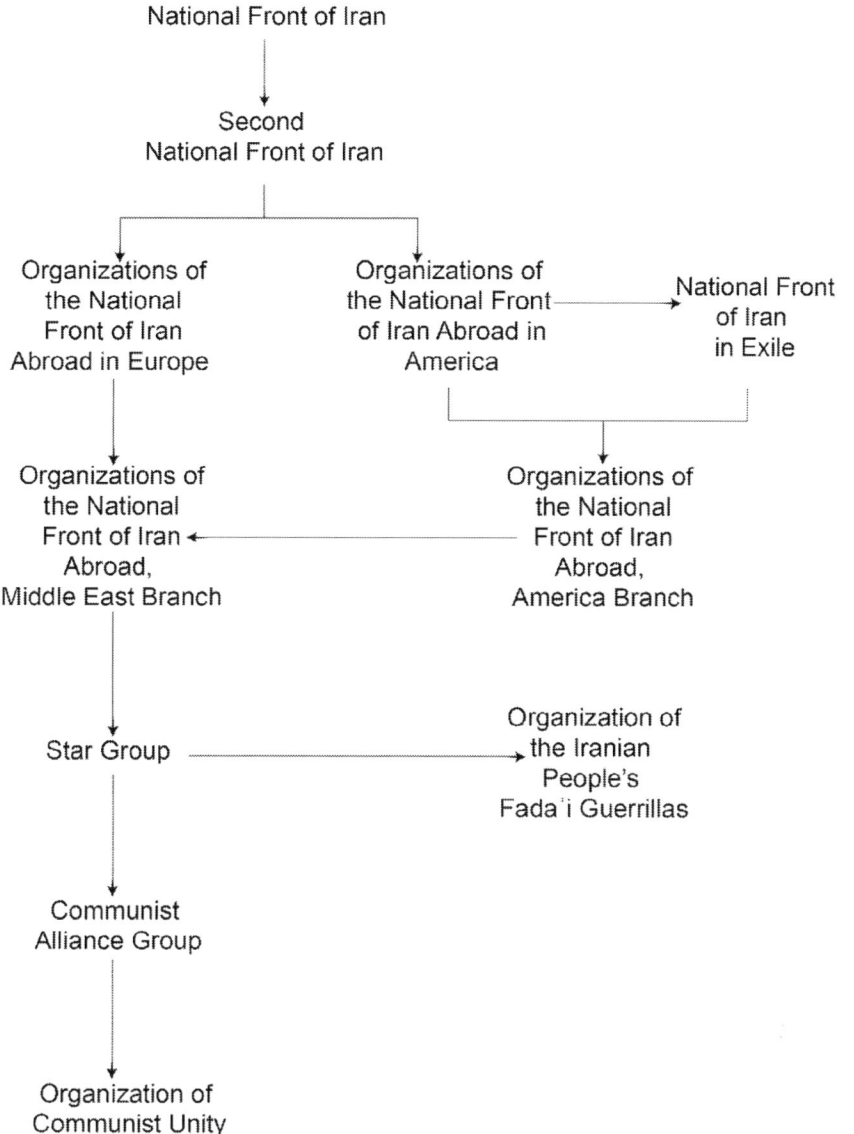

Figure 1. Mapping the origins of the Organization of Communist Unity.

after 5 years [since the 1972 congress] it will be observed that the only activity under the name of the National Front was from those who belonged to the group [namely, the Star Group, later Communist Alliance Group]. The others did not take a single step for the National Front. During the last five years, the council did not even hold a single meeting.[119]

Those elected to the committees of the Front's foreign-based organizations were overwhelmingly criticized for their general inactivity, lackadaisical attitude and the absence of any sense of genuine accountability within the organization itself. As a direct result, CAG/OCU argued

---

[119]*Chih nabayad kard?*, 30.

the NFI was susceptible to manipulation as an inherently 'temporary coalition',[120] whereas parties, at least the archetypal party they had in mind, were synonymous with ideology, strategy, tactics and a practical programme.[121]

'Homogenization process', the Star Group and the emergence of Communist Unity

As mentioned briefly earlier, in the spring of 1973 a constellation of independent Marxist activists associated with the ONFME entered into the 'homogenization process'[122] with the OIPFG under the name of the 'Star Group', and thus effectively dissolved their organizational structure into that of the Fada'i Guerrillas.[123] It was Hamidi who was chosen and agreed to covertly return to Iran as the Star Group's representative in this process and aid its progress.[124] According to a former member of the OIPFG, Haydar Tabrizi, the *nom de guerre* of Muhammad Dabiri Fard, who was involved in the organization's foreign relations and operations during the latter half of the 1970s, the Star Group, under the cover of the Organizations of the National Front Abroad played a vital part in the distribution of OIPFG propaganda and political literature in Europe and the United States.[125] Within the clandestine Star Group there also appears to have been a dilemma between preserving its hidden identity as an organization, which advocated and partook in armed struggle and facilitated the operations of the OIPFG, while continuing to work under the banner of the Organizations of the National Front.[126] It, nevertheless, acted as an essential intermediary and interlocutor with militant Palestinian organizations inside Lebanon and representatives of the Iraqi state.[127] According to Tabrizi, the members of the National Front in the Middle East acted as the OIPFG's representatives in the region during this time.[128] Though the OIPFG was undoubtedly the larger, more famous organization, with active professional cadres inside Iran, the Star Group's extensive logistical and political networks in the Arab world harboured valuable political, military and symbolic capital. This capital was sorely needed by the OIPFG in the face of an unrelenting state campaign against it. ONFME's relations with revolutionary movements and governments in Lebanon, Iraq, Syria and Turkey, and their pronounced influence within the Confederation of Iranian Students in Europe and the United States, therefore proved indispensable to the OIPFG's propaganda and logistical networks abroad.[129]

While we can take CAG/OCU's account of the Organizations of the National Front of Iran Abroad as a generally accurate appraisal by virtue of the other evidence marshalled here and being confirmed in the few alternative accounts at our disposal, by their own tacit admission, the process of unification they had undertaken with the OIPFG only served to

---

[120]An identifiably Leninist view. See, V.I. Lenin, *Essential Works of Lenin* (New York: Dover, 1987), Loc 1975, 2185.

[121]*Chih nabayad kard?*, 37.

[122]This article cannot expand at length on the 'homogenization process' which has been tackled elsewhere in the extant scholarship: see, Vahabzadeh, *A Guerrilla Odyssey*, Loc 2020; Maziar Behrooz, *Rebels with a Cause: The Failure of the Left in Iran* (London: I.B. Tauris, 2000), 66–7; Afshin Matin-asgari, *Iranian Student Opposition to the Shah*, 139–40.

[123]*Nukati dar barah-yi purusah-yi tajanus*, 10, 18.

[124]Masali, *Nigarishi bih guzashtah va ayandah*, 364.

[125]Tabrizi, *Ravabit-i burun marzi*, 25.

[126]*Nukati dar barah-yi purusah tajanus*, 31.

[127]Tabrizi, *Ravabit-i burun marzi*, 29.

[128]Ibid., 26.

[129]*Nukati dar barah-yi purusah-yi tajanus*, 29.

further aggravate the already serious differences in outlook and approach between and within the respective branches of the Organizations of the National Front Abroad.[130] The very idea of continuing as part of the National Front had in their estimation ceased to be tenable after revising their one-time adherence to the notion of 'national-democratic revolution' (inqilab-i dimukrat-i milli), the conditions for which in late 1970 they still believed to obtain, and would be led by none other than a revitalized National Front.[131] But when the core of the Star Group, later Communist Alliance ceased to endorse the thesis of national-democratic revolution, and began instead to advocate fully fledged socialist revolution with the Iranian working class as its basis and chief driver,[132] the notion of a Front cutting across classes appeared misguided and a betrayal of Leninist theory.[133] They came to explicitly reject the 'two stage theory of revolution', and now stated that the 'dictatorship of the proletariat' would effectively commence with the revolution's inception. This circumvented the 'national bourgeoisie', since they argued that the post-revolutionary democratic phase and dictatorship of the proletariat would overlap and entail one another.[134] How exactly socialist revolution would be achieved under the current circumstances and in the absence of powerful, antagonistic workers' unions and organic relationships with the Iranian proletariat was a theoretical and practical question for which they were aware they still had little answer.

Hamid Ashraf's (d. June 1976) dominant role in the leadership of the OIPFG, as well as the ideological shadow cast by Hamid Mu'mini and his Stalinist and Maoist tendencies, led relations between the Star Group and OIPFG to be strained.[135] CAG alleged the OIPFG's nascent theoretical and political Stalinism motivated the internal executions which took place within the OIPFG;[136] subsequently they claimed the latter were decisive in the homogenization process's failure by 1976.[137] Consonantly, it was also in this period that members of the Star Group authored substantial theoretical criticisms of Stalinist and Maoist proclivities within the organizational modus operandi and theoretical armoury of the OIPFG.[138] It was in late 1975 that troubling revelations emerged of the OIPFG's involvement in the execution of two of its members deemed to pose a 'security risk', as well as the exaction of corporal punishment at their safe houses as they sought to prepare themselves for the

---

[130]Chih nabayad kard?, 40.

[131]Nukati dar barah-yi purusah-yi tajanus, 42.

[132]Ibid., 34.

[133]A position which came to be held by a number of communist organizations during this period. The fortunes of 'Leninism' in the broadest of terms witnessed something of a revival amongst elements within the New Left opposed to established socialist parties, which were regarded as compromised and prone to opportunism and détente vis-à-vis American imperialism. Max Elbaum, Revolution in the Air: Sixties Radicals Turn to Lenin, Mao and Che (London: Verso, 2006), 51.

[134]Nukati dar barah-yi purusah-yi tajanus, 34.

[135]A member of OIPFG has also confirmed Mu'mini's decisive role in the disagreement. Tabrizi, Ravabit-i burun marzi, 48.

[136]This is implied by CAG/OCU in Chih nabayad kard?, 39–40, when it is said that the problem of Stalinism in the OIPFG did not merely exist at a theoretical level.

More contemporary accounts confirm that members of the Star Group were apprised of internal executions within the OIPFG outside of Iran by individual Fada'is such as Muhsin Nurbakhsh. The Star Group held it was due to the ascendancy of Stalinism in the OIPFG, while others in the OIPFG contended it was due to 'security' concerns. Masali, Sayr-i tahavul-i junbish-i chap-i Iran, 129–30; Tabrizi, Ravabit-i burun marzi, 49.

[137]CAG/OCU also contend that another reason for the failure of the unification process was SAVAK's raids against the OIPFG in May–June 1976, which provoked the demotion of the theoretical opus of Ahmadzadah and Amir Parviz Puyan as the basis of political praxis, and the adoption of Bizhan Jazani's perspective instead. CAG/OCU were later critical of Jazani, contending that his analysis of Iran's political situation was too closely aligned with that of the Tudah Party. Masali, Nigarishi bih guzashtah va ayandah, 381.

[138]See, Guruh-i ittihad-i kumunisti, Istalinism: tabadul-i nazar dar purusah-yi tajanus bayn-i sazman-i chirikha-yi fada'i-yi khalq va guruh-i ittihad-i kumunisti, Bahar 1356 [Spring 1977].

prospect of torture at the hands of SAVAK. It was news which deeply shocked the Star Group.[139] The death of Hamidi, one of the Star Group's founders and most accomplished partisans, in a flurry of SAVAK raids on safe houses (*khanah-ha-yi timi*) in Rasht, Karaj and Tehran, also had a decisive impact on the process's feasibility as the OIPFG struggled for survival.[140]

Following the homogenization process's final breakdown, the ONFME activists decided to reorganize themselves to form the CAG. It should, however, be made clear that not all of those who were members of the Star Group, for example K.K. (Ahmad), K.F. (Tahir), Iftikhari and Rusta, joined the OCU, despite their initial participation in this new-formation Communist Alliance. Rusta would claim in a 1995 interview that he and 20 of his comrades broke with the latter due to its refusal to abandon 'Leninism', which he claimed was 'dogmatic', 'anti-humanist' and 'anti-communist'.[141] Following the revolution, all the members and close sympathizers of CAG returned to Iran and joined their comrades who were already inside the country. Though we still require more information apropos the process which led to the change of name to OCU, it ostensibly signified the organization's ambition and desire to inaugurate a new level of activities in an Iran which had just overthrown one of the United States' must powerful and trusted allies in the region. While some notable activists such as Rusta and Iftikhari parted ways with the new organization over ideological and political disagreements, the newly named Organization of Communist Unity was intended to indicate the deeper ideological affinity binding its cadres together and a more ambitious political platform on the post-revolutionary political stage. Soon after the fall of the *ancien régime*, OCU began recruiting new members from among its sympathizers and developed a new party structure at the first assembly of the membership in March 1979.[142]

But as already mentioned, during the 1970s and until the revolution of 1978–1979, the ONFME undertook significant collaboration with Palestinian Fateh, and furthermore the Popular Front for the Liberation of Palestine, and the Popular Front for the Liberation of Palestine (General Command). According to Masali, it was in this way that they established close relations with these groups' leaders, including Yasir Arafat, Khalil Ibrahim al-Wazir (better known as Abu Jihad) and George Habash.[143] This cooperation continued apace despite the homogenization process's unravelling.[144] Members of the ONFME/Communist Alliance not only received military training in the camps of the Palestinian guerrillas,[145] but a few also participated directly in the conflicts inside Dhufar, Oman during the first half of the 1970s, in which armed revolutionaries attempted to overthrow the British-backed Sultan Qaboos,[146] and the Lebanese Civil War (1975–1991).[147] They also fought the Israeli invasion to drive the Palestine Liberation Organization out of Southern Lebanon in the context of Operation Litani

---

[139]Masali, *Nigarishi bih guzashtah va ayandah*, 372.

[140]Ibid., 364; Tabrizi, *Ravabit-i burun marzi*, 54.

There has even been speculation that Hamidi may too have been purged, but there is no concrete evidence of this. Mahmud Nadiri, *Chirik-ha-yi fada 'i-yi khalq: az nukhustin kunish-ha ta bahman 1357*, vol. 1 (Tehran: Mu'assissah-yi mutala'at va pazhuhish-ha-yi siyasi, 1390), 653.

[141]Rusta and Ahmadi, Interview with Rusta, *RAIOA*, Part 5.

[142]Correspondence with Mahmud Irani, 25 June 2017. I address OCU's post-revolutionary activities in a forthcoming article.

[143]Masali, *Nigarishi bih guzashtah va ayandah*, 318.

[144]'9 sal-i mubarizah 'alayhah impiriyalism va dast nashandaganish: zindigi namah-yi mukhtasar-i rafiq Murtaza Sayyid Isma'il (Abu Shahin)', *Raha 'i*, no. 31 (29 April 1980 [9 Urdibihisht 1359]).

[145]Masali, *Sayr-i tahavul-i junbish-i chap-i Iran*, 128.

[146]See, Abdel Razzaq Takriti, *Monsoon Revolution: Republicans, Sultans, and Empires in Oman, 1965–1975* (Oxford: Oxford University Press, 2013).

[147]*Nukati dar barah-yi purusah-yi tajanus*, 11.

of March 1978.[148] These collaborative efforts emerged not only out of the desire to have a base of operations closer to Iran and acquire training from some of the pre-eminent guerrilla movements within the region, but also from a genuine conviction and belief in the collective liberation of all colonized peoples. Taken together they should be regarded as a form of South–South solidarity in the name of collective emancipation against imperial penetration and neo-colonialism.

By the time of Communist Alliance's (post-1979 Communist Unity) maturation in the second half of the 1970s their stated principles and outlook were enumerated thus:

(1) Scientific communism (*kumunism-i 'ilmi*).[149]

(2) Only under a classless society are the conditions for human liberation capable of realization.

(3) Capitalism is a global system predicated on the exploitation of the dispossessed and is currently in the monopoly imperialist stage; an obvious iteration of Lenin's *Imperialism: The Highest Stage of Capitalism*.[150] It is only by means of a socialist revolution that the yoke of colonial oppression might be overturned, where the dictatorship of the proletariat was synonymous with the masses' re-appropriation of their collective destiny.[151]

(4) Proletarian internationalism. Irrespective of nationality, race, language, religion or culture, the global working class is bound together by its antithetical relation to capital and must therefore support each other's struggle against the predations of global capitalism.

(5) In the numerous debates between Iranian leftists revolving around whether Iran had ceased to be a 'feudal' society, CAG/OCU, like a number of other Marxist organizations, had concluded late Pahlavi Iran had indeed become a capitalist country and that the fundamental contradiction characterizing Iranian society was that of capital against labour.[152]

(6) The violence inherent in the maintenance of empire and the ruling class makes armed resistance key to the liberation of the oppressed. They concurred with Guevara's contention that 'imperialism is a world system, the final stage of capitalism, and that it must be beaten in a great worldwide confrontation'.[153]

(7) Revisionism and parliamentarianism had led the working class astray as had political parties which resort to either ignoring or glossing over class conflict.

(8) Maoism, Trotskyism and Stalinism were all deviations (*inhirafat*) within the communist movement.[154]

(9) Like other New Left trends at the time they did not, in their own words, recognize any *ka'ba* as the privileged 'homeland' (*mihan*) of socialism and therefore refused to be subject to the dictates or geo-political realpolitik of any external power, explicitly rejecting 'nationalism under the guise of socialism' in a clear swipe at both the U.S.S.R. and People's Republic of China.[155]

---

[148] Jibhah-yi azadi bakhsh-i filastin va Guruh-i ittihad-i kumunisti, 'Jang-i labnan' (Spring 1357); Tabrizi, *Ravabit-i burun marzi*, 25–7.

[149] Sazman-i vahdat-i kumunisti, *Dar tadaruk-i inqilab-i sawsiyalisti* (Azar 1357 [November/December 1978]), 2–3.

[150] V.I. Lenin, *Imperialism: The Highest Stage of Capitalism: A Popular Outline* (London: Penguin Books, 2010 [1916]), chapter 7.

[151] *Chih nabayad kard?*, v.

[152] Jazani, for example, had concluded that Iran's was indeed a dependent capitalist regime: Jazani, *Tarh-i jami'ih shinasi*, 61.

[153] Che Guevara, *Che Guevara Reader: Writings on Politics & Revolution*, 2nd expanded ed. (North Melbourne, VIC: Ocean Press, 2003), 358.

[154] *Nukati dar barah-yi purusah-yi tajanus*, 40.

[155] The critique of Chinese foreign policy vis-à-vis the Pahlavi regime was publicly evident as early as 1972. 'Dar barah-yi siyasat-i kharijah-yi chin', *Bakhtar-i imruz* 4, no. 33, Day 1351 [January 1972–December 1973].

Apart from the discernible influence of the Tri-continental Moment and its profound emphasis on 'internationalist proletarian solidarity',[156] the importance of CAG/OCU's anti-imperialist lineage in the National Front and Musaddiq's advocacy of 'negative equilibrium' should not be underestimated. Preceding Bandung and Non-Alignment by some years, this distinguished inheritance impacted the group's political trajectory and insistence on the pursuit of an independent revolutionary policy along the lines of comparable movements in Asia, Africa and Latin America.[157] This lineage also arguably shaped their inveterate hostility to Stalinism and the repression of dissenting voices internal to their organization, propelling them instead to partake in vigorous self-criticism, democratic discussion and critical reflection.

Despite holding revolutionary views, many of which would have undoubtedly been wholly foreign to the Qajar aristocrat and statesman, Musaddiq, they continued to operate under the banner of the ONFME, only irrevocably parting ways with the National Front in the autumn of 1977. As this article has tried to demonstrate, this process of disillusionment and eventual break with the National Front Abroad, though not Musaddiq's legacy, was a complex and circuitous one: in organizational terms moving from a plural, amorphous front to Marxist-Leninist vanguardism, and in geographical scope shifting from the national frame to internationalist class struggle, albeit with considerable emphasis upon solidarity with like-minded struggles in the Global South.

Conclusion

The activists of the Organizations of the National Front Abroad (Middle East Branch) and Communist Alliance/Communist Unity continued to see themselves as perpetuating Musaddiq's legacy, if not radicalizing its logic altogether.[158] They sought not only to establish an independent and democratic government free from imperial meddling, but to overturn capitalist exploitation and class oppression by founding a more humane and equitable socialist society. Just as importantly, they located Iran's liberation in the collective emancipation of the Global South and, to this effect, collaborated and fought alongside national liberation movements throughout the West Asia and North Africa.

It would be facile to blame the National Front in the Middle East/Communist Alliance for the internal divisions and dysfunction of the National Front Abroad, which as we have seen in many respects mirrored the disagreements over organization which had plagued the Second National Front. Indeed, one could even make the case that this challenge which faced the National Front had dogged it from its inception, including during Musaddiq's tenure as premier. In later years, in addition to issues of organization, serious political and ideological cleavages also began to arise. These were to some extent the outcome of a consequential generational gap, as a younger class of dissidents grew frustrated with the Shah's entrenched authoritarian security state and the support it received from the United

---

[156]*Che Guevara Reader*, 360–2.
[157]For an account of the impact of Musaddiq's visit to Egypt in November 1951 and its wider significations for anti-colonial politics in the Arab world, see Lior Sternfeld, 'Iran Days in Egypt: Mosaddeq's Visit to Cairo in 1951', *British Journal of Middle Eastern Studies* 43, no. 1 (2016): 1–20.
[158]Mu'azzami, 'Az tajrubah-yi Musaddiq', 361.

States during the 'global Cold War'. As has been recounted, this period also saw the exposure of a sizeable body of Iranian students to radical anti-colonial and leftist thought and activism in Graz, Berlin, Munich, Paris, New York, Berkeley and elsewhere in the United States against the backdrop of the Vietnam War and the worldwide revolt of 1968.[159]

Though recent scholarship has argued that Cold War power politics was experienced by many in the Third World as merely another iteration of European-style colonialism,[160] this insight had already been acutely understood by a generation of dissidents, which had preserved and upheld the anti-imperialism of its forebears, most notably the Musaddiq government of 1951–1953. This was achieved while striking an independent revolutionary path that repudiated the American capitalist imperium and its Soviet and Chinese rivals whose espousal of communist internationalism was given short shrift.

Exceeding the immediacy of Iran's own political and economic conditions, it was also the outcome of a larger struggle and politico-ideological shift on an international scale, where the erstwhile colonized nations of Asia, Africa and Latin America witnessed and participated in the emergence of a plethora of armed liberation movements, many of which had reached the conclusion that the only way to achieve their objectives was by force of arms. The committed were bound to take the lead and help engender the conditions whereby a popular revolutionary process could unfurl.

The National Front in the Middle East and Communist Alliance/Communist Unity, despite their diminutive size, exercised a disproportionate influence on dissident and student activists abroad, as part of the Organizations of the National Front Abroad and the Confederation of Iranian Students. But arguably even more crucial was its transnational network across the Arab world, encompassing Beirut, Tripoli (Lebanon), Libya, Baghdad, Dhufar, Aden[161] and Damascus.[162] The need for a transnational network with like-minded regional movements had also been recognized by leading Fada'i theoretician, Bizhan Jazani, who wrote from his prison cell to Musaddiq's grandson, Hidayatullah Matin-Daftari, that 'The next practical phase is that organizations…gather together in Palestine or Iraq and as councils (*shura'i*)…bring the national liberation movement of Iran into being.'[163] This was in 1972 and Jazani would never again experience freedom, as he would be extra-judicially executed at the hands of SAVAK on the hills behind Evin Prison in April 1975. The letter, however, was written some two years after the activists of ONFME had already begun to make their way and establish themselves in the Middle East. The ONFME was by no means alone in trying to realize this objective, but the fact remains that the invaluable networks it created in the Arab world evinced a spirit and concrete exemplar of South–South internationalism few other Iranian political organizations could match.[164]

---

[159]The global moment of '1968' is explicitly adduced by Bizhan Iftikhari when retelling the story of his political formation as a student activist along with Kambiz Rusta in Graz, Austria. Iftikhari and Ahmadi, Interview with Bizhan Iftikhari, *RAIOA*, Part 3.

[160]Odd Arne Westad, *The Global Cold War: Third World Interventions and the Making of Our Times* (Cambridge: Cambridge University Press, 2007), 5;
   Robert J.C. Young, 'Postcolonialism: From Bandung to the Tricontinental', *Historein* 5 (2005): 15.

[161]Masali, *Nigarishi bih guzashtah va ayandah*, 399.

[162]Correspondence with Mahmud Irani, 2 April 2017.

[163]Jazani, 'Namah bih yak dust', 338.

[164]The Mujahidin-i khalq (M-L) perhaps being the chief exception in this regard.

Finally, because of the CAG and later OCU's critical stances on what it regarded as the lack of internal democracy within the Fada'i Guerrillas as well as its theoretical sophistication and progressive stances on a host of pressing issues following the revolution, it was commended and received plaudits within Iran's left-wing intelligentsia, and was thereby able to further distinguish itself both politically and intellectually from the larger and better-established Iranian Marxist organizations.[165] While it is important not to overstate this group's significance or impact upon Iranian politics and society, the story of its activists' evolution, embrace of a transnational revolutionary politics and preservation of democratic criticism, both recovers and illuminates a neglected vantage point on opposition to Pahlavi authoritarianism during the 1960s and 1970s.

Acknowledgements

The author would like to thank Homa Katouzian, Ervand Abrahamian, Nasser Mohajer, Afshin Matin-asgari, Siavush Randjbar-Daemi, Abdel Razzaq Takriti, Mehrdad Vahabi, Behrooz Moazami, Naghmeh Sohrabi, Peyman Vahabzadeh, Khalil Rostamkhani, Roham Alvandi, Touraj Atabaki, Ala Jazayeri and Houchang E. Chehabi, whose comments and suggestions greatly helped improve and strengthen previous drafts of this article.

Disclosure statement

No potential conflict of interest was reported by the author.

---

[165]One example of their post-revolutionary interventions is their pamphlet unambiguously repudiating capital punishment: 'Havadaran-i sazman-i vahdat-i kumunisti dar urupa', *Dar nafy-i i'dam* (Autumn 1988).

8   Political Parties and Women's Rights in Turkey

Zehra F. Kabasakal Arat

ABSTRACT

Political parties are important political actors, but they are seldom studied in relation to human rights. This article examines the human rights discourse of political parties in Turkey by focusing on women's rights. The content analysis of party programmes issued by major political parties between 1923 and 2007 reveals significant differences and changes in parties' approach to women, ranging from no mentioning of women to addressing women's issues from a feminist perspective. Women's rights and issues, once neglected practically by all political parties, have gained attention during the last few decades, largely due to women's activism. While conservative, religious, and Turkish nationalist parties started to display a dualist approach that combines traditionalism with gender equality, social democrat, socialist, and pro-Kurdish parties increasingly employ feminist terminology and analysis.

Introduction[1]

Political parties are important political actors, the discourse and action of which can have significant political consequences. However, human rights research has neglected political parties' role and approach. This is particularly the case for the Middle East, for which studies tend to focus on governing parties and examine them usually as 'regimes'.

This study examines the human rights discourse of political parties in Turkey, focusing on women's rights. The content analysis of political party programmes issued by the major political parties in Turkey between 1923 and 2007 reveals that women's rights and issues, once neglected by practically all political parties, have been gaining attention during the last few decades, but both the type and level of attention have varied according to the ideology of the party. The increased references to women and women's rights, especially since the 1980s, can be ascribed to the development of autonomous women's organizations and the rise of a new women's movement, which have invoked international human rights norms and treaties and rallied external support.

[1]This article reports partial findings of a larger project, which examines the human rights discourse and policies in Turkey since the 1920s and was sponsored by grants from the International Research & Exchanges Board, the National Endowment for the Humanities, the United States Institute of Peace, as well as the Human Rights Institute and the Alan R. Bennett Fund of the University of Connecticut. I am grateful for their support but should note that the article does not necessarily represent the views of these institutions. I would also like to thank Lauren Banko and the anonymous reviewer for their valuable comments and my undergraduate assistants, Rubayet Lasker and Emma Morelli, for their help with the library research, tables, and editing.

The paper starts with a brief discussion of the importance of political parties and continues with information on political parties in Turkey. The last sections present the methodology and research findings.

Importance of Political Parties

Political parties are important political machinery that perform crucial functions, including: political socialization; interest articulation and aggregation;[2] political participation and recruitment; agenda setting; debating and formulating policies; and implementing or monitoring government policies. Serving as mediators and communication channels between the state apparatus and the public at large,[3] 'they transmit popular preferences into policy'.[4] These functions, no matter how ineffectively fulfilled, make political parties important players in shaping the political agenda, discourse, and policies of the country in which they operate.

Recognizing the influence of political parties on human rights, Amnesty International called on 'all political parties of Pakistan to honestly commit themselves to upholding respect for and protection of human rights' and proposed a 12-point plan.[5] Pointing to the increased attention to the human rights responsibilities of non-state actors such as transnational corporations, scholars argue for the need to hold political parties accountable as well.[6] However, parties are seldom studied for their approach to and impact on human rights. Although a body of literature, collectively called 'the manifesto studies', examines the correlation between issues raised in party manifestos and government policy priorities and spending, it pays no attention to human rights.[7]

Political parties' approach to women's *rights* and *issues* is also an under-explored topic.[8] Feminist scholarship on parties tends to focus on the extent to which they include women in governance, nominate women in elections, and adopt electoral quotas,[9] or on parties established by women.[10]

[2]Gabriel Almond and Bingham Powell, *Comparative Politics: A Developmental Approach* (Boston, MA: Little, Brown and Co., 1966).

[3]Leon D. Epstein, *Political Parties in Western Democracies* (New York: Praeger, 1967), pp. 31–45; Richard Hofferbert and Ian Budge, 'The Party Mandate and the Westminster Model: Election Programmes and Government Spending in Britain 1948–85', *British Journal of Political Science*, 22(2) (1992), pp. 151–182, here p. 157; Michael Johnston, *Political Parties and Democracy in Theoretical and Practical Perspectives* (Washington, DC: National Democratic Institute for International Affairs, 2005).

[4]S. C. Stokes, 'Political Parties and Democracy', *Annual Review of Political Science*, 2 (1999), pp. 243–267, here p. 250.

[5]Amnesty International, 'Amnesty International's Call to Political Parties to Commit Themselves to Uphold a 12-Point Plan on Human Rights', 14 February 2008, https://www.amnesty.org/en/documents/asa33/004/1993/en/ (accessed 2 June 2009).

[6]Tim Wood, 'Reinforcing Participatory Governance through International Human Rights Obligations of Political Parties', *Harvard Human Rights Journal*, 28(1) (2015), pp. 147–203.

[7]Ian Budge, Richard Hofferbert, and H.-D. Klingemann, *Parties, Policies and Democracy* (Boulder, CO: Westview Press, 1994).

[8]Amrita Basu, 'Women, Political Parties and Social Movements in South Asia', *Occasional Paper 5* (Geneva: UN Research Institute for Social Development [UNRISD], July 2005).

[9]Jessica Fortin-Rittberger and Berthold Rittberger, 'Nominating Women for Europe: Exploring the Role of Political Parties' Recruitment Procedures for European Parliament Elections', *European Journal of Political Research*, 54(4) (2015), pp. 767–783; Mona Lena Krook and Pippa Norris, 'Beyond Quotas: Strategies to Promote Gender Equality in Elected Office', *Political Studies*, 62(1) (2014), pp. 2–20; Manon Tremblay, *Women and Legislative Representation: Electoral Systems, Political Parties, and Sex Quotas* (New York: Palgrave, 2008); Sheri Kunovich and Pamela Paxton, 'Pathways to Power: The Role of Political Parties in Women's National Political Representation', *American Journal of Sociology*, 111(2) (2005), pp. 505–552.

[10]Kimberly Cowell-Meyers, 'Women's Political Parties in Europe', *Politics & Gender*, 12(1) (2016), pp. 1–27.

Political Parties in Turkey

Party politics emerged in Turkey at the turn of the twentieth century, under Ottoman rule.[11] The leaders of the resistance (independence) war against the states that occupied the country after World War I established the Grand National Assembly in April 1920. As ideological and political rivalries emerged within the Assembly, a month before the proclamation of the Republic in October 1923, Mustafa Kemal and other founders reorganized their group as a political party and named it Halk Fırkası (HF).[12] This marked the beginning of the one-party regime, which lasted until 1945, when the multi-party electoral system was adopted. Even under the one-party rule, however, there were attempts to establish other parties. Writing in the 1960s, Fredrick Frey asserts that 'Turkish politics are party politics'.[13]

Turkey's democratic experience has been interrupted by four military interventions (in 1960, 1971, 1980, and 1997) that reinforced the military's oversight of politics. Nevertheless, political parties have been arguably the most institutionalized political entities, after the military and courts.[14] Despite the military interventions and frequent Constitutional Court decisions to close parties and ban leaders, political parties have proved resilient and managed to reorganize under new names. They remained connected to their constituencies and played important roles in agenda setting and framing issues, albeit in varying degrees.

Given political parties' important roles, it is important to understand their approach to gender and women's rights. Without a close examination of political parties' perception of women and their role in society, we cannot understand the limitations of policies in addressing women's needs and issues.

Political Party Programmes and Women's Rights

Both the single-party and multi-party regimes in Turkey have followed the basic characteristics of a parliamentary regime. Thus, political parties have issued programmes that articulated their main principles, issue concerns, and policy alternatives.

This study analyses the programmes issued by all political parties that were represented in the parliament during the 1923–2007 period, as well as a few parties that failed to secure seats in the parliament but enjoyed media coverage and contributed to the policy debates. A total of 92 programmes issued by 53 political parties are included in the study. (See the Appendix for a list of parties and the dates of programmes.)

The programmes were subjected to both manifest and latent content analyses. For the manifest content analysis, three key terms—women's rights, women's freedoms, and equal pay for equal work—were selected, and the frequency of each term is tallied for each programme.[15] The latent content analysis is employed to examine the parties' overall approach to women, as reflected in programmes, and to contextualize the use of key terms if they are mentioned. This close reading of programmes with attention to the wording in reference to

[11]Tarık Zafer Tunaya, *Türkiye'de Siyasi Partiler*, 3 vols. (Istanbul: İletişim Yayınları, 1998).

[12]Following the recent practice, all political parties are referred to by their Turkish name and acronym throughout the article. HF continued to exist under different names and with the acronyms of CHF and CHP.

[13]Frederick W. Frey, *The Turkish Political Elite* (Cambridge, MA: MIT Press, 1965), pp. 301–303.

[14]Ergun Özbudun, 'Turkey: How Far from Consolidation?', *Journal of Democracy*, 7(3) (1996), pp. 123–138, here p. 126.

[15]'Women's rights' and 'women's freedoms' are a part of the human rights language and identify women as the subject of 'rights and freedoms'. 'Equal pay for equal work' has been recognized as a human right—first in International Labour Organization (ILO) resolutions, and then in other international human rights treaties.

women reveals the level of importance assigned to women, as well as the parties' under-standing of gender roles, women's rights, and the state's obligations.

The study has two main goals. In addition to identifying the general pattern of change in the political parties' gender discourse, it is concerned with the variation displayed by ideologically distinct political parties. Thus, time is a variable and is measured in decades. The second variable, party ideology, is more complex.

Traditionally, political parties' ideologies are sorted out on a *left–right* spectrum that accounts for polarization on the issues of economic production and regulation (reliance on market vs planned economy), redistribution, traditional morality, and national defence and security.[16] Students of Turkish politics, however, treated the left–right classification as sec-ondary, if not inappropriate, in capturing the differences of parties in Turkey; they treated the central cleavage as *centre–periphery*, which identified the centre as occupied by a nation-alist-modernist elite in charge of the state apparatus and the periphery as a heterogeneous group, including shopkeepers, peasantry, and farmers that resist *étatism* and the top-down modernization by the founding party.[17]

However, this cleavage does not hold for the post-1960 period, when Cumhuriyet Halk Partisi (CHP) assumed a social-democratic platform that fits to the traditional left–right par-adigm, and social and geographic mobility, rapid urbanization, and the development of modern communication networks have integrated the periphery to the centre to a great extent.[18] A factor analysis of 35 political party election manifestos issued during the 1950–1995 period led Ali Çarkoğlu to identify two cleavages for political parties in Turkey: (1) local/traditional vs universalist, which tends to address differences in moral and cultural values; and (2) government-controlled economy vs market system/civil society, which tends to address economic policy choices, freedoms, human rights, and concerns of youth and women.[19] A cross-tabulation of parties on these two cleavages can yield at least four different ideological groups of parties.

Focusing on the continuity in the *core issue* for the long-lasting political parties, this project employs an alternative, 'nominal'-level ideological classification of parties: (1) religious, emphasizing religious morality and Islam as an identity; (2) economic conservative, display-ing a pro-business attitude; (3) Turkish nationalist, promoting Turkish identity and culture; (4) modernizing-redistributive/social democrat, seeking modernization and distributive justice through policy intervention; (5) socialist, subscribing to conventional socialist prin-ciples; and (6) pro-Kurdish/Kurdish nationalist, seeking an end to the marginalization of the Kurdish population. In this scheme, there may be overlaps. Parties categorized as religious, for example, may be pro-business or redistributive in terms of their economic policy prefer-ences, but they are classified as 'religious' because it is their distinct and dominant identity. Yet, we may roughly place the first three categories on the right and the last three on the left on the conventional left–right spectrum. (See the Appendix for the ideological classifi-cation of parties.)

The following sections report the findings of both manifest and latent content analyses, with attention to the change over time and party ideologies.

---

[16]M. Laver and I. Budge, eds., *Party Policy and Coalition Governments in Western Europe* (London: Macmillan, 1993).
[17]Şerif Mardin, 'Center-Periphery Relations: A Key to Turkish Politics', *Dædalus*, 102 (Winter 1972), pp. 169–190.
[18]Binnaz Toprak, 'Islam and the Secular State in Turkey', in Ç. Balim et al., eds., *Turkey: Political, Social and Economic Challenges in the 1990s* (Leiden: E. J. Brill, 1995), pp. 90–96.
[19]Ali Çarkoğlu, 'The Turkish Party System in Transition: Party Performance and Agenda Change', *Political Studies*, 46(3) (1998), pp. 544–571.

Women's Rights

The manifest content analysis reveals that 'women's rights' has not been a salient issue for political parties in Turkey. The term is mentioned only in 33 (about one-third) of the 92 programmes studied and for a total of 59 times.

In fact, during the first decade of the Republic, we see no references to the word *women* in party programmes. Serbes Cumhuriyet Fırkası (SCF), established in 1930, was the first party to mention women in its programme, as it promised to 'advocate the expansion of political rights to women' (Art. 11).[20] The governing party Cumhuriyet Halk Fırkası (CHF), on the other hand, first granted women the right to vote in municipal elections in 1930, by amending the law of municipalities, and then included the right in its 1931 programme: 'Our Party observes citizens' political rights without any distinction to sex. … considers its duty to prepare the conditions necessary for women to exercise their political rights in parliamentary elections, as it has been the case in municipal elections' (Art. I.4). After women's rights to vote and run for office in all elections became the law in 1934, CHP's 1935 programme notes that 'The Party does not make a male–female distinction in assigning citizens [their] rights and duties' (Art. 4-B).

As illustrated in Table 1, the number of political parties that mention women's rights in their programmes increased over the years. The diversity of parties that incorporated the term into their programmes has also increased during the last two decades.

Party programmes from the earlier decades mention women's rights by linking them to traditional gender roles that enshrine the family and value women for their reproductive function, childcare, and household responsibilities. When CHF/CHP promoted the principle of equality in rights and duties in the 1930s, for example, the principle appeared to apply to only a few rights, such as the right to vote.[21] The 1931 programme also notes that 'The privacy of family is the principal element in Turkish domestic life' (VI.1) and promises to take measures that would stimulate population increase (VII.3).

Demokrat Parti (DP), which functioned as the main opposition party when the multi-party regime was established in 1945 and then ruled the country throughout the 1950s, mentioned 'women' in none of its programmes, but all of its programmes define 'Turkish society' as one 'that is based on family and the principle of [private] property'. Its successor Adalet Partisi (AP) acknowledged women and women's rights in its first programme (1961), but in a single sentence and with an emphasis on domestic responsibilities: 'The Party recognizes all rights in all areas held by men for women [as well], and it views the need to provide all forms of assistance to them, especially to facilitate fulfilling their duties in [sustaining] family health and social life' (Art. 23).

In addition to enshrining the family, some right-wing party programmes take a pro-natalist position, because they see population increase as essential to economic development.[22] According to the Liberal Demokrat Parti (LDP), 'every citizen should consider raising a family as a national and sacred duty' (1946, Art. 19), and İslâm Demokrat Partisi (İDP)

---

[20]The translation of all quotations from programmes is mine.

[21]In practice, even the principle of 'equality before law' failed, since the laws were essentially biased and discriminated against women. See, Zehra F. Arat, 'Kemalism and Turkish Women', *Women and Politics,* 14(4) (1994), pp. 57–80.

[22]R. T. Erdoğan, who has led Adalet ve Kalkinma Partisi (AKP) in government since 2002, also subscribes to this approach. Addressing women in Uşak, on the 2008 International Women's Day, he called on every young woman to have three children to keep the population young and stimulate the economy. *Hurriyet* (7 Mart 2008) http://www.hurriyet.com.tr/erdogan-en-az-uc-cocuk-dogurun-8401981 (accessed February 3, 2017). Despite protests from women's groups, he has been repeating the same call and promoting policies that would curb women's reproductive rights and access to abortion.

Table 1. Political Party Programme References to Women's Rights by Decade and Party Ideology.

				Party Ideology			
Decade	Total*	Religious	Conservative	Turkish Nationalist	Modernizing-Redistributive/ Social Democrat	Socialist	Pro-Kurdish/ Kurdish Nationalist
1930	3		SCF 1930		CHF 1931 CHF 1935		
1940	0						
1950	2			CMP 1954	CHP 1954		
1960	4		AP 1961 AP 1964	CKMP 1965 MHP 1969			
1970	1					TBP 1972	
1980	5		MDP 1983	MÇP 1988	SODEP 1983 SHP 1985	TBP 1980	
1990	7		DYP 1998	MHP 1993	CHP 1994 SHP 1993	ÖDP 1996	HEP 1990 HEP 1992
2000	11	AKP 2002 SP 2001	GP 2002 HYP 2005	MHP 2000	SHP 2002 YTP 2002 CHP 2002 CHP 2004	ÖDP 2006	DTP 2006

*Total number of programmes that mention women's rights.

seeks penalizing those who ignore their reproductive duty: 'Marriage and birth are our national issues. We will facilitate both. For those who refrain from marriage, their taxes will be increased; and, if they are civil servants, they will be held back in promotions' (1952, Art. 18).[23]

The pro-natalist approach is prevalent in the programmes of religious and Turkish nationalist parties, which share interest in promoting a 'Turkish-Islamic' synthesis. The programme of Milli Selamet Partisi (MSP), established in 1972, lacks explicit references to women but unequivocally states: 'Our party opposes the idea of population planning. It will encourage the increase of our population' (1973, Art. 87). Milliyetçi Çalışma Partisi (MÇP) and Milliyetçi Hareket Partisi (MHP), in their 1988 and 1993 programmes, respectively, object to abortion and artificial insemination, reject women's right to choose, and propose placing family planning under the state's control.

Until the 1980s, all political parties tended to women as mainly mothers and homemakers. Right-wing parties continued to emphasize women's critical role in the family even when they assumed more inclusive and egalitarian language in the later decades.

When we examine the frequency of women's rights references employed in each programme, it is evident that the left-of-centre parties tend to mention women's rights more frequently. Table 2 shows that if there is any mention of women's rights in party programmes, it is typically mentioned only once. Multiple references appear in left-wing party programmes.

The HF/CHF/CHP, which incorporated women's rights into its programmes in the 1930s, had been quiet on the topic until its reestablishment in 1993. Then, it started to address a range of women's issues by employing the language of rights. Its 1994 programme, which mentions women's rights four times, notes that 'Women's rights should be claimed, not only in law and economy'. The 1994 and 2006 programmes define 'the main goal' of the new Turkey as 'having men and women share together both the benefits and burdens of life in

---

[23]Since the workforce was mainly male, imposing a penalty on men, the programme legitimizes men's control over women's reproductive function.

Table 2. Frequency of Women's Rights References in Political Party Programmes by Ideology.

			Party Ideology			
Frequency	Religious	Conservative	Turkish Nationalist	Modernizing-Redistributive/ Social Democrat	Socialist	Pro-Kurdish/Kurdish Nationalist
1	AKP 2002	SCF 1930	CMP 1954	CHP 1954	TBP 1980	HEP 1990
		AP 1961	MHP 1969	SHP 1985		HEP 1992
	SP 2001	AP 1964	MÇP 1988	SHP 1993		DTP 2006
		DYP 1998	MHP 1993	CHP 2002		
		GP 2002				
		HYP 2005				
2		MDP 1983	CKMP 1965	CHF 1931	TBP 1972	
				SODEP 1983		
			MHP 2000	SHP 2002		
3				CHF 1935		
				YTP 2002		
4				CHP 1994		
				CHP 2006		
5					ÖDP 1996	
6					ÖDP 2006	

family and society'. Including a section entitled 'A Society in which Men and Women are Equals', they assert the party's commitment to 'change the country from being a male-dominated society and transform it into a society of free individuals' (Section 1.4B). Sosyal Demokrasi Partisi (SODEP), which was established in 1983, preceded CHP in employing a comprehensive approach. Its programme mentions women's rights twice and treats gender equality as a prerequisite of social equality at large. The socialist Özgürlük ve Dayanışma Partisi (ÖDP) not only refers to women's rights in its programmes more frequently but also employs a feminist discourse and brings up women's freedoms.

Education

Although not recognized as a right, education of women is an issue that is frequently mentioned in party programmes and usually in a favourable light. Soon after the establishment of the Republic of Turkey, in 1923, the ruling primary education as a constitutional right for both sexes and made it both free and mandatory.[24] CHP's 1943 programme introduces new proposals that support women's education: 'Providing, renewing, and enhancing the knowledge of every citizen, man or woman, in an educational institution, now take place among the duties of the State' (Art. 9). The party also sought women's public engagement and desegregation of sexes by promising to establish adult education and cultural centres (Halkevi or Halkodasi) only if they include 'a meeting hall *for men and women to assemble together*, a library, and activities of fine arts' (Art. 9, emphasis added).

However, women's education is often supported as a means to train mothers to raise healthier and properly socialized children. The programmes issued by Türkiye Köylü Partisi (TKP) promise to help women to fulfil 'their duties within the family heart' (1952, Art. 15) and declare that it is the party's duty 'to bring up Turkish women in a way that appreciates and teaches their duty and responsibilities in family and society' (1961, Art. 45). The programme of the religious Milli Nizam Partisi (MNP) reveals the same approach:

---

[24]Z. Arat, 'Kemalism and Turkish Women'.

> Our party, believing in the principle that everyone, man or woman, has the right to be learned, considers it necessary to equip our children, who are tomorrow's parents, with the necessary pedagogical knowledge, and ... to provide—especially for the future mothers, our daughters who are housewives—[instructions on] home economics and information on the physical, spiritual, moral, and religious training of children. (1970, Art. 24).

The conservative Cumhuriyetçi Güven Partisi (CGP) also draws attention to women's 'very important status within family and society in terms of the spirit and manners that will be conveyed to Turkish children who constitute the future of the nation'; thus, it stresses the need to 'raise Turkish women' as fully able to 'comprehend their duties and responsibilities within family and society' and fulfil them 'with precision' (1971, 81–82).

The only programme issued by the religious Refah Partisi (RP, 1983) fails to mention women and it omits sex in its equality clause, promising to 'treat everyone as equals without distinction to religion, language, race, or sect'. Its successor Fazilet Partisi (FP) repeats the same non-discrimination statement but mentions women briefly; indicating that women are 'the foundational pillar of society', the party promises 'special attention to women's education and training' to enable them 'to be more successful in economic and public life' (1997).

Supporting women's education for the sake of women and as a means of improving women's employment opportunities and independence appears as a goal after 1980. It is included mainly in the social democratic, socialist, and pro-Kurdish parties' programmes.

Women's Work and the Principle of 'Equal Pay for Equal Work'

Although political parties in Turkey tended to view women's lives as anchored in the home, especially in earlier decades, they also appreciated the fact that some women have to work. Thus, programmes promise jobs, maternity leave, and day care, but with an understanding that women's primary domain is the home and childcare is women's responsibility.

As CHF/CHP recognized some women's need to work first in its 1931 programme by promising more 'institutions that take care of children when female labourers are at work' (VII.3), its 1935 programme included 'The protection of working mothers and their children' (Art. 56-C) and 'opening nurseries in business areas for women who have the responsibility of earning a living' among the party's goals (Art. 58).

Some party programmes indicate that women, like children, should be spared from 'harmful' work and designate certain occupations as inappropriate for women. According to AP's 1964 programme, it is 'appropriate to have women and children among the working population to be protected by special provisions' (Art. 68). This paternalistic approach, which leads to occupational segregation, is more overt in Turkish nationalist parties' programmes. The 1965 programme of Cumhuriyetçi Köylü Millet Partisi (CKMP) emphasizes protecting 'children, the youth, and women ... from [dangerous and difficult] work conditions' (1965, Art. 242). The same sentiments resurface in the programmes of the nationalist Millet Partisi (MP) and MHP. MHP's 1969 programme problematizes women's subordination (Art. 30) but elevates paternalism to essentialism, as it commits to 'ensure that male and female characteristics are scientifically observed in the national educational system' (Art. 56) and tied to appropriate occupations.

In the transition to civilian rule in 1983, Anavatan Partisi (ANAP) came to power and ruled either alone or as a coalition partner for most of the 1980s and 1990s. However, it ignored women in both programmes, issued in 1983 and 2002. The programme of Milliyetçi Demokrasi

Partisi (MDP), established in 1983 and later merged into ANAP, follows a traditionalist approach. Displaying both essentialism and paternalism, it pledges to protect mothers, along with family and children (Art. 56), and promises to 'ensure that the *work conditions are appropriate for the age, sex, and strength of the working person* and that *children, women, and the mentally or physically disabled individuals* are under special protection' (Art. 44, emphasis added).

Even social democratic and socialist parties gendered work and emphasized marriage and motherhood. The 1972 programme of Türkiye Birlik Partisi (TBP), for example, includes a section that is entitled 'Women's Rights' and speaks to women's importance. It 'recognizes woman's right to develop her own individuality', as well as the need to achieve women's full legal equality, along with social and economic equality. At the same time, the party 'considers married women's work in occupations relevant to their skills as a social and economic necessity, and motherhood as a public service'. Opposing women's being 'forced to work in hard and improper jobs due to low [family] income', the party promises 'to facilitate marriages', promotes women's right to have 'vacations with their husbands', and 'finds the protection of women from excessive work and fatigue as crucial to their ability to perform their duties as mothers and homemakers' (TBP 1972, 62).

Türkiye İşçi Partisi (TİP) has been the only socialist party that managed to acquire seats in the parliament. TİP declared its opposition to all forms of discrimination, including discrimination based on sex, and became the first party that incorporated the 'equal pay for equal work' principle into its programme. Its 1972 programme includes several progressive measures, but its promise to take 'measures to tackle working women's difficulties related to motherhood' invokes some traditional notions.

Despite embracing a social democratic identity in the 1960s, CHP kept circulating its 1954 programme, which addressed women in one article that declares the party's mission as ensuring that 'all Turks, men and women, freely apply their ability and reach an advanced and affluent living standard, as equals in rights and duties and as confident about their status and future' (Art. 1). When a new programme was issued in 1976, less than one page was spared to women (p. 103) and only to promise equal pay, a healthy working environment, childcare, increased union participation, and maternal leave.

The attitude towards women's education and economic participation started to change in the 1980s. Although the left-of-centre Halkçı Parti (HP), established in 1983, still demonstrated a traditionalist and home-centred approach, a social democratic party (SODEP), established in the same year, set the path for a more progressive discourse. In a section entitled 'Women's Problems', SODEP's programme addresses women's rights and freedoms, advocating women's participation in the workforce regardless of financial need. Being 'cognizant that *a free and egalitarian system can be realized only if all individuals in the society have free and equal rights* without any male-female distinction', the party supports educational programmes 'that enable a woman ... to claim her rights', and 'considers it a duty to remove the obstacles faced by *women who desire to work*, [and plans to fulfil it] by opening childcare centres and nurseries, and taking similar measures' (1983, 37–38, emphasis added).

When SODEP and HP merged into Sosyal Demokrat Halkçı Parti (SHP), SODEP's progressive outlook was maintained. SHP's programmes, issued in 1985 and 1993, emphasize the causes of discrimination in 'our social structures and cultural conditioning' and call for removing 'all obstacles placed before women for being women' (1985, 46).

Table 3. Party Programme References to Equal Pay for Equal Work by Decade and Ideology.

Decade	Party Ideology					
	Religious	Conservative	Turkish Nationalist	Modernizing-Redistributive/ Social Democrat	Socialist	Pro-Kurdish/ Kurdish Nationalist
1960					TİP 1964	
1970		MNP 1970		CHP 1976	TİP 1974	
					TSİP 1976	
1980						
1990				CHP 1994	ÖDP 1996	
2000	SP 2001		MHP 2000	YTP 2002	ÖDP 2006	DEHAP 2003
	AKP 2002			CHP 2006		DTP 2006

When the International Labour Organization (ILO), of which Turkey has been a member since 1932, adopted the Equal Remuneration Convention (No. 100) in 1951, it did not reso-nate in Turkey. Political parties, with one exception, remained silent on the issue until after the country ratified the Convention in July 1967. As illustrated in Table 3, TİP was the only party that mentioned the equal pay for equal work principle in its programme in the 1960s. Even after the ratification of the Convention, only two more parties, Türkiye Sosyalist İşçi Partisi (TSİP) and MNP, joined TİP in supporting the principle in their programmes in the 1970s. Equal pay for equal work became a dormant issue in the subsequent years, until the mid-1990s.

In the 2000s, more parties with different ideologies mentioned the equal pay for equal work principle in their programmes. However, right-wing parties continued to frame women's employment as a forced necessity and lamented pulling women away from their true work as mothers. For example, the religious Saadet Partisi (SP)'s 2001 programme supports the equal pay principle but also notes that the cost of women's employment outside the home should not be the neglect of children or family (Section III.14). On the other hand, ÖDP programmes state that 'The goal being the elimination of male-domination' in all areas, 'women should not be confined to house work', and 'work without pay or for low pay should be ended; women's right to be equal in all areas and right to work for equal pay should be warranted; and the principle of positive discrimination should be supported by law' (ÖDP 1996 and 2006).

Women's Freedoms

References to women's freedoms did not enter the lexicon of political parties until the 1980s, and even then infrequently. As shown in Table 4, only six parties mention the term in their programmes.

Promoting women's freedoms indicates a commitment to women's rights that go beyond anti-discrimination and creating opportunities for women that are equal to those of men. Women's freedoms, which may include liberating women from the traditional gender roles, allowing them to decide for themselves, as well as freedoms of sexuality and sexual orien-tation, speak to women's subjectivity and agency more directly. The incorporation of this term into party programmes after 1980 points to the influence of the women's movement that emerged also in the 1980s and involved women's groups that subscribed to a range of feminist theories.

Table 4. Party Programme References to Women's Freedom by Decade and Ideology.

				Party Ideology		
Decade	Religious	Conservative	Turkish Nationalist	Modernizing-Redistributive/ Social Democrat	Socialist	Pro-Kurdish/Kurdish Nationalist
1980					TBP 1980	
1990		DYP 1998			ÖDP 1996	
2000		GP 2002			ÖDP 2006	DEHAP 2003 DTP 2006

Table 5. Frequency of References to Women's Freedom in Political Party Programmes by Ideology.

				Party Ideology		
Frequency	Religious	Conservative	Turkish Nationalist	Modernizing-Redistributive/ Social Democrat	Socialist	Pro-Kurdish/ Kurdish Nationalist
1		DYP 1998 GP 2002			ÖDP 1996 ÖDP 2006 TBP 1980	
2						DTP 2006
3						
4						DEHAP 2003

Programmes issued by the conservative parties Doğru Yol Partisi (DYP, 1998) and Genç Parti (GP) (2002) explicitly limit their reference to women's economic freedom and independence. Pro-Kurdish parties start to include women's freedoms in the new millennium but then use the term more frequently (Table 5) and broadly. Demokratik Halk Partisi (DEHAP)'s 2003 programme, which mentions women's freedoms four times, notes that 'In the twenty-first century, freedom of women will be important just like human rights'. Its successor Demokrat Türkiye Partisi (DTP) reintroduces DEHAP's gender equality measures and mainstreams women's issues as systemic problems connected to the hierarchical structure of social and state systems, militarism, capitalism, globalization, and patriarchy. The DTP programme sets a female quota of 40% within the party and proposes a 33% quota to be set by law for all political parties. Moreover, it suggests the expansion of the quota system for the executive boards of trade unions and associations.

The ÖDP programmes mention the term 'women's freedom' once but in a subheading that reads 'Freedom for Women!' The title then leads to the discussion of a range of women's issues, suggesting that neglecting these issues inadvertently restricts women's freedoms.

Coexistence of Traditionalism and Feminism since 1980

The gender analysis of political party programmes issued since the 1920s shows a pattern of gradual change from no mention of women to explicit feminist treatment of women's subordination. Although the early 1980s may appear to be a major turning point, the change has been neither linear nor unanimous. While the trend has been towards accepting women's participation in economy and politics and treating equality as more than equality before the law, several powerful parties remained committed to preserving the traditional family structures and gendered division of labour. Moreover, a few parties, some of which became ruling parties in majority or coalition governments, failed to mention women, let alone women's rights (i.e. ANAP 1983 and 2002, MP 1983, RP 1983, and MÇP 1986).

Progressive and feminist discourses started to appear and spread, especially since the 1990s, but the importance assigned to family, emphasis placed on motherhood, and proposals to restrict women's employment opportunities in order to protect them did not vanish. Most parties continued to display a dualistic approach, as exemplified by the pro-business DYP. The party's 1983 programme does not address the female electorate directly, but by promising 'nurseries and day care centres for working fathers and mothers', it presents a rather gender-neutral approach towards childcare. Its 1998 programme pledges to provide women with education and training opportunities, secure women's property rights, and increase penalties for domestic violence and sexual harassment. Arguing for women's economic independence and integration into social life, the programme calls for measures that involve 'well-meaning discrimination' (1998, 14). On the other hand, it treats women as home-bound by emphasizing women's 'important place in our family structure' and by promising arrangements and credit opportunities that would 'allow women to work at home' (1998, 14).

This dualism is more pronounced in Turkish nationalist parties' programmes that call for putting women's legal right into practice but also stress women's role within the family. The 1988 programme of MÇP, later adopted by MHP (1993), spares a section to 'family', which seeks 'the advancement of mothers' in its effort to 'mount family ... on healthy bases'. Then, it continues in bold text: 'We fiercely reject attacks directed at family and its social functions under the disguise of feminism. Nevertheless, we believe in the defence of women and women's rights, as well as the necessity of protecting women as respected beings along with men.' MHP's 2000 programme continues to address women and children together and anchors women at home, but it drops the explicit rejection of feminism and pledges to remove 'all actual and legal discrimination against women' and to elevate 'women's social status' by improving their education level, as well as their participation in the development process, work life, and decision-making mechanisms. Büyük Birlik Partisi (BBP), which split from MHP in 1993, maintains a traditionalist approach, as all of its programmes repeat the following: 'Family is the foundation of society. The society and state take every measure to preserve the power of traditional Turkish-Islamic family. ... All forms of activities that would damage the order and health of family structure would be banned.'

Kurdish nationalist parties' programmes tend to display a progressive approach and commitment to gender equality. However, they also refer to motherhood as 'a social and natural duty' and promise its protection (DEP 1993, 11; HADEP 1994, 12; DEHAP 1997, 14). Upholding motherhood continues to be more prominent in religious parties' programmes. Both SP (2001) and Adalet ve Kalkınma Partisi (AKP, 2002) appear as more inclusive and progressive than FP, from which they split. They acknowledge women's low social status and hardship and support for the equal pay principle but also express concerns about employment being a distraction from childcare. Compared to SP, AKP takes a more comprehensive and progressive approach. Its 2002 programme promises to improve women's education, employment opportunities, social security, work conditions, participation in public life, and involvement in the party and in politics at large. It also pledges to take measures to prevent violence against women, assist the victims of violence, uphold 'international standards on rights and freedoms regarding women, children, and work life', and to implement all principles and requirements of the United Nations' Convention on the Elimination of All Forms of Discrimination against Women (CEDAW). Yet, it also reveals elements of a traditionalist approach, such as justifying support for women for 'being the most effective [actors] in bringing up healthy generations'. It promises 'new employment opportunities' by adding a qualifier: 'but the respect for [women's] work at home will be upheld.' Social security and work conditions are promised to be improved 'with a consideration of women's work life and responsibilities regarding children and family'.

Several programmes acknowledge that the right to run for office does not guarantee women's equal political representation. The left-of-centre Demokratik Sol Parti (DSP)'s programmes promise to encourage 'women's active participation in party work ... to enhance the verity of male–female equality' (1985, 35 and 2003). The conservative DP's 1998 programme pledges to remove 'All legal, administrative and traditional obstacles that prevent our women ... from playing a more active role in all areas, but especially in politics and work life' (42). Statements such as 'equality before law is not enough' (MHP 1993) or the need to employ a comprehensive approach to women's hardship and exclusion become increasingly common. A few programmes problematize women's unequal burden and status within the family. For example, the short-lived Yeni Türkiye Partisi (YTP) notes that 'Women do not share [the joys of] life; they carry the heaviest burdens of the family' (2002, 7–8). The silence on gender-based violence, domestic violence, and sexual harassment is also broken.[25] Some programmes also make explicit references to the CEDAW and promise to uphold and implement its provisions,[26] and a few promise ensuring gender equality through positive discrimination.[27]

The most comprehensive and consistent approaches to gender inequalities and women's rights are presented in the later programmes of left-wing parties.[28] In addition to addressing inequalities in the private domain, they challenge patriarchal norms, and address women's lower status by employing feminist analyses and terminology, including: gender gap, male-dominance, male-dominant society, sexism, sexist, patriarchy, and feminism. They stand out also for integrating women's subordination into the discussion of practically all issues. ÖDP and DTP also oppose discrimination based on sexual orientation.

Discussion and Conclusions

The longitudinal analysis of party programmes issued since the 1920s shows some significant differences and changes in political parties' approaches towards women. The positions of parties vary from complete disregard for women to addressing their problems and concerns from a feminist perspective.

The overall change from ignoring women or assuming pro-natalist and patronizing attitudes to recognizing women as citizens and the need to end their subordination can be largely attributed to women's activism. Turkey experienced two major feminist movements— in the late Ottoman era and in the 1980s. Women's rights activists of the Ottoman era continued to work and affect the public discourse and certain reforms of the Republic. Turkish

---

[25]Programmes that address violence against women: CHP 1994 and 2006; ÖDP 1996 and 2006; DYP 1998; AKP 2002; YTP 2002; DEHAP 2003; and DTP 2006. Programmes that problematize sexual harassment: CHP 1994 and 2006; DYP 1998; YTP 2002; DTP 2006; and ÖDP 2006.

[26]CHP 1994 and 2006; AKP 2002; DEHAP 2003; and DTP 2006. HP's 1983 programme alludes to the CEDAW: 'It will be ensured that our women's pre- and post-natal leaves are in compliance with the UN principles' (28).

[27]ÖDP 1996 and 2006; DYP 1998; YDP 2002; DEHAP 2003; and DTP 2006.

[28]ÖDP, CHP 1994 and 2006; DEHAP 2003; and DTP 2006.

Women's Union, established in 1924, pressed for women's political rights and acquired them for municipal elections in 1930 and national elections in 1934.[29] Then, the leaders of the Union dissolved it upon achieving these main goals of the organization. Other groups were marginalized or co-opted, first by the regime and later by socialist organizations in which women became active.[30]

The second wave of feminism emerged in the 1980s and included a range of groups with distinct perspectives, which can be labelled Kemalist, socialist, Islamist, Kurdish nationalist, liberal, etc.[31] They not only pressured their immediate ideological groups to recognize women's rights[32] but also collaborated with each other to pressure the government.[33] They embraced Turkey's ratification of CEDAW in 1985 and used the treaty as leverage. When Turkey sought European Union (EU) membership in the late 1990s, they lobbied both the government and political parties to ensure that women's rights were not ignored in the legislative reforms carried out to harmonize Turkey's laws with those of the EU. Similarly, they did not hesitate to rally the EU agencies to their cause when the domestic political mechanisms failed to respond.[34]

The incorporation of the equal pay for equal work principle into some party programmes in the 1970s can be attributed to the increase in unionization and women's emerging presence in unions. Nevertheless, the significant increase in references to this principle during the last two decades also points to the power and pressure of the women's movement rather than those of unions.

Left-wing parties' relatively earlier incorporation of women's issues into their programmes and higher support for women's rights are in line with the global data, which show that women have been represented in parliaments at higher rates in countries with strong left-wing parties.[35] However, it should be noted that such parties in Turkey displayed a dualistic approach towards women's roles and rights until the 1980s. Their discourse changed only after women's groups sought autonomous organizations and collaborated with the governing and other parties without sacrificing their independence.[36] Further research on women's work within political parties and strategies to advance women's rights and achieve gender equality would allow us to understand the politics and process of human rights better.

Disclosure statement

No potential conflict of interest was reported by the author.

---

[29]Yıldız Ecevit, 'Women's Rights, Women's Organizations and the State', in Zehra F. Kabasakal Arat, ed., *Human Rights in Turkey: Policies and Prospects* (Philadelphia: University of Pennsylvania Press, 2007), pp. 187–201.

[30]Ecevit, 'Women's Rights, Women's Organizations'.

[31]Yeşim Arat, 'Toward a Democratic Society: The Women's Movement in Turkey in the 1980s', *Women's Studies International Forum*, 17(2) (1994), pp. 241–248; Zehra F. Kabasakal Arat, ed., *Deconstructing Images of 'the Turkish Woman'* (New York: St. Martin's Press, 1998).

[32]Yeşim Arat, *Rethinking Islam and Liberal Democracy: Islamist Women in Turkish Politics* (Albany: State University of New York Press, 2005); Aynur İlyasoğlu, 'Islamist Women in Turkey: Their Identity and Self-Image', in Z. Arat, ed., *Deconstructing Images of 'the Turkish Woman'* (New York: St. Martin's Press, 1998), pp. 225–240.

[33]Zehra F. K. Arat, 'Women', in Metin Heper and Sabri Sayarı, eds., *Routledge Handbook of Modern Turkey* (Abingdon: Routledge, 2012), pp. 259–270; Ecevit, 'Women's Rights, Women's Organizations'.

[34]Z. Arat, 'Women'; Ayşe Güneş Ayata and Fatma Tütüncü, 'Party Politics of the AKP (2002–2007) and the Predicaments of Women at the Intersection of the Westernist, Islamist and Feminist Discourses in Turkey', *British Journal of Middle Eastern Studies*, 35(3) (2008), pp. 363–384.

[35]Jean Jaquette, 'Women in Power: From Tokenism to Critical Mass', *Foreign Policy*, 108 (1997), pp. 23–37; Krook and Norris, 'Beyond Quotas', pp. 2–20; Tremblay, *Women and Legislative Representation*; Kunovich and Paxton, 'Pathways to Power', pp. 505–552.

[36]Ecevit, 'Women's Rights, Women's Organizations'.

Appendix. The List of Parties Included in the Study, Programme Dates and Ideology Coding (IC)

Party Acronym and Name	IC	Programme Date	Party Acronym and Name	IC	Programme Date
ACF—Ahali Cumhuriyet Fırkası	4	1930	LCİÇF—Lâyik Cumhuriyetçi İşçi ve Çiftçi Fırkası	4	1931
AKP—Adalet ve Kalkınma Partisi	1	2002	LDP –Liberal Demokrat Parti	2	1946
ANAP—Anavatan Partisi	2	1983; 2002	MÇP—Milliyetçi Çalışma Partisi	3	1986; 1988
AP—Adalet Partisi	2	1961; 1964; 1969; 1974	MDP—Milliyetçi Demokrasi Partisi	2	1983
BBP—Büyük Birlik Partisi	3	1993; 1999; 2002	MHP—Milliyetçi Hareket Partisi	3	1969; 1973; 1993; 2000
BP—Birlik Partisi	5	1967	MKP—Milli Kalkınma Partisi	2	1945
MGP/CGP—Milli/Cumhuriyetçi Güven Partisi	2	1971	MNP—Milli Nizam Partisi	1	1970
CHF—Cumhuriyet Halk Fırkası	4	1927; 1931	MP—Millet Partisi	3	1948; 1963; 1967
CHP—Cumhuriyet Halk Partisi	4	1935; 1939; 1943; 1947; 1953; 1954; 1959; 1976; 1994; 2002; 2006	MSP—Milli Selamet Partisi	1	1973
CKMP—Cumhuriyetçi Köylü Millet Partisi	3	1961; 1965	MTSP—Müstakil Türk Sosyalist Partisi	5	1948
CMP—Cumhuriyetçi Millet Partisi	3	1954	MuP—Muhafazakar Parti	3	1983
DEHAP—Demokratik Halk Partisi	6	1997; 2003	ÖDP—Özgürlük ve Dayanışma Partisi	5	1996; 2006
DEP—Demokrasi Partisi	6	1993	RP—Refah Partisi	1	1983
DİP—Demokrat İşçi Partisi	4	1950	SCF—Serbes Cumhuriyet Fırkası	2	1930
DP—Demokrat Parti	2	1946; 1951; 1998	SHP—Sosyaldemokrat Halk Partisi	4	2002
DSP—Demokratik Sol Parti	4	1985; 2003; 2007	SHP—Sosyal Demokrat Halkçı Parti	4	1985; 1993
DtikP—Demokratik Parti	2	1970	SODEP—Sosyal Demokrat Parti	4	1983
DTP—Demokrat Türkiye Partisi	2	1997	SP—Saadet Partisi	1	2001
DTP—Demokratik Toplum Partisi	6	2006	TBP—Türkiye Birlik Partisi	5	1972; 1980
DYP—Doğru Yol Partisi	2	1983; 1998	TCAÇP—Türk Cumhuriyet Amele ve Çiftçi Partisi	5	1930
FP—Fazilet Partisi	1	1997	TCF—Terakkiperver Cumhuriyet Fırkası	2	1924
GP—Genç Parti	2	2002	TİÇP—Türkiye İşçi ve Çiftçi Partisi	5	1946
GP—Güven Parti	2	1967	TİP—Türkiye İşçi Partisi	5	1964; 1975
HADEP—Halkın Demokrasi Partisi	6	1994	TKP—Türkiye Köylü Partisi	3	1952
HEP—Halkın Emek Partisi	6	1990; 1992	TSDP—Türk Sosyal Demokrat Partisi	4	1946
HF—Halk Fırkası	4	1923	TSEKP—Türk Sosyalist Emekçi ve Köylü Partisi	5	1946
HP—Halkçı Parti	4	1983	TSİP—Türkiye Sosyalist İşçi Partisi	5	1976
HuP—Hürriyet Partisi	2	1956	TSP—Türkiye Sosyalist Partisi	5	1946
HYP—Halkın Yükseliş Partisi	2	2005	YTrP—Yeni Türkiye Partisi	2	1961
İDP—İslâm Demokrat Partisi	1	1952	YTP—Yeni Türkiye Partisi	4	2002
			YVİP—Yalnız Vatan İçin Partisi	4	1946

Note: Ideology Coding (IC): (1) religious; (2) conservative; (3) Turkish nationalist; (4) modernizing-redistributive/ social democrat; (5) socialist; (6) pro-Kurdish/Kurdish nationalist.

9 The historical emergence and transformation of the Moroccan political party field

Khalil Dahbi

ABSTRACT

This article offers a historical analysis of the emergence of the political party field in post-independence Morocco and makes the case for a bottom-up approach that pays close attention to actors' cultural dispositions, capabilities and the constraints imposed upon them by emergent fields. It starts by briefly introducing the conceptual toolbox of Bourdieusian field theory, underscoring the analytical strengths of the concepts it includes. Drawing on a qualitative analysis of both primary and secondary sources, the article then deploys the aforementioned concepts to trace the historical processes that shaped the emergence of the Moroccan political party field. In doing so, this article suggests a novel approach to the study of political parties that emphasizes the importance of adopting a bottom-up perspective, and the need to go beyond mono-causal explanatory accounts.

Introduction

This article aims to contribute to the understanding of the emergence and development of political parties, particularly in the case of early post-independence Morocco. While addressing the case study, Pierre Bourdieu's field theory will be employed in order to uncover the processes through which a political field emerges, and its rules are negotiated and decided. The reason behind this methodological choice is that Bourdieu's field theory is particularly apt at exploring political processes due to its ability to take into account multiple actors' agency and their agendas and horizons for political action, while embedding these actors in the historically emergent arena of political action where their actions are structured by material and symbolic constraints collectively made and experienced. Therefore this article can be read both as a statement about the explanatory power of Bourdieusian field theory and as an attempt to revisit and offer a novel reading of a determinative period in Morocco's political history, armed with a conceptual framework that has not been employed for this empirical material before. Based on both theoretical insights derived from Bourdieu's conceptual toolbox, and productive empirical observations derived from a detailed empirical study, this paper offers new conceptualizations of Moroccan political parties, the political party field that they are embedded in, and the political field in its entirety. It also highlights the dynamic connections between the struggle over the rules of the political field in question, and the developments in other proximate fields. Finally, it illustrates how the relative autonomy of fields affects the way in which struggles are reflected within them.

The dominant scholarly approach to the study of political systems in the Middle East and North Africa is to adopt a 'top-down' approach when setting up analytical questions and framing the relevance of particular national cases. The conventional method is to first adopt a 'big-picture' perspective and categorize the political systems in the region under the 'authoritarian' category, as opposed to 'democratic' political systems in the West. From this large-scale perspective the question is set up as one of explaining the resilience of the region's authoritarian regimes. Explanatory variables are also imagined in this fashion, as ingredients making a political system that eventually falls under the category of authoritarian or democratic. Some scholars focus on the cultural 'ingredients', using the region's cultural specificities to explain the prevalence of authoritarian political systems in the region. Other scholars adopt the universalistic narrative of modernization theory, and focus on variables that they relate with 'development'. Their explanatory accounts often centre on a 'political development' inducing ingredient that is missing in the region, or in a specific country, and prevents it from democratizing.

In this article, I propose that we move away from this 'top-down' approach and adopt a 'bottom-up' approach which I attempt to develop based on Bourdieu's theory of fields and the case of early post-independence Morocco. Instead of starting with an assumed political entity such as 'an authoritarian political system' and investigating its 'ingredients' retrospectively, I work my way towards the bigger picture, that is the Moroccan political field, by exploring and studying the processes which bring into existence this holistic entity, the role of various actors, how these actors were constrained by rules and positions of the very field that they are piecing together and how in the emergence and development of political party systems, one cannot single out 'cultural' or developmental 'ingredients' as these aspects manifest themselves in the everyday details of actions taken by certain actors and woven together in an inseparable manner with material, symbolic, collective and in-group factors.

The 'bottom-up' approach proposed in this article is derived from Bourdieu's theory. For this reason, before delving into the case study itself, an overview of the theoretical framework, along with a succinct introduction of field theory's conceptual toolbox, is offered in the next section. The following section deploys that framework within a historical analysis of the struggles taking place in post-independence Morocco, highlighting their impact on the emergence and development of the country's political field in general, and its political party field in particular.

Conceptual framework

The work of Bourdieu is quite vast and expansive, though if one had to single out its most distinctive feature, it would have to be its struggle to overcome dichotomies, especially the structure and agency one. The relevance of this dichotomy to the question of 'authoritarian political systems' and the importance of overcoming it have been alluded to in the introduction. Bourdieu's approach, which offers a unique solution to the structure–agency dilemma, allows for an exploration of the emergence and development of political parties that pays attention simultaneously both to the actor's agency, and to the ways in which the relevant arena of action, the field, structures, shapes, enables and constrains their actions, all the while emphasizing that the field itself is emergent from the cumulative and historical product of this interplay. Here lies the power of the 'bottom-up' approach that works towards the whole and offers an alternative to the 'top-down' and dichotomous approaches prevalent in the study of political systems in the Middle East and North Africa region.

The structure–agency dilemma is overcome in Bourdieu's theory by virtue of a triad of concepts: *habitus*, field, and capital, which are often deployed in combination with a historical genealogy of the object studied. These concepts can only be adequately understood in relation to one another, so this paper will briefly introduce each and will try to show how they all fit together. This task is also essential in order to clarify how the empirical case in this article is treated in a way that weaves together the 'cultural' and material influences and resources available to actors, with the constraints imposed upon their actions due to their positioning relative to their peers, as all these interwoven 'variables' are manifested in actors' choices, strategies and shortcomings at every decisive moment during the unfolding of post-independence Moroccan political history. As readers will see in the following section, the unfolding of this history is couched in Bourdieusian vocabulary in order to reap the analytical powers of his approach.

The first concept is the *habitus* which refers to the internalized and embodied effects of structures on an individual, shaping his dispositions.[1] The *habitus* affects how the individual perceives the social world, his position within it, and the range of possible courses of action available to him. The concept operates without 'presupposing a conscious aiming at ends or an express mastery of the operations necessary to attain them'.[2]

The second element in the conceptual triad is the idea of *forms of capital*. Capital comes in various forms, principally economic, social, cultural, and symbolic capital.[3] These different forms of capital can be converted into one another at variable exchange rates, which are set through the meta-capital acquired within the field of power.[4]

While the concept of habitus refers to an actor's dispositions, the concept of *field* empha-sizes an actor's relational position. Fields are quite central to Bourdieu's approach, as it is through them that the two other concepts are brought together. In the broad sense, a field can be defined as the space formed by 'a network, or configuration of objective relations between positions'.[5] Actors vie for positions constantly within a field, with better positions granting access to more benefits in terms of status and power. As Bourdieu and Wacquant[6] put it, the positions that actors compete over are:

> objectively defined, in their existence and in the determinations they impose upon their occu-pants, agents or institutions, by their present potential situation (*situs*) in the structure of the distribution of species of power (or *capital*) whose possession commands access to the specific profits that are at stake in the field, as well as by their objective relation to other positions.[7]

---

[1]Pierre Bourdieu, *The Logic of Practice* (Stanford, CA: Stanford University Press, 1990).
[2]Ibid., p. 53.
[3]Pierre Bourdieu, 'The Forms of Capital', in Nicole Woolsey Biggart, ed., *Readings in Economic Sociology* (Oxford, UK: Blackwell, 2002), pp. 280–291, http://doi.wiley.com/10.1002/9780470755679.ch15.
[4]Pierre Bourdieu, *Sur l'État: Cours Au Collège de France, 1989–1992*, ed. Patrick Champagne, Cours et travaux (Paris: Raisons d'agir: Seuil, 2012).
[5]Pierre Bourdieu and Loïc J. D. Wacquant, *An Invitation to Reflexive Sociology* (Chicago, IL: University of Chicago Press, 1992), p. 97.
[6]Bourdieu and Wacquant, *An Invitation to Reflexive Sociology*.
[7]Ibid., p. 97.

A field can be viewed both as a space within which positions are organized by the 'forces' of capital and reflect the capital distribution, and as a space of struggle between the dominant and the dominated.[8] In addition to their constant jockeying for position, actors are often engaged in a struggle over what is at stake in a given field, over the rules of the game itself, and over who belongs within it. Thus, one of the advantages of using the concept of fields as an analytical tool is that it helps in avoiding a reification of official categories and boundaries. A field can refer to specific formal institutions, or they can be 'inter- or intra-institutional in scope; they can span institutions, which may represent positions within fields.'[9] Furthermore, fields vary in their degree of relative autonomy. The more relatively autonomous a field is, the less its internal balance of power is affected by changes to the forces in the social space surrounding it, and the more the struggles within it take place following its own internal logic.[10] For instance, Bourdieu considered that the literary and artistic fields were relatively autonomous from the forces of the economic field.

Finally, there are two more important variations on the concept of field. The first one is the 'field of power', wherein a set of actors highly endowed with various forms of capital, or in more colloquial terms, the powerful elites of a given society, struggle with one another over dominance. The struggle within the field of power is the main determinant of the exchange rates among the various forms of capitals and their relative power.[11] The second one is the notion of field as it refers to a national social space, which encompasses all the other fields, and is the space where class struggle occurs and the relations between classes are defined.[12]

Building upon these concepts, this article tackles political parties as collective actors located within an organized social space, a *field*, in which they must compete with one another. It refers to that specific field as the *political party field*, and views it as being in turn embedded within a larger *political field*. This larger *political field* includes a number of other actors aside from political parties, both collective and individual, all of which compete over the positions and benefits to be gained within it. The *political field* is principally characterized by the prominent role of the political capital available and circulating within it. Competition within this field is done, amongst other ways, through the production of political ideas, mobilization of popular support, and the claims of representation of more or less large social categories.

In the case of post-independence Morocco, the vacuum created by the end of the protectorate within the political field opened the possibility for a radical reorganization of the field itself, and of the relative weight and autonomy of the sub-fields it encompassed. The ripples caused by the resulting struggle reverberated widely throughout the Moroccan social space. This article will principally analyse the repercussions that were observed within the political field, by tracing the processes through which different struggles over the rules of the political field have unfolded and how these processes were dynamically related to the developments in connected fields.

---

[8]Pierre Bourdieu, *Sociologie Générale*, ed. Patrick Champagne et al., Cours et travaux (Paris: Raisons d'agir: Seuil, 2015).
[9]David Swartz, *Culture & Power: The Sociology of Pierre Bourdieu* (Chicago, IL: University of Chicago Press, 1997) p. 120.
[10]Ibid.
[11]Ibid.
[12]Bourdieu, *Sur l'État*.

Foundational struggle

As Morocco regained its independence, the Alaouite monarchy found itself in a much better situation than, for instance, its Tunisian counterpart. The Sultan Mohammed ben Youssef (the future king Mohammed V), seen as the institution's embodiment, accumulated a high amount of both social and symbolic capital. The preservation and use of the monarchic institution and its forms of capital by the French protectorate to bolster its own legitimacy stands as a testimony to the privileged position enjoyed by the palace within the Moroccan field of power. The protectorate also gave the monarchy access to significant social capital accruing from the connections it was allowed to maintain and develop both with the traditional elites, and within the more modern institutions that the protectorate had created. By 1955, the monarchic institution had regained a significant amount of social and symbolic capital, mainly through the political positioning of the Sultan in support of the nationalist movement. The Sultan's late opposition to the protectorate authorities' policies, and the connections he developed with nationalist leaders laid the bridges for the cooperation of the two factions against the French authorities, especially following his deposition by the French authorities and exile in 1953.[13] The nationalist movement actively used the return of the Sultan as a central frame to mobilize the population.

The decision of the *Parti de l'Istiqlal* (hereafter PI) to centre its mobilization campaign on the return of the Sultan was not fortuitous. Rather, it was in great part motivated by the party's realization of its limited reach beyond the major urban centres. They viewed the Sultan as an actor that could give them access to the traditional and religious forms of symbolic capital that they were lacking, and that were highly valued especially in those parts of the country that were hard to penetrate for the party. The view that the Sultan was the religious embodiment and the symbolic representative of the *umma* was a notion deeply rooted in the local culture and widely spread. Therefore, for the PI, the plan was to use the monarchy as a tool to further its efforts at dominating the post-independence political field and the state apparatus.[14] The PI itself had a heterogeneous membership and leadership, with a diversity in terms of *habitus* that gave it, especially during the struggle for independence, the capacity to navigate efficiently around a number of fields. Some of its leaders were more proficient at mobilizing workers or students, while others had, from their traditional aristocratic upbringing, access to the embodied forms of cultural and symbolic capital that allowed them to feel at ease in some other social settings.

The PI's mobilization campaign against the protectorate was very effective. The party succeeded in increasing its membership significantly, and began a coordinated armed resistance campaign. Faced with the general escalation of violence around its colonies, especially

---

[13]With the support of a number of *Grands Caids* (traditional feudal leaders and large landowners that were empowered by the protectorate, such as El Glaoui) who opposed the Sultan's cooperation with the PI, the French authorities orchestrated the deposition and replacement of Ben Youssef by Mohamed ben Arafa. The deposed Sultan and his family were then sent into exile, first to Corsica, and then to Madagascar.

[14]Paul Chambergeat, 'Le Référendum Constitutionnel Du 7 Décembre 1962 Au Maroc', *Annuaire de l'Afrique Du Nord*, 1 (1964), pp. 167–205; Octave Marais, 'La classe dirigeante au Maroc', *Revue française de science politique*, 14(4) (1964), pp. 709–737; Maâti Monjib, *La Monarchie Marocaine et La Lutte Pour Le Pouvoir: Hassan II Face À L'opposition Nationale, de L'indépendance À L'état D'exception*, Collection 'Histoire et perspectives méditerranéennes' (Paris: L'Harmattan, 1992); Michael J. Willis, *Politics and Power in the Maghreb: Algeria, Tunisia and Morocco from Independence to the Arab Spring* (London: Hurst, 2012). Paul Chambergeat and Octave Marais are both pseudonyms used by the famous French political scientist Remy Levau to publish his work during the time when he was a legal councilor at the Moroccan Ministry of Interior, from 1959 until 1965 as reported by Valérie Amiraux, Mounia Bennani-Chraïbi, and Hamit Bozarslan, "Hommage à Rémy Leveau," Critique internationale 27, no. 2 (2005), p. 12.

in neighbouring Algeria, the French authorities decided to enter into negotiations with the National movement.[15] The negotiation process culminated in Morocco regaining its independence, and in the triumphant return of the Sultan Muhammad ben Youssef. This foundational moment laid the ground for the definitional struggle over the political field that characterized the period from 1955 to 1965, which would in turn deeply impact the future evolution of Morocco's political system.

The nascent political field

Even though it was by far the largest and most influential organized actor, the PI was not alone on the emerging political party field. As far as political parties went, there was also the *Parti Democratique de l'Independance* (PDI), the *Parti Communiste Marocain* (PCM), and the later-organized *Mouvement Populaire* (MP). The PDI was in no way comparable to the much larger and better organized PI. It mostly represented an urban and bourgeois constituency. The PCM was an old party, which was banned under the protectorate, and operated mostly underground. Its reappearance on the post-independence political field was to be short-lived, as it was banned again in 1959. As for the MP, its growth was supported by the monarchy, and it regrouped a number of actors whose *habitus* and pre-colonial political field positions put them at odds with the PI and the nationalist movement as a whole. A considerable number of rural notables chose to be part of this regrouping. Among these rural notables who eventually formed the backbone of the MP were those who were relatively supportive of the protectorate prior to independence and those who were not supportive but resented the domination of the urban-based PI. This feeling of resentment was partially an expression of the mismatch notables felt between their 'ways' and the modernizing goals espoused by the PI. Some of these significant differences can arguably be traced back to the differences in education as well. The protectorate authorities had prior to independence, since 1923, established a separate educational system aimed at the Berber population, with the goal of insulating them from the nationalist discourses that had already started spreading in the cities. On that matter, a very prescient report written in 1930 by the commander of Dar el-Beida, the elite military school in Meknes designed principally to train the sons of rural notables, mentions that one of the institution's main goals was the creation of a loyalist bloc that would serve as a counterweight to the nascent nationalist faction.[16]

The main leaders of the MP were Mahjoubi Aherdane and Abdelkrim Khatib. They were both involved with the *Armée de Liberation* (AL, Liberation Army). Aherdane was a captain in the French army known for his very pro-Berber and pro-rural positions, and was later appointed as a *Caid* by the protectorate.[17] As for Dr Khatib, he was especially close to the palace and was born into a wealthy family. He was married into a prominent Rif family, and was the first Moroccan to train as a surgeon in France. Under the protectorate, he was supporting the resistance with fundraising amongst Moroccan workers in Europe.[18] Both were

---

[15]It is worth pointing out that the PI was not able to impose itself as the sole (or even principal) representative of the Moroccan side during the negotiations. Though it was much larger than the other actors, the French made sure that representatives of the traditional rural notability would be represented as well.

[16]As quoted in Pierre Vermeren, *La Formation Des Élites Marocaines et Tunisiennes: Des Nationalistes Aux Islamistes, 1920–2000*, Collection 'Recherches' (Paris: Découverte, 2002), p. 32. See also Elbaki Hermassi, *Leadership and National Development in North Africa: A Comparative Study* (Berkeley: University of California Press, 1972).

[17]Ignace Dalle, *Les Trois Rois: La Monarchie Marocaine, de L'indépendance À Nos Jours* (Paris: Fayard, 2004).

[18]See ibid., pp. 126–130 for a more detailed interview with Abdelkrim Khatib.

known as staunch monarchists without any deep relations with the PI, and were thus able to gain the support of those dissatisfied with its policies.

Within the PI, the MP was viewed as an assemblage of 'cooperators' if not outright traitors to the nationalist cause. Through its closeness to the monarchy and its ability to use traditional social networks to mobilize the rural population, especially in Berber areas, the MP was increasingly viewed as a threat by the PI.

Soon after independence, the relationship between the PI and the monarchy started to become more antagonistic. At stake was the definitional struggle over the rules of the Field of Power. The central disagreement was over the claim to represent the nation. In other words, the question they were debating was: Which form of capital would have more purchase, the nationalist symbolic capital accruing from closeness to the party and the nationalist movement, or the traditional and religious symbolic capital embodied by the monarch and earned from closeness to him? The PI viewed itself as the principal force that led the country towards independence, and most of its leadership considered that it should be able to continue the process by being able to govern alone. The palace was wary of such demands, especially given how a similar process led to the side-lining of the monarchy in neighbouring Tunisia.[19] Allowing the PI to single-handedly control the state apparatus at this point would have led to an increase in its appeal, augmenting its reach and membership. It would become the dominant actor in the national political field, and from the perspective of potential new recruits the party would be seen as the main gateway to achieve social ascension by acquiring positions within the state bureaucracy. As the Moroccan monarchy was not willing to be pushed into a position that would at best be secondary to the party, if not outright ceremonial, it entered into a conflict with the PI.

The monarchy had many advantages in the struggles that followed. First, its claim to represent the nation was bolstered by the fact that the PI had used the institution's appeal for its mobilization campaign during the phase leading up to independence. Second, the monarchy actively engaged in what could be labelled a strategy of dilution. It 'diluted' the PI's claim by actively supporting the alternative actors that the party was trying to side-line.[20] It also granted them disproportionately large representation within the first government at the expense of the PI.[21] The insurrectionary reactions of local traditional elites[22] to the PI's attempts at asserting its authority over Berber and rural areas, through the state bureaucracy, gave more support to the monarchy's efforts.[23]

To drum up support for its reform plans, the PI, very early on, used the governmental positions that it controlled to appoint its members into administrative posts in various rural areas. This could have proved to be a fruitful move. However, the young, educated, and modern party members who were dispatched to rural areas as part of the agrarian reform plans substantially failed at their task. And in their failure, it is possible to read a fine

---

[19]Khalil Dahbi, "The Historical Emergence and Transformation of Political Fields: A Strategic Action Fields Approach to the Case of Tunisia," in *Global and the Local: New Concepts and Approaches: Proceedings of the Papers Presented at Consortium for Asian and African Studies (CAAS) 6th International Conference, Hankuk University of Foreign Studies,* 27–28 October 2015, ed. Nobuaki Kondo (Tokyo, Japan: International Office, Tokyo University of Foreign Studies, 2016), pp. 241–248.

[20]Through legal means, as well as less than legal ones, such as the use of kidnappings and assassinations.

[21]'Documents Maroc', *Annuaire de l'Afrique Du Nord,* 1 (1964), pp. 742–782.

[22]Especially the Addi ou Bihi rebellion in the Tafilalet, and the Rif rebellion. In both the Rif and the Addi ou Bihi cases, the monarchy gained a lot of credit by appearing as the actor fixing the mistakes caused by the PI's assertiveness and maintaining the unity of the country, whether by using its social and symbolic capital or through coercion.

[23]Monjib, *La Monarchie Marocaine.*

demonstration of the importance of *habitus* and the decisive effect it has on social actions and capabilities. These young party members often displayed condescension towards the regressive traditional norms and mundane concerns of the mostly illiterate peasants. What they cared more about were the national-level reform plans, as set up by the party leadership. It was part of their *habitus* to display this condescension, and never in their usual social circles was this attitude challenged or questioned, so it simply manifested in the way they spoke, in the way they interacted.[24]

The local administrators came principally from within the ranks of the PI, except in the northern provinces where many of the appointees belonged to the local factions of the AL. They were generally from a lower-class urban background. They often failed to display the leadership traits required to gain and maintain the respect of the villagers. The villagers were until then used to dealing with local French administrators representing the protectorate, who were often very well trained and had a deep knowledge of the social and cultural features of the villages that they oversaw.[25] Furthermore, a number of the new PI administrators overseeing Berber-speaking areas had reportedly 'no knowledge of the local Berber dialect or customs'.[26] The fact that these low-level positions were not very prestigious or appealing made it even more difficult for the new administration to find enough qualified appointees.

At the provincial level, communication and understanding between the administrators and the rural people were not any smoother; the rural notables who would at times convey the villagers' grievances to the provincial-level authorities often found themselves in what they viewed as the uncomfortable position of having to be lectured by young French-speaking and Westernized bureaucrats about the primacy of national-level goals over the more practical needs of their villages.[27] This reportedly made the rural people often feel that their whole existence and lifestyle were targeted, and that the administration (and therefore the PI) ultimately aimed at making them leave their villages for the sprawling shantytowns surrounding the main cities.[28]

Thus, the rural notables would have what they viewed as their legitimate demands for modern infrastructure and services dismissed. Peasants, in turn, were very familiar with what they deemed a Westernized demeanour and modern values and often reciprocated with contempt for these young urban party members.[29] In many cases, the villagers would often end up circumventing the new local administrators, leaving them at times so isolated from the population that some would reportedly end up abandoning their posts after a few months.[30] In other cases, they would react violently, drawing upon a repertoire that has been compared to those of the pre-colonial rural rebellion patterns against the *Makhzen* authority.[31]

---

[24]This form of *habitus*-related condescension, which can still be noticed in contemporary Morocco, was not unique to the PI but is a feature that can be found across numerous social boundaries (ethnic, regional, linguistic, educational, etc.).

[25]Rémy Leveau, *Le Fellah Marocain Défenseur Du Trône* (Paris: Presses de Sciences Po, 1985), p. 45.

[26]Douglas E. Ashford, *Political Change in Morocco*, Princeton Oriental Studies 3 (Princeton, NJ: Princeton University Press, 1961), p. 215.

[27]Leveau, *Le Fellah Marocain Défenseur Du Trône*, p. 46.

[28]Leveau, *Le Fellah Marocain Défenseur Du Trône*.

[29]Maâti Monjib, *La Monarchie Marocaine*.

[30]Leveau, *Le Fellah Marocain Défenseur Du Trône*, p. 45.

[31]Octave Marais, 'Les relations entre la monarchie et la classe dirigeante au Maroc', *Revue française de science politique*, 19(6) (1969), pp. 1175–1176.

The concept of *habitus* explains well the cultural setting of these interactions. The other factor, which, could be associated with the concepts of forms of capital and fields, was the fact that at the local level, the young PI administrators were pitted against rural notables. The latter were perfectly at ease in their environment and had a lifetime of experience and an accumulation of field-specific capital on their side, all of which young PI administrators fell short of. The notables had large clientelistic networks in their areas, and would often be respected and/or feared by the villagers as powerful local leaders. They often combined this social capital with economic capital, as many of the notables had acquired large private agricultural land holdings under the protectorate, which they were able to efficiently deploy to protect their positions when needed.[32] So they, and not the young party members, were the ones who succeeded in mobilizing the dominated peasantry against the outsiders, and ironically against peasants' own material interests.

These events further supported the impression that the monarchy was crucial for the maintenance of a national unity that was endangered by what appeared to be the PI's dangerous power-plays. The monarchy took advantage of this favourable conjuncture to pass the *Charte des Libertes Publiques* (Public Liberties Charter) in 1958, which paid some lip service to ideals such as democracy and freedom, but at the same time shattered the party's hopes of domination by defining the structure of the emerging Political Party Field as a multiparty system. The fact that the palace had already created security forces whose loyalty it could count on was another important development tipping the balance of power in its favour.[33] It still however made sure to neutralize potential contestation from the PI's most important ally on the political field, the large and powerful *Union Marocaine du Travail* (UMT), by granting it some of its demands for official recognition.[34] A similar strategy was used when granting the PI the *homogeneous government* that it had campaigned for since independence, a few months before the passing of the charter. Though it granted the PI control over most ministerial posts, the monarchy made sure that those appointed came principally from the conservative and monarchist members of the party. These moves made it so that any attempts by the PI to dominate either the political field or the political party field would face staunch opposition not just from the monarchy, but from a number of relatively autonomous actors who would view such domination as a threat to their positions within their respective fields.

The effects of the monarchy's successful campaign to dominate the field of power, its establishment of a multiparty system in the political party field, and its opening of the political field to alternative actors such as unions and other forms of associations, impacted the internal dynamics of the PI. Given its heterogeneous composition, the party had a number of dormant internal fault lines, and the loss of the prospect of a unified political field under its control led to their activation.

The main division pitted the progressive and conservative wings of the party against each other. Control over the political and bureaucratic fields would have been a necessary step towards the implementation of the party's ambitious reform programme, which aimed at implementing an agrarian land redistribution programme and the achievement of territorial

[32]Marais, 'Les relations entre la monarchie'; for a more detailed analysis highlighting the importance of local field-specific forms of capital in ensuring political success, see the review of legislative elections' candidates in Leveau, *Le Fellah Marocain Défenseur Du Trône*, pp. 146–240.

[33]Willis, *Politics and Power in the Maghreb*.

[34]Dahir n° 1-57-119 (16 Juillet 1957) on professional syndicates.

integrity. The appointment of the Balafrej (PI) government in May 1958 further complicated matters internally, and the political line that it followed led to growing discontent within the party's left wing. Ahmed Balafrej, who grew up in an aristocratic background, was the secretary general of the PI since its foundation. He was respected as an intellectual figure, and was reportedly known to be a very diplomatic person. He disliked open confrontation, and some regarded him as the palace's man inside the PI.[35] The more radical faction of the left, in association with the UMT, was very active in spearheading the opposition to the Balafrej government, organizing a number of labour strikes. Mehdi ben Barka and Allal al Fassi were still focused on by maintaining a united front, and both factions at first avoided the levelling of direct critiques at each other and at the Balafrej government. A few months later, in December 1958, the monarchy appointed Abdallah Ibrahim, one of the closest PI leaders to the labour movement, to lead the government.[36] This move further exacerbated the tensions within the party, while also putting its more leftist wing to the test of governance. As Ben Barka[37] was to observe later on, being in the government did not necessarily mean that the PI had the power to apply its programme. It still had to deal with an increasingly assertive monarchy, especially with the then Prince Hassan, who was at the time very involved in organizing the forces opposed to the PI. The King was uncooperative as well, at times using a tactic that he had previously resorted to against the protectorate, refusing to sign bills that he disapproved of.

Within the PI, taken as a field of its own, the confrontation turned around the rules of the game, and the lines of demarcation between those wanting to reform the internal functioning of the central organs of the party were aligned with the actors' positions within the larger social space. At the level of the party leadership, both Mehdi ben Barka and Allal al-Fassi, while situated on different sides of the issue, still kept in mind their party's position within the larger field, and reportedly preferred the avoidance of a split that would principally benefit the monarchy at the expense of the national movement.[38] Yet, while it was a reflection of the on-going struggle for domination within the larger political field between the monarchy and the nationalist movement, the relative autonomy of the PI field meant that the struggle would be played out through the field's own internal dynamics.

Internal strife accelerated soon after the appointment of the Ibrahim government. By late December, the dispute transitioned from the more limited circle of the leadership to become a more public issue at the level of the whole party.[39] The left wing considered that the internal organization of the party had to be rethought. More specifically, they were pushing for a more democratic mode of selection for party delegates. The conservative wing was opposed to that proposal, and adamantly insisted on maintaining a number of seats for unelected notables. A compromise that would have granted the notables the status of observers was rejected as well.[40] Following this disagreement, the leftist faction started mobilizing the provincial sections for a move against the central leadership.

---

[35] According to an interview with his son, Anis Balafrej, Ahmed Balafrej was 'not a convinced monarchist, but a monarchist by interest', even if he enjoyed good relations with the palace; see Dalle, *Les Trois Rois*, p. 143.

[36] 'Documents Maroc'.

[37] Mehdi Ben Barka, *Option Révolutionnaire Au Maroc : Suivi de Écrits Politiques 1960–1965*, Cahiers libres (Ézanville, impr. Gouin: F. Maspero, 1966).

[38] Monjib, *La Monarchie Marocaine*.

[39] Ashford, *Political Change in Morocco*.

[40] Monjib, *La Monarchie Marocaine*.

Opposition membership within the PI struggle reflected and coincided with the positions occupied by the many protagonists within the Moroccan social space. Without delving into too much detail, endowments in various forms of capital, as well as the *habitus* factor, as reflected in one's age, social origin, and education, all coincided quite well with the positions adopted by the actors in the struggle.[41] Some exceptions to this observation were noted, for example the actors primarily involved in the internal struggles of other fields, and who viewed their position within the PI's internal game as secondary, such as in the case of the regional/ethnic and economic rivalry between businessmen from Fez and Sūs which was instrumental in making the latter throw their weight behind the progressive wing.[42]

Within the labour movement field, the PI's internal frictions were reflected and mediated through its own internal dynamics. The field was dominated by the UMT, headed by Mahjoub Benseddik since its founding in 1955. It was very close to the PI's left, especially to Abdallah Ibrahim. Throughout the tenure of the Balafrej government, the UMT engaged in a strong opposition campaign, organizing a number of strikes, and publishing a number of critical articles, some of which were penned by Ibrahim himself. However, politically motivated strikes did not come cheap, and opposition to the union leadership increased as some of its membership viewed that the purely political use of strikes against the Balafrej government was not in the labour movement's best interests. For instance, the conservative wing managed to mobilize the dock workers of Casablanca against the union leadership, in favour of a potential split, by challenging the leadership on the priority they often granted to the games occurring in the larger political field at an economic cost to the workers.[43]

Events accelerated quickly afterwards. Despite their stated personal disapproval of the scission, the divided party membership coalesced around the charismatic figures of Mehdi Ben Barka and Allal al Fassi. In 1959, the rivalry culminated with the schism that led to the foundation of the *Union Nationale des Forces Populaires* (UNFP). The new party regrouped the leftist factions of the PI, and was closely aligned with the labour movement, under Ben Barka's leadership. The conservative faction remained united around Allal al Fassi within the old PI.

The split was a major victory for the monarchy, as this development strengthened its claims to be the main representative of national unity, and granted it sole access to the symbolic capital that accrues from that role. This also increased the monarch's share of the symbolic capital that came to be associated with the struggle for independence, as the independence-related symbolic capital held by the nationalist movement was now split between the PI and UNFP and was even further eroded by the fierce competition and trading of blame between the two parties.

Building upon the gains it reaped from that victory, the monarchy solidified its dominant position within the field of power, and dramatically increased its autonomy from the now subordinate political party field.[44] However, autonomy did not mean withdrawal. The monarchy still partook in the political party field through the tacit or sometimes explicit support it provided to the eclectic range of parties opposing the PI and UNFP.

---

[41] Ashford, *Political Change in Morocco*; Monjib, *La Monarchie Marocaine*; Willis, *Politics and Power in the Maghreb*.

[42] Marais, 'La classe dirigeante au Maroc'; Monjib, *La Monarchie Marocaine*; Frédéric Vairel, *Politique et mouvements sociaux au Maroc: la révolution désamorcée?* Sociétés en mouvement (Paris: Presses de Sciences Po, 2014) pp. 54–56.

[43] Monjib, *La Monarchie Marocaine*.

[44] John Waterbury, *Le Commandeur Des Croyants: La Monarchie Marocaine et Son Elite*, trans. Catherine Aubin, Etudes d'Outre-Mer 11 (Paris: Presses Universitaires de France, 1975).

In a process that paralleled the internal struggles within the PI field, the monarchy had also managed to monopolize the legitimate use of force, by dissolving the AL, and integrating a portion of its members into the newly established *Forces Armées Royales* (FAR, Royal Armed Forces), the police, and the bureaucracy. The presence of a number of veterans from the French and Spanish colonial militaries within these institutions ensured their continued hostility towards both the PI and the UNFP. Moreover, within the local administration, anyone suspected of sympathy to the PI or UNFP was swiftly purged.[45]

Therefore, when King Hassan II ascended to the throne after the death of his father in 1961, the monarchy was already in a dominant position within the field of power. Within the political field, this was reflected in the marginalization of the UNFP by the monarchy in the creation of the 1962 constitution. The PI, though present in government, was relatively pushed aside too and expressed some reservations over the increasing concentration of powers that was engaged in by the new King. Having played a central role in the foundation of the FAR and the police force, Hassan II could rely on their indefectible support in any rivalry pitting him against the PI/UNFP. That relation was made stronger given that most of the Moroccan officer corps in that period came from the French or Spanish armies. William Zartman describes them as 'aristocrats, frequently sons of merchants or pashas and caids who had occupied their tribal posts with the favor of the protectorate'.[46] They reportedly displayed a staunch monarchism, and preferred to keep the military institution out of politics, resisting the attempts that the PI reportedly made to infiltrate its ranks.[47]

Conclusion

The account provided in this article hints at the analytical shortcomings of top-down explan-atory accounts, that tend to advance singular isolated variables, such as cultural dispositions[48] or 'segmented politics',[49] as their main explanatory factors. These variables cannot sin-gle-handedly account for and adequately explain the complex dynamics that are revealed by rigorous process-tracing. There are of course cultural influences affecting actors' choices but these should be understood as *habitus*, multiple, co-existing sets of habits, familiarities, and insights that render the actors capable of some actions in certain settings and not so skilful in others. *Habitus* also determines what is imaginable to them as an 'action horizon', and also what counts as an acceptable political manoeuvre. Yet despite its influence, *habitus* should not be understood as a cultural ingredient that can be isolated, because at any given moment the social actions of actors, along with *habitus*, are determined simultaneously by forms of capital and the affordances of the field, and actors' relative positions within the field.

The emergent character of the political field and the political party field does not manifest a region-specific feature throughout its history. How the system eventually turned out to

---

[45]I. William Zartman, *Morocco: Problems of New Power*, American Association for Middle East Studies Series (New York: Atherton Press, 1964); Leveau, *Le Fellah Marocain Défenseur Du Trône*.

[46]Zartman, *Morocco: Problems of New Power*, p. 75.

[47]Only the MP, through its networks within the officer corps and the troops that previously belonged to the AL, combined with its monarchist positions, managed to have a relatively significant level of support within the institution according to Zartman, *Morocco: Problems of New Power*. He also mentions in a footnote that the PI was rumoured to have encouraged some of its youths to enrol into the FAR.

[48]Abdellah Hammoudi, *Master and Disciple: The Cultural Foundations of Moroccan Authoritarianism* (Chicago, IL: University of Chicago Press, 1997).

[49]Waterbury, *Le Commandeur Des Croyants*.

be, that is authoritarian, can only be accounted for by carefully assessing the dynamics unfolding at certain decisive moments, along with the relative positioning of the significant actors involved, and what made sense to them within the immediate frame of the struggles that they were embedded in.

In other words, the devil is in the detail. Without understanding actors' cultural dispositions, capabilities (i.e. their agency), and the constraints imposed upon them by the emergent field, it is unlikely that a satisfactory explanatory account will be developed. This article argued that one way to achieve such an explanation is to marry a comprehensive historical account, attentive not only to the unfolding of big historical processes, but also to the history of everyday life as in the case of what happens in interactions between peasants and party members, as well as the personal background of the actors, with the field theoretical approach, overcoming the structure–agency dilemma through its triad of concepts (*habitus*, forms of capital, and fields).

Disclosure statement

No potential conflict of interest was reported by the author.

10   The Popular Front for the Liberation of Palestine during the First Intifada

From Opportunity to Marginalization (1987–1990)

Francesco Saverio Leopardi

ABSTRACT

In understanding the decline of the Popular Front for the Liberation of Palestine (PFLP), the analysis of its political agency allows the identification of a pattern of policy fluctuation that recurs throughout several critical phases of its trajectory. In this regard, the First Intifada is a case in point. The new geographical setting, the strong network of affiliated organizations and the more favourable balance of power with Fatah represented a major opportunity for the PFLP to revive its political initiative and increase its political weight. However, the PFLP was unable to grasp this opportunity due to its inconsistencies in confronting the main challenges posed by the Intifada, namely Fatah's diplomatic agenda, the relations with the PFLP's branch in the Territories, the fragmentation of the Palestinian Left and the rise of the Islamist movement. Resorting to a systematic study of the PFLP's official publications and to interviews with former and current militants, this article identifies the pattern of policy fluctuation that transformed the First Intifada into a turning point in its weakening process. This pattern acquires further relevance since it illustrates the basic poles of tensions behind the fluctuation of the PFLP's political conduct throughout the following decades.

Introduction

Today, the Popular Front for the Liberation of Palestine (PFLP), the most prominent Palestinian leftist faction, is a marginalized political actor. The scholarly literature on the Palestinian national movement attributes this condition to a wide range of factors. Strict adherence to Marxism-Leninism and political intransigence,[1] lack of agenda and leadership renewal,[2] professionalization of party membership and consequent cases of corruption and rent seeking are often indicated as the main reasons behind the PFLP's decline.[3] A closer analysis of the PFLP's policies highlights how shortcomings in its conduct contributed to the dilution of its

---

[1] Ali Jarbawi, 'Palestinian Politics at a Crossroads', *Journal of Palestine Studies*, 25(4) (1996), pp. 37–38; Harold M. Cubert, *The PFLP's Changing Role in the Middle East* (London: Frank Cass, 1997), pp. 182–194.

[2] Jamil Hilal, *Al-Yasar al-Filastini. Ila ayna?* [The Palestinian Left. Where To?] (Ramallah: Rosa Luxemburg Foundation, 2009), pp. 58–76.

[3] Asʿad AbuKhalil, 'Internal Contradictions in the PFLP: Decision Making and Policy Orientation', *The Middle East Journal*, 41(3) (1987), pp. 369–371.

political weight. The inability to overcome the long-standing factionalism of the Palestinian Left, the lack of a coherent line encapsulating the nationalist and socialist agendas[4] or the inability to stand up to the Islamist challenge in the social and cultural spheres[5] emerge as controversial points that the PFLP failed to address properly. Particularly, fluctuation in policy orientations at the Palestinian, Arab and international levels apparently undermined the effectiveness of the PFLP's agenda.[6]

This article resorts to the concept of policy fluctuation and applies it to the turning point of the First Intifada, and in particular to its first three years. The goal is to outline how the inconsistencies in the PFLP's response to the challenges that emerged between 1987 and 1990 contributed notably to its marginalization. The focus on the PFLP's conduct does not aim to minimize external factors that had a direct, negative impact on the organization. For instance, Israel's repressive campaigns or the concentration of power into Arafat's hand that accompanied the pursuit of his diplomatic goals both undermined the PFLP's own agenda. On the regional and international level, the Palestine Liberation Organization (PLO) support to Iraq during the 1991 Gulf War and the gradual demise of the Soviet Union had an overall backlash on the Palestinian factions that the PFLP felt deeply.

Nonetheless, a comprehensive analysis cannot underestimate the role of the PFLP's active agency, particularly in the peculiar context of the first Intifada. This approach appears even more significant as it allows the delineation of a pattern of fluctuation recurring beyond the framework of the uprising. Consequently, the PFLP's own conduct acquires a major relevance in the production of its current situation.

The PFLP was able throughout the 1980s to develop its network of trade unions and associations in the Occupied Palestinian Territories (OPT). Consequently, once the uprising broke out, the PFLP managed to gain representation in the Unified National Leadership of the Uprising (UNLU), avoiding the irrelevance that the smaller PLO factions experienced ever since. The PFLP also had the opportunity to benefit from the new political scenario that the unprecedented mass revolt shaped. In particular, the lack of significant interferences from any Arab country and the different political balances existing among the PLO factions in the OPT represented two positive developments. Therefore, the PFLP could exploit such circumstances to start filling the gap with Fatah and acquire further political relevance. Moreover, the PFLP displayed a certain pragmatism during the first year of the Intifada in adapting to the political priorities of the new phase, its new means of struggle and in fitting into the debate on how to support the uprising diplomatically.

However, these opportunities came alongside outstanding challenges and the PFLP's unclear response to them is pivotal in understanding its marginalization. Fatah's diplomatic agenda, the tensions between the PFLP's diaspora leadership and its base in the OPT, the inability to overcome the Left's factionalism and finally the rise of the Islamist camp were dilemmas that the PFLP confronted inconsistently. Drawing from official publications and interviews with former and current cadres, this article aims at outlining how such inconsistent response had a major negative impact on the PFLP that turned the First Intifada from an opportunity into a landmark of its marginalization.

---

[4]Hasan Ladadwe, 'Al-Yasar al-Filastini: al-Waqi' wa al-Tahaddi [The Palestinian Left: Realities and Challenge]', in Jamil Hilal and Katia Herman, eds., *Itlala Awalliyya 'ala al-Yasar fi-l-Mashriq al-'arabi* [Mapping of the Arab Left. Contemporary Leftist Politics in the Arab East] (Ramallah: Rosa Luxemburg Foundation, 2014), pp. 54–69.
[5]Salim Tamari, 'Left in Limbo: Leninist Heritage and Islamist Challenge', *Middle East Report*, no. 179 (1992), pp. 17–18.
[6]AbuKhalil, 'Internal Contradictions in the PFLP', pp. 374–376.

The Development of PLO, PFLP Networks in the OPT

The preconditions for the mass uprising which exploded in December 1987 largely lie in the intense activism that characterized the OPT's political life in the preceding decade. Such activism ensued from the three main PLO factions' efforts, namely Fatah, the PFLP and the Democratic Front for the Liberation of Palestine (DFLP), to develop their networks in the OPT. Alongside the PLO factions, also the long-standing presence of the Palestinian Communist Party (PCP)[7] and the nascent Islamist movement contributed to the growing mass mobilization.[8] When the PLO started to turn its attention to the OPT in the late 1970s, the PFLP was initially marginalized and did not enjoy any representation in the PLO-affiliated organizations. The PFLP's opposition to the two-state solution as envisioned in the 1974 PLO interim programme limited its popularity. This position conflicted with the priorities of the national movement in the OPT who saw in the end of the occupation its main goal and was less interested in total liberation.[9] Nonetheless, the PFLP was the first PLO faction to address labour force organization with the creation of the 'Voluntary Work Committee' in 1976. Starting this new endeavour, the PFLP broke the PCP's monopoly over unionization as well as set a pattern of mobilization that was fundamental in the politicization of the Palestinian population in the OPT.[10] By 1979, the PFLP created a local organization in the OPT called Jabhat al-ʿAmal, around which spread a wide range of trade unions, students, women's and professional associations. Fatah and the DFLP moved likewise, establishing respectively the Harakat al-Shabiba and the Kutlat al-Wahda. Indeed, the 1980s saw a multiplication of trade unions and popular associations due to the high degree of political competition. Each of the PLO factions as well as the PCP-controlled al-Kutla al-Taqaddumiyya established its own organization for each sector of the Palestinian society, despite the fact that the agenda and the ideology of such organizations changed little. The goal was not to present a political alternative but to achieve the highest number of members possible.[11]

Despite this general trend, a more evident division emerged in the late 1970s between the Palestinian Left and Fatah. This latter faction, thanks to its rapprochement with the Jordanian regime, had the upper hand on the control of the Arab League's funds. A Palestinian–Jordanian Joint Committee managed the allocation of these financings to the PLO-affiliated organizations reuniting the factional associations. Consequently, the Joint Committee favoured those local organizations that displayed their support for Fatah and its agenda.[12] While Fatah and Jordan tried to buy the loyalty of the OPT leadership, the leftist factions focused on developing their grassroots presence among the Palestinian masses. This approach helped reshuffle the power balance among the Palestinian factions, limiting Fatah's supremacy.[13]

---

[7] The PCP was established in 1982. Previously the Palestinian Communists in the OPT were active within different organizations. Although this article touches also the pre-1982 period, the acronym PCP is preferred for the sake of clarity.

[8] Joost R. Hiltermann, *Behind the Intifada* (Princeton, NJ: Princeton University Press, 1991), pp. 174–176.

[9] Weldon Matthews, 'The Rise and Demise of the Left in West Bank Politics: The Case of the Palestine National Front', *Arab Studies Quarterly*, 20(4) (1998), pp. 14–18.

[10] Joost Hiltermann, 'Mass Mobilization under Occupation: The Emerging Trade Union Movement in the West Bank', *MERIP Middle East Report*, no. 136 (1985), p. 19.

[11] Islah Jad, 'From Salons to the Popular Committees: Palestinian Women 1919–1989', in Jamal R. Nassar and Roger Heacock, eds., *Intifada: Palestine at the Crossroads* (New York: Praeger, 1990), pp. 131–132; Hiltermann, *Behind the Intifada*, pp. 132–135.

[12] Hiltermann, *Behind the Intifada*, pp. 50–51, 78–79.

[13] Muhammad Muslih, 'Palestinian Civil Society', *Middle East Journal*, 47(2) (1993), p. 262.

The efforts to mobilize the Palestinian population resisted several Israeli campaigns aimed at annihilating the PLO presence in the OPT. In fact, the rise of activists arrested, notably since the 1985 launch of the Iron Fist policy, turned the Israeli prisons into veritable political schools where the detainees organized themselves according to their political affiliation. Younger detainees received training from more experienced militants in ideology, resistance activities and structure of the Palestinian national movement. The Israeli prisons thus shaped a new generation of leaders, the generation that constituted the backbone of the Intifada.[14]

After the outbreak of the uprising, the PFLP managed to gain equal representation alongside Fatah, the DFLP and the PCP in the UNLU. This was a direct result of the PFLP's political investment in the OPT during the previous decade. Conversely, the smaller PLO factions such as the Syrian-controlled Popular Front-General Command, unable to develop a significant presence in the Territories, were sidelined. This ensured more freedom of manoeuvre to the four main organizations.[15] The OPT as a new space of action and the new balance of power among the Palestinian factions were both positive developments for the PFLP that had the chance to renew its political initiative and come out from the stalemate experienced since 1982.

The First Year of the Intifada

The PLO factions' work to develop a solid presence in the OPT provided the local population with the infrastructure needed to sustain a long-term insurrection. This, coupled with the deteriorating living conditions of the Palestinian population and the Israeli Iron Fist policy, ensured the outbreak and continuation of an unprecedented uprising that challenged the Israeli occupation.[16] Despite spearheading political mobilization in the OPT, the PLO did not plan the uprising. After the 9 December 1987 car accident that sparked popular protests, it took at least two weeks before the Palestinian leadership gained control over the Intifada.[17] After the initial confusion, the PFLP realized the relevance of the uprising by defining it as a 'qualitative landmark' in the history of the Palestinian national movement.[18] The new priority was to achieve a 'mass civil disobedience' in the OPT, by widening the popular mobilization and empowering the Palestinian institutions such as the Popular Committees. All the efforts should focus on challenging the occupation through the institutionalization of the protests and the boycott of Israeli products and institutions.[19] The PFLP showed the ability to adapt its agenda to the new circumstances, by dropping the call for long-term armed struggle that recurred in its discourse until the very eve of the uprising.[20]

The PFLP also shifted its position towards the involvement of the international community, notably the United Nations (UN), in the Arab–Israeli conflict, in order to meet the priorities of the national movement in the OPT. As the Intifada managed to attract global attention, the UN Security Council issued three different resolutions between December 1987 and

---

[14]Rashid Khalidi, 'The Uprising and the Palestine Question', *World Policy Journal*, 5(3) (1988), p. 500.
[15]Helena Cobban, 'The PLO and the "Intifada"', *The Middle East Journal*, 44(2) (1990), pp. 211–212; Yezid Sayigh, 'Struggle within, Struggle without: The Transformation of PLO Politics since 1982', *International Affairs*, 65(2) (1989), pp. 262–268.
[16]Jamal R. Nassar and Roger Heacock, eds., *Intifada. Palestine at the Crossroads* (New York: Praeger, 1990), pp. 15–72.
[17]Yezid Sayigh, *Armed Struggle and the Search for State: The Palestinian National Movement, 1949–1993* (Oxford: Clarendon Press, 1997), p. 614.
[18]*Al-Hadaf*, no. 893, 24 December 1987, pp. 4–5.
[19]*Al-Hadaf*, no. 895, 17 January 1988, p. 9.
[20]*Al-Hadaf*, no. 891, 7 December 1987, p. 4.

January 1988 to condemn Israel's violations of the Palestinians' human rights.[21] The PFLP grasped the potential of human rights and international law that had emerged as crucial tools to pursue the goals of the national movement.[22] Consequently, its Politburo called the UN to dispatch a team of observers to testify to Israel's breach of UN resolutions as well as international charters and laws which concerned the protection of human rights.[23] Additionally, the PFLP changed its position on a possible political settlement of the conflict, showing its alignment with the OPT leadership. The UNLU called for an international peace conference, with the participation of all the parties involved in the Arab-Israeli conflict.[24] Before the uprising, the PFLP had only accepted the idea of an international conference as the minimum denominator to preserve the PLO's unity. Subsequently, the international conference became a systematic demand as the PFLP believed that the Intifada gave new bargaining weight to the PLO in relation to both the US and Israel.[25] In a bid to gain more support, the PFLP displayed its closeness with the movement in the OPT and tried to differentiate itself from the other factions. In this context, the pro-Syrian PLO factions maintaining an all-out rejectionist position were labelled as 'nihilist'. In the PFLP's view the Syrian proxies were unable to acknowledge the positive developments the Intifada made possible.[26] Similarly, the PFLP condemned those ready 'to rush into negotiations with the enemy'. Their goal was to 'capitalize' on the Intifada and exploit its momentum, although the balance of power still favoured Israel: only by escalating the uprising to a generalized civil disobedience, could the Palestinians accept to start negotiating.[27]

In this context, the PFLP was particularly critical towards some personalities, who emerged as unofficial representatives of the Palestinians, and who had become the de facto mediators between Israel, the US and Arafat. Such personalities, including Birzeit University professor Sari Nusseibeh, reported directly to the PLO Chairman. The positions of these individuals did not reflect that of the UNLU or the rest of the PLO factions.[28] Their hints at the possibility of opening bilateral talks with Israel met with the PFLP's harsh condemnation.[29] The PFLP knew that the PLO Chairman was exploring possibilities of solution outside the agreed framework of the international conference. To these Fatah-aligned intellectuals, the PFLP preferred the representatives of the OPT grassroots leadership such as Bassam al-Shakʿa, the 'legitimate' Mayor of Nablus deposed by the Israeli government. Their 'nationalist' positions received much attention from the PFLP that wanted to underline the common views it shared with the popular base of the Intifada.[30]

The PFLP's initial grassroots-focused approach influenced its position over the issue of forming a Government in Exile (GiE). The idea found supporters among exponents of the

---

[21]United Nations Security Council, 'Resolution 605' 1987, https://goo.gl/K0ntWi (accessed 11 March 2016); United Nations Security Council, 'Resolution 607' 1988, https://goo.gl/4Dbi5d (accessed 11 March 2016); United Nations Security Council, 'Resolution 608' 1988, https://goo.gl/cAjulH (accessed 11 March 2016).

[22]Nicola Perugini and Neve Gordon, *The Human Right to Dominate* (Oxford: Oxford University Press, 2015), pp. 38–39.

[23]*Al-Hadaf*, no. 893, 24 December 1987, p. 7.

[24]*Wafa Info*, 'Bayan Raqm 10 (Leaflet N. 10)', 1988, http://www.wafainfo.ps/pdf/bayan_10.pdf (accessed 11 March 2016).

[25]*Al-Hadaf*, no. 917, 3 July 1988, p. 16.

[26]*Al-Hadaf*, no. 924, 8 August 1988, pp. 4–6.

[27]*Al-Hadaf*, no. 917, 3 July 1988, pp. 16–18.

[28]Ziad Abu-Amr, 'The "Personalities" of the Occupied Territories: Notes on Palestinian Political Leadership', *MERIP Middle East Report*, no. 154 (1988), pp. 24–25.

[29]*Al-Hadaf*, no. 898, 7 February 1988, pp. 4–8.

[30]Abu-Amr, 'The "Personalities" of the Occupied Territories', p. 24; *Al-Hadaf*, no. 897, 31 January 1988, pp. 12–13; *Al-Hadaf*, no. 919, 18 July 1988, pp. 26–27; *Al-Hadaf*, no. 921, 7 August 1988, pp. 8–11.

rightist current within Fatah and likely in Arafat himself.[31] Although the PFLP did not oppose the motion in principle, it pointed out that burdening the PLO with the task of forming a GiE was not in the best interest of the Intifada. The PLO should strengthen the existing institutions in the OPT and continue to gain international recognition thanks to the impact of the uprising. This would enable the PLO to reach an equal representative status to Israel.[32]

However, the evolving political scenario of the Intifada forced the PFLP to reconsider its positions. In August 1988, Jordan's King Hussein decided to break all administrative, economic and political ties with the West Bank, and drop Hashemite claims to it. According to King Hussein, this step complied with PLO wishes and allowed it to exert fully its role of sole Palestinian representative.[33] For the PFLP, although the Intifada had pushed Jordan to cut its ties with the West Bank, this positive result also entailed some risks. As the PFLP's Secretary-General George Habash clarified, King Hussein aimed to hamper the PLO through the creation of an institutional vacuum. The dissolution of the Jordanian-run administrative bodies and the cancellation of economic development plans were all measures that Jordan took to drive the PLO to a stalemate and show its inability to manage such a critical situation alone. To respond to this challenge, the PLO had to resort to new institutional frameworks and possibly reconsider the issue of a GiE.[34]

Months of debate led the PLO factions to convene in November 1988 an extraordinary session of the Palestine National Council (PNC) to vote on the adoption of a Declaration of Independence. The PFLP supported such a step as an effective reply to Jordan's withdrawal. However, the PFLP warned of those 'Palestinian circles' who might consider the declaration as overcoming the PLO programme and as a sufficient institutional cover to recognize Israel and to start bilateral negotiations.[35] Despite this concern, the PFLP's acceptance of the Declaration of Independence represented a concession to the moderates within the PLO. The direct reference to the 1947 UN Partition Plan featured in the text was per se an implicit recognition of Israel's right to exist.[36] In addition, the moderates' agenda was further strengthened by the adoption of a Political Statement that formally accepted UN Security Council (UNSC) Resolutions 242 and 338, and therefore the concept of land for peace as a base for negotiations. The PFLP opposed the adoption of such a statement exactly for its explicit recognition of these resolutions but was unable to impose a veto.[37] As a result, its position appeared ambiguous. The PFLP supported a text accepting a two-state solution and the negotiations but at the same time, it rejected another document which defined a more explicit but similar stance, given the acceptance of the UNSC.

The extraordinary 19th PNC and the documents approved during this session represented the basis for the PLO leadership's efforts to open a dialogue with the US and Israel. These

---

[31]Sayigh, *Armed Struggle and the Search for State*, p. 616.

[32]'Bayan Sadir 'an al-Maktab al-Siyasy li-l-Jabha [Political Communique Issued by the PFLP's Politburo]', *Al-Hadaf*, no. 895, 17 January 1988, pp. 4–6.

[33]'King Hussein, Speech on the West Bank, Amman, 3 July 1988', *Journal of Palestine Studies*, 18(1) (1988), pp. 279–283.

[34]*Al-Hadaf*, no. 922, 14 August 1988, pp. 4–10.

[35]*Al-Hadaf*, no. 928, 25 September 1988, pp. 4–5.

[36]'Palestine National Council, "Palestinian Declaration of Independence", Algiers, 15 November 1988', *Journal of Palestine Studies*, 18(2) (1989), pp. 213–216; 'Palestine National Council, "Political Communique", Algiers, 15 November 1988', *Journal of Palestine Studies*, 18(2) (1989), pp. 216–223.

For an in-depth analysis of the 19th PNC resolution see: Rashid Khalidi, 'The Resolutions of the 19th Palestine National Council', *Journal of Palestine Studies*, 19(2) (1990), pp. 29–42.

[37]Sayigh, 'Struggle within, Struggle without: The Transformation of PLO Politics since 1982', p. 255.

efforts posed a dilemma for the PFLP: on the one hand, the popular base pressured the PFLP to respect its traditional role of hard-line opposition, fighting against unfavourable settlement plans and specifically against the betrayal of the Intifada demands. On the other, the unwillingness to provoke a major split in the PLO and the consequent marginalization, as happened in the mid-1980s, led the PFLP to look repeatedly for an understanding with Fatah to safeguard the PLO's unity. Indeed, these two poles of tension can be seen as the main source of the PFLP's policy fluctuation.

Losing the Intifada Momentum

Following the outcome of the 19th PNC, Arafat decided to launch a 'peace offensive'. The PLO Chairman started touring several countries to gain recognition for the new State of Palestine in a bid to open a dialogue with the US and Israel, despite the PLO's official commitment to the framework of the international peace conference.[38] Such dialogue started in early 1989, and occurred through the mediation of the OPT-based personalities. The base for such talks was a plan drafted by the Israeli Prime Minister (the Shamir plan) that called for elections in the OPT in order to identify a Palestinian negotiating team. The US subsequently supported this initiative through the Baker Plan. It followed the Israeli one but also envisioned a series of tailor-made talks on specific issues to avoid forcing the parties, especially Israel, to make excessive concessions on sensitive questions.[39]

The PFLP's response to Arafat's peace offensive appeared confused. Ambiguity marked the PFLP's policies throughout this second phase of the uprising, negatively affecting its political fortunes. According to the PFLP's analysis, the beginning of the indirect US–PLO talks underscored the capability of the Intifada to impose the PLO-as-representative role. After refusing such status for decades, the US had been forced to recognize the PLO as a negotiating partner in order to try to broker a settlement to the conflict.[40] However, in order to comply with the stance displayed during the 19th PNC, the PFLP could not give its total support to the US–PLO dialogue. It had to 'hold in check' the PLO Right's 'concession' to the 'enemy'.[41] The PFLP showed its distrust towards the US, affirming that its actions would always be in favour of Israel, hence the need to escalate the Intifada to tip the balance of power. Habash went as far as to say that he bet on a time to see the failure of Arafat's line on the US.[42] However, the PFLP's verbal commitment to restrain the PLO Chairman did not produce meaningful results. Throughout 1989, Arafat and other senior Fatah exponents such as Salah Khalaf displayed their readiness to make further steps to meet US and Israeli requirements. From hoping for direct, bilateral negotiations with Israel to announcing that the Palestinian National Charter's article that called for the destruction of Israel was an obsolete document, the PLO leadership repeatedly breached the alleged PLO consensus over the framework for negotiations.[43] The PFLP systematically condemned these 'violations' and declared its

---

[38] Sayigh, *Armed Struggle and the Search for State*, p. 638.

[39] Joe Stork and Rashid Khalidi, 'Washington's Game Plan in the Middle East', *Middle East Report*, 164/165(1) (1990), p. 11.

[40] *Al-Hadaf*, no. 942, 10 January 1989, pp. 18–21.

[41] *Al-Hadaf*, no. 944, 29 January 1989, pp. 6–11.

[42] Ibid.

[43] 'Salah Khalaf, Address (via Video Tape) to the International Center for Peace in the Middle East, Jerusalem, 22 February 1989', *Journal of Palestine Studies*, 18(4) (1989), pp. 153–155; 'Yasir Arafat's "Caduc" Interview, Paris, 2 May 1989', *Journal of Palestine Studies*, 19(2) (1990), pp. 144–146.

willingness to fight those who did not respect the official PLO line. These condemnations were coupled with the PFLP's statement of resolve to escalate the Intifada, forcing Fatah to adhere to the positions that the masses in the OPT and the UNLU expressed.[44] Notwithstanding such declarations, the PFLP's actual conduct highlighted its willingness to keep internal PLO divisions to a minimum. On the one hand, the PFLP's leaders avoided direct attacks against the PLO Chairman, and Habash continued to declare his trust in Arafat's adherence to the national line.[45] On the other, the PFLP responded positively to Fatah's attempts to appease the internal opposition during the meetings of the PLO Executive Committee or Central Council. For the PFLP, Fatah's reassertion during such occasions of its attachment to the escalation of the Intifada and the framework of the international peace conference was sufficient to guarantee the 'minimum denominator' of Palestinian unity.[46] The struggle to preserve the 'correct line' had to be waged within the boundaries of national institutions; breaking away from the PLO to both mark the difference from a 'deviating' leadership and embody the right, nationalist line of Palestinian struggle was no longer an option, as it had been during the 1970s and 1980s.[47] In the PFLP's view, the Intifada and the new political scenario imposed on the Palestinian factions a 'tactical flexibility' to ensure the success of the 'Palestinian peace project'.[48]

The PFLP's softer position towards the PLO leadership had a negative impact on its popularity in the OPT. The local branches of the PLO factions, especially the PFLP's (PFLP-OPT), were increasingly sceptical about the PLO Chairman's dialogue with the US. In particular, as such dialogue failed to produce concrete results, the perception that the exiled PLO leadership sacrificed the original demands of the Intifada to strike a peace deal with Israel started to spread widely.[49] In this context, the PFLP-OPT started urging its leadership in exile to adopt a harsher position towards Fatah and continue to work for the escalation of the Intifada outside the limits posed by the PLO consensus. Unlike the official PFLP's evaluations, the PFLP-OPT did not see real possibilities to restrain the PLO leadership from pursuing its diplomatic agenda and believed in the impossibility of reforming the PLO internally.[50] The disappointment towards Arafat's initiative as well as a new Israeli repressive campaign unleashed in early 1989 fostered the radicalization of the uprising and led to an increased number of armed clashes and guerrilla-style attacks.[51] The PFLP, instead of exploiting such radicalization to challenge Fatah's primacy, preferred to remain in the role of loyal opposition, alleging its ability to reform the PLO from inside.

Indeed, besides the fear of marginalization ensuing from a major split within the national movement, the PFLP's external leadership did not want to excessively empower the new generation of the PFLP's leaders in the OPT by bringing them over to their line. In effect, all the PLO factions' leaders of the 'outside' were concerned that an alternative leadership issued from the uprising could substitute them. Such concern made the 'outside' eager to assert its

---

[44]*Al-Hadaf*, no. 950, 12 March 1989, pp. 4–5.
[45]*Al-Hadaf*, no. 959, 21 May 1989, pp. 8–9.
[46]*Al-Hadaf*, no. 955, 16 April 1989, pp. 12–13.
[47]*Al-Hadaf*, no. 959, 21 May 1989, pp. 8–9.
[48]*Al-Hadaf*, no. 1005, 6 May 1990, p. 5.
[49]Salim Tamari, 'Limited Rebellion and Civil Society: The Uprising's Dilemma', *MERIP Middle East Report*, no. 164/165 (1990), p. 5.
[50]Interview with former PFLP-OPT cadre Issam Hijjawi, Edinburgh, November 2015.
[51]Joost Hiltermann, 'Israel's Strategy to Break the Uprising', *Journal of Palestine Studies*, 19(2) (1990), p. 87; F. Robert Hunter, *The Palestinian Uprising. A War by Other Means* (London: I.B. Tauris, 1991), pp. 202–203.

control on the 'inside' from the first phases of the Intifada onwards. Moreover, the exiled PLO leadership feared that their adversaries might look for alternative Palestinian representatives among the local leaders.[52] In the PFLP's case, the inside–outside divide surfaced clearly from the second year of the Intifada whereas earlier Habash's faction tried to show its alignment with the movement in the OPT. The little space that the PFLP-OPT enjoyed in the PFLP's official press underscored the growing distance with the external leadership. Between 1989 and 1990 only two communiques issued by the PFLP-OPT were published in the official mouthpiece *Al-Hadaf*, while Politburo statements and top-leaders' interviews were reported in great evidence.[53]

The PFLP's leadership ultimately acted inconsistently on two fronts at the same time. It was unable to restrain and influence Fatah towards a less pliant diplomatic line while it started alienating its base in the OPT for its unwillingness to prompt a confrontation with the PLO leadership. Such fluctuation did not come without costs and, ultimately, this undermined its grassroots popularity and led to a loss of its political capital.

The PFLP and the Palestinian Left

Alongside the inconsistencies in tackling the coordination with the PFLP-OPT and the confrontation of Fatah's policies, the divisions within the Palestinian Left contributed to undermining the PFLP's efforts to counter the PLO leadership policies and increase its political weight. The lack of a more institutionalized coordination with the DFLP and the PCP appears particularly meaningful in the light of the specific balance of power among the PLO factions in the OPT. The UNLU remained the main framework regulating the relations among the Palestinian factions and the local branches of the leftist organizations did not develop closer ties among themselves. Similarly, the leadership of such factions did not coordinate their policies within the PLO institutions to limit Fatah's supremacy.

The reasons for the absence of a leftist coalition during the uprising lay partly in the history of ideological and strategic divergences that shaped inter-leftist relations. The DFLP was formed in 1969 out of the PFLP's left-wing split from the right-wing. At that time, divergences in terms of ideological and military orientations as well as personal rivalries between representatives of the two trends made any coexistence impossible.[54] After the secession, the PFLP remained tied to the legacy of its predecessor, the Arab Nationalists Movement (ANM), and retained its Pan-Arab and anti-imperialist dimension of the struggle for Palestine. Furthermore, in the wake of the split, Habash enjoyed undisputed authority over the PFLP and his own views had an unmatched weight within the PFLP. Consequently, his staunch nationalism was one of the main factors behind the PFLP's intransigence on solutions to the conflict that did not include total liberation.[55] Conversely, the DFLP's position over these issues evolved more quickly over time, often spearheading change in the political debate. The DFLP was the first faction to recognize Israeli nationhood as well as the first to articulate a two-state solution through the establishment of a 'national authority' on parts of 'liberated

[52]Ziad Abu-amr, 'The Palestinian Uprising in the West Bank and the Gaza Strip', *Arab Studies Quarterly,* 10(4) (1988), p. 396.
[53]'Bayan Sadir 'an al-Jabha al-Sha'biyya fi al-Dakhil [Communique of the PFLP in the Occupied Territories]', *Al-Hadaf,* no. 956, 26 March 1989, pp. 32–33; *Al-Hadaf,* no. 996, 25 February 1990, p. 16.
[54]Walid Kazziha, *Revolutionary Transformation in the Arab World: Habash and His Comrades from Nationalism to Marxism* (New York: St. Martin's Press, 1975), pp. 100–101.
[55]AbuKhalil, 'Internal Contradictions in the PFLP', pp. 363–365.

territory'. Moreover, Hawatmeh's faction remained politically closer to Fatah from its inception as Arafat ensured military protection during the 1969 split.[56] Finally, the Communist movement in the OPT consistently supported a two-state solution and never joined the PLO on armed struggle. This peculiar position was a consequence of the alignment with the USSR and the PCP inherited such a line.[57] These differences fostered the factionalism that afflicted the Palestinian Left throughout its history and resurfaced during the Intifada.

In addition to long-standing rifts, the failed attempts to build a 'coalition of democratic forces' between 1983 and 1986 made this option less attractive during the uprising.[58] At a local level, the intense competition that characterized contacts among popular organizations, particularly trade unions, throughout the 1980s, represented a further obstacle to a tighter coordination within the Palestinian Left.[59]

The distance among the leftist factions is well reflected in the exchange of criticism that appeared in the official press of the parties in the first months of the uprising. For instance, the PFLP harshly condemned the PCP's Secretary-General Bashir Barghouti for his 'propensity to make concessions' in order to start negotiations with Israel. Abu Ali Mustafa accused Barghouti of disrespecting the official PLO line sanctioned during the 'reconciliatory' PNC held a year earlier. The PCP endorsed mutual recognition as a precondition to start bilateral negotiations and it accepted the UNSC Resolutions 242 and 338. Furthermore, it supported the idea of elections in the OPT to determine a suitable Palestinian representative and preferred majority rule over the consensus principle within PLO institutions. These aspects were at odds with the PFLP's outspoken support for the international conference scheme. Similarly, they clashed with the PFLP's belief in the necessity of escalating the Intifada to tip the balance with the enemy before launching a peace process. According to the PFLP, the PCP aimed at rushing into negotiations by making 'gratuitous concessions' and covering them under the pretext of proposing the 'necessary tactical steps' towards the strategic goal of establishing a Palestinian state.[60]

The PFLP directed its criticisms at the DFLP too, despite the fact that Hawatmeh's organization held a more nuanced position between the 'moderates' and the PFLP. Debating the convenience to form a GiE, the DFLP repeatedly expressed its favour concerning such a step. The PFLP saw this position as evidence of the DFLP leaders' opportunism as they supported the GiE only to increase their chances to gain representation in the Palestinian government.[61] Such accusations, besides reflecting the different understandings of PLO political support to the Intifada, underscore the factionalism that influenced inter-leftist relations and especially PFLP–DFLP relations. The argument that political selfishness drove the DFLP's leaders had always been present in the PFLP's discourse. Still today, the PFLP's cadres of all levels highlight the DFLP's opportunism as the main cause behind the fragmentation of the PLO Left and its manifestations throughout history, from the 1969 split to the lack of unity during the Intifada.[62]

---

[56]Alain Gresh, *The PLO. The Struggle within* (London: Zed Books, 1988), pp. 40–42, 138–143.

[57]Tareq Y. Ismael, *The Communist Movement in the Arab World* (Abingdon: RoutledgeCurzon, 2005), pp. 57–79.

[58]'PFLP-DFLP Joint Statement on the Formation of a Joint Political and Military Command', *Journal of Palestine Studies*, 13(1) (1983), pp. 226–227; Al-Hadaf, no. 705, 1 February 1984, pp. 26–27.

[59]Hiltermann, 'Mass Mobilization under Occupation', pp. 30–31.

[60]*Al-Hadaf*, no. 921, 7 August 1988, pp. 11–18.

[61]Sayigh, *Armed Struggle and the Search for State*, p. 623.

[62]Interviews with PFLP's Representative in Lebanon Marwan ʿAbd al-ʿAl, Beirut, May 2015; and with former PFLP-OPT cadre Issam Hijjawi, Edinburgh, November 2015.

The 19th PNC session enshrined the diverging views of the leftist factions. The DFLP and the PCP voted in favour of both the Declaration of Independence and the political statement formalizing the PLO acceptance of UNSC Resolutions on the Arab–Israeli conflict. Conversely, the PFLP rejected the latter document, underscoring its disagreement with Fatah's readiness to satisfy the US requirements before the start of dialogue.[63] The factionalism affecting the Palestinian Left (and especially the PFLP and the DFLP) throughout the Intifada appears particularly ill-fated in the light of the Oslo accords, the main outcome of this historical phase. While the PFLP and the DFLP demonstrated little interest in coordinating their efforts, Arafat managed to marginalize both on multiple levels. Not only did he control the Palestinian delegation in Washington after the 1991 Madrid peace conference, but he was also able to keep the Oslo talks a secret from the DFLP and the PFLP's leaderships. Apart from his closest advisors, the PLO Chairman informed only some PCP (renamed Palestinian People's Party at this stage) high cadres and some members of the DFLP that seceded from Hawatmeh's faction in 1991.[64] The PFLP and the DFLP were left dealing with the fait accompli and pondering on their future strategy in the post-Oslo phase, increasingly overwhelmed by Fatah's rise to state party and Hamas' emergence as a radical actor.

The PFLP and the Islamist Camp

The last major political development of the First Intifada was the rise to prominence of political Islam within the Palestinian national movement. The PFLP met this challenge too inconsistently. In this case, the PFLP's ambiguous response stemmed from its misunderstanding of the political significance of the Islamists' rise. Furthermore, this inconsistent stand resulted in a pattern that resurfaced well beyond the dynamics of the Intifada.

By the early 1980s the Palestinian branch of the Muslim Brotherhood (MB) had developed a strong presence in the OPT. This was the result of long-term work started in the late 1960s, the goal of which was spreading Islamic doctrine and morale among the Palestinian public. Israel turned a blind eye to the MB's activities as it hoped that the Islamists would form an effective counterweight to the PLO. The MB's initial disregard for nationalist activism encouraged the Israeli authorities to avoid intervention in their affairs. As a result, the MB set up a large number of educational and charitable organizations, acquiring a solid entrenchment in the OPT.[65] In the 1980s, pressures on the MB to join active resistance against Israel mounted as the younger members disagreed with the traditional quietist approach of the organization. In this context, former MB members founded the Islamic Jihad Movement in Palestine (Islamic Jihad), eager to revive armed struggle in the OPT. Around the mid-1980s the MB's leadership too decided that the times were ripe for joining the confrontation with the enemy, paving the way for the creation of the Islamic Resistance Movement (Hamas) in the early days of the Intifada. Ultimately, the Islamists' efforts to assert their presence in the OPT contributed to increasing political mobilization and allowed them to crystallize their role in the Palestinian political arena.[66]

---

[63]'Habash fi Mu'tamar sahafi [Habash in a Press Conference]', *Al-Hadaf*, no. 936, 20 November 1988, pp. 7–8.
[64]Sayigh, *Armed Struggle and the Search for State*, p. 653.
[65]Ann M. Lesch, 'Prelude to the Uprising in the Gaza Strip', *Journal of Palestine Studies*, 20(1) (1990), pp. 9–12.
[66]Ziad Abu-Amr, 'Hamas: A Historical and Political Background', *Journal of Palestine Studies*, 22(4) (1993), pp. 5–7; Azzam Tamimi, *Hamas. A History from within* (Northampton, MA: Olive Branch Press, 2011), pp. 43–47.

The emergence of the Islamist camp represented a challenging development for the whole PLO since, for the first time, a genuinely Palestinian movement outside its framework gained increased popularity and legitimacy among the population of the OPT.[67] Hamas, for instance, manifested its intention to defy the authority of the PLO from the earliest phases of the Intifada. The publication of its own leaflets and the calls for different strike days were all measures meant to challenge the PLO control over the uprising.[68] The emergence of strong Islamist actors represented a double challenge for the PFLP. Besides defying the leadership and the representative role of the PLO, the Islamists threatened the PFLP's popular support, quickly emerging as the new radical opponents to the moderate Fatah's leadership within the wider Palestinian national movement, a role attributed historically to the PFLP itself. However, the PFLP's response to the emergence of the Islamist camp was rather unclear and paralleled the ambiguity displayed towards other political challenges that emerged with the Intifada.

Interestingly, the PFLP, or at least its official press, seemed to ignore the most important Islamist faction, namely Hamas, for almost the entire first year of the Intifada. The first mention is featured in an interview with Abu Ali Mustafa, in October 1988. At this stage, Hamas' competition started to concern the PFLP. Indeed, Abu Ali Mustafa criticized Hamas for acting outside the framework of the UNLU while the national consensus was with the slogans outlined by the Unified Leadership. The PFLP's leader also displayed the ostensible superiority of the PLO, affirming that Hamas' involvement and effectiveness in the Intifada were retreating as the uprising continued.[69] The resurfacing of Hamas in the PFLP's consideration proved the falsity of such claims. As Hamas' competition continued to concern the PFLP, it tried to discredit the Islamist movement by pointing to its alleged readiness to open contacts with the Israelis in order to sideline the PLO. While the political debate focused on the Shamir Plan, the PFLP affirmed that some Hamas representatives had already met with Israel's Defence Minister Rabin. In addition, the PFLP criticized Hamas' leader, Shaikh Yassin, for considering elections in the OPT under international supervision the only way to choose the representatives of the Palestinian people, a measure that Israel supported to undermine the PLO's authority.[70]

However, the initial distrust towards the Islamist movement was gradually abandoned as the extent of Hamas' entrenchment and popularity became clearer to the PLO factions, especially in light of the Israeli repressive campaigns against the movement. Furthermore, as the Palestinian peace initiative reached a stalemate and caused increased discontent among the Palestinian population, the containment of Hamas became a urgent priority.[71] Despite its criticisms of the PLO's diplomatic line, the PFLP shared the goal of limiting Hamas' ability to present itself as the radical alternative. Moreover, the co-optation of both Hamas and Islamic Jihad could increase the political weight of the opposition within the national movement. Thus, the PFLP's leadership started to invite Hamas to join the PLO-controlled institutions, especially the UNLU, in order to ensure the protection and the continuation of

---

[67]Khaled Hroub, 'Hamas: Conflating National Liberation and Socio-Political Change', in Khaled Hroub, ed., *Political Islam: Context versus Ideology* (London: Saqi Books, 2010), pp. 163, 170–172.
[68]Hunter, *The Palestinian Uprising. A War by Other Means*, pp. 116–117.
[69]*Al-Hadaf*, no. 929, 2 October 1988, pp. 4–9.
[70]*Al-Hadaf*, no. 951, 19 March 1989, pp. 20–21.
[71]Tamimi, *Hamas. A History from within*, pp. 57–61, 187–190.

the Intifada.[72] The PFLP's repeated calls for the Islamists to join the PLO indicated that the PFLP envisioned its relations with them through the traditional patterns of PLO politics: the shared nationalist interest represented the base to build consensus. However, if this approach was obsolete concerning relations with Fatah, as the outcome of the 19th PNC demonstrated,[73] this was true also for Hamas as it rejected the PLO and Fatah supremacy. Indeed, Hamas' unwillingness to accept the PLO umbrella was to be confirmed during inter-Palestinian talks held in spring 1990, supposed to prepare the 20th PNC session. On this occasion, the Islamist movement required 40–50 seats for its representatives at the Council, demonstrating its bid for equality with Fatah and de facto compromising any chance of inclusion in the PLO.[74]

The appearance in the PFLP's vocabulary of references to Islamist rhetoric accompanied the attempts to find common ground with Hamas. The PFLP's leaders started to invoke figures like 'Omar ibn al-Khuttab and, notably, 'Izz al-Din al-Qassam alongside the representatives of the PFLP's pantheon. Such rhetorical devices, just like the inclusion of Islamic feasts in the PFLP's political calendar, aimed at underscoring how Islamist models and references were a legitimate part of the Palestinian nationalist tradition. Moreover, they represented the PFLP's attempt to appeal to an allegedly more Islamized Palestinian public.[75]

The overview of the PFLP's attitude towards the Islamists highlighted that the PFLP misunderstood this epochal political development at the time of its emergence. The ambiguity in addressing the Islamist camp testified to the PFLP's inability to evaluate the challenge that Hamas mounted against the PLO.[76] Consequently, Hamas' strong positioning towards the PLO forced the PFLP to be the junior party in the leftist–Islamist coalition established to oppose the 1993 Oslo accords.[77] Furthermore, the PFLP continued to display its loyalty to the PLO and to prioritize its maintenance and reform. As evidenced earlier, the PFLP was adhering to the role of 'loyal opposition' to the Fatah-led PLO.[78] However, such a position appeared mostly deprived of its political and operative meaning in the light of Hamas' emergence as a new radical competitor. In the mid-1980s, the split within the PLO due to Arafat's diplomatic turn and the ensuing conflict over PLO legality and nationalist legitimacy provided the rationale for the PFLP's claim of embodying the 'correct line' in contrast with the Fatah leadership's 'deviations'.[79] With the re-centring of the Palestinian national movement in the OPT and the Islamists' rise, the PLO was no longer the unrivalled reference framework of Palestinian politics. In addition, after the advent of the Oslo era and the subsequent failure of the PLO to achieve statehood in the OPT, popular attachment to the PLO started to shrink in Occupied Palestine, while the diaspora communities were de facto sacrificed to allow the negotiations and the implementation of the accords.[80] In this context, little space remained

---

[72]*Al-Hadaf*, no. 1004, 22 April 1990, pp. 9–11; *Al-Hadaf*, no. 1012, 1 July 1990, pp. 18–19.

[73]Sayigh, 'Struggle within, Struggle without', pp. 253–258.

[74]Sayigh, *Armed Struggle and the Search for State*, p. 657.

[75]*Al-Hadaf*, no. 1012, 1 July 1990, p. 5; *Al-Hadaf*, no. 1014, 22 July 1990, pp. 8–9.

[76]Wendy Kristianasen, 'Challenge and Counterchallenge: Hamas' Response to Oslo', *Journal of Palestine Studies*, 29(3) (1999), pp. 20–21.

[77]Anders Strindberg, 'The Damascus Based Alliance of Palestinian Forces: A Primer', *Journal of Palestine Studies*, 29(3) (2000), pp. 60–63.

[78]Sayigh, 'Struggle within, Struggle without', p. 248.

[79]*Al-Hadaf*, no. 705, 2 January 1984, pp. 26–27; 'I'lan Al-Barnamaj al-Siyasi wa al-mabad'i al-tanzimiyya al-asasiyya li-jabha al-inqadh al-watani al-filastini [Announcement of the Political Programme and Foundative Organizational Principles of the Palestine National Salvation Front]', *Al-Hadaf* no. 764, 1 April 1985, pp. 8–11.

[80]Rashid Khalidi, *The Iron Cage. The Story of the Palestinian Struggle for Statehood* (Oxford: Oneworld Publications, 2007), pp. 180, 199–201.

for a policy centred on the respect of national institutions; the PFLP's political initiative was increasingly stuck in between Fatah's endeavour of state building and the challenge Hamas presented to this project. The shortcoming of the PFLP's policies towards Hamas set the pattern for its relation with the Islamist camp in the following decades. Fluctuation between opposition and coordination resurfaced regularly during the 1990s and 2000s, highlighting an unresolved point in the PFLP's line.

Conclusions

This analysis evidenced how the PFLP's agency ultimately determined its inability to benefit politically from the opportunities that emerged during the Intifada. More precisely, policy fluctuation appears central in shaping this outcome.

First, the PFLP did not formulate a clear line concerning Arafat's agenda on exploiting the uprising to start negotiations and approach a political settlement. While moderating its historical intransigence, the PFLP was not ready to totally relinquish its rejectionist tradition. From this stemmed its ambiguity towards the resolutions of the 19th PNC, the US–Israel–PLO dialogue and Fatah leaders' alleged violations of the PLO consensus.

Secondly, the PFLP lacked clarity in approaching its base in the OPT. Notwithstanding the official goal of achieving a full-fledged national disobedience and the commitment to the escalation of the Intifada, the PFLP's leadership did not pursue a real policy of radicalization of protests and it did not challenge Fatah's liquidatory policies. Conversely, the PFLP-OPT favoured a harsher position towards Fatah and the radicalization of the Intifada, especially after the stalemate of the PLO–US dialogue started to fuel resentment among the militants in the OPT. The PFLP's leadership feared a loss of relevance in case of an open challenge to Fatah and a consequent disengagement from official PLO politics.[81] This, coupled with its adversity towards the emergence of an alternative group of leaders from the OPT, led the leadership in exile to neglect the demands that its base expressed and to maintain the role of loyal opposition within the PLO, notwithstanding the meagre effectiveness of such a stance.

Ambiguity also characterized the PFLP's response to the emergence of the Islamist camp, as the PFLP passed from almost total neglect, to aversion and finally to attempts of co-optation. In this case, the PFLP's fluctuations stemmed from its misinterpretation of the Islamists' goals and strategy, particularly concerning Hamas. By envisioning its relations with Hamas through the consensus-building processes, the PFLP apparently failed to understand the extent of Hamas' challenge and its bid for prominence within the Palestinian national movement. As Hamas increasingly embodied the main opposition pole to the PLO leadership, the PFLP's commitment to the national institutions, democratic reform, and to the restoration of the 'correct nationalist line' had lost much of its appeal to the Palestinian public.

Finally, the persistence of factionalism and of major differences over the political praxis prevented tighter collaboration among the leftist organizations and particularly between the PFLP and the DFLP. The fear of losing relevance, at a factional level in this case, prevented the leaders of the Palestinian Left from relinquishing a share of their power and independence for the sake of the struggle against marginalization.

---

[81]Osamah Khalil, "'Who Are You?': The PLO and the Limits of Representation', 2013, https://al-shabaka.org/briefs/who-are-you-plo-and-limits-representation/ (accessed 15 March 2016).

These problems resurfaced in the years following the Intifada. This underscores their centrality. After 1993, the PFLP's position towards the Palestinian National Authority (PNA) continued to fluctuate between acceptance and opposition to the so-called Oslo institutions. Ambiguity marked its stance towards Hamas, particularly as demonstrated during the events that followed the 2006 legislative elections. The PFLP, after welcoming Hamas' victory during the elections, finally sided with Fatah and the PNA in condemning the Islamists' takeover of the Gaza Strip. Moreover, the PFLP's subsequent attempts to mediate between Fatah and Hamas recall its unsuccessful efforts to bring this latter movement into the fold of the PLO during the First Intifada. In addition, fragmentation continued to affect the Palestinian Left, even as its factions reached their lowest points in terms of popularity. This was exemplified by the inability of the Palestinian Left to coalesce on the occasion of the 2006 legislative elections.[82] Ultimately, the PFLP's failure to address these issues raises long-term questions on whether the Palestinian Left might be rebuilt within the framework of its historical representatives or solutions should be sought outside the PLO factions.

Acknowledgements

I would like to thank Anthony Gorman, Thomas Pierret and Lauren Banko for their help and comments as well as the *BJMES* reviewers. My appreciation also goes to the Council for British Research in the Levant for the Travel Grant that allowed me to conduct part of my archival research and fieldwork in Lebanon.

Disclosure statement

No potential conflict of interest was reported by the author.

---

[82]On this subject see: Manal a. Jamal, 'Beyond Fateh Corruption and Mass Discontent: Hamas, the Palestinian Left and the 2006 Legislative Elections', *British Journal of Middle Eastern Studies*, 40(3) (2013), pp. 273–294.

Index

Note: Page numbers in **bold** refer to tables.

'28 Murdad' (Musaddiq coup, Iran) 90, 92

Adalet Partisi (AP), Turkey 121, 124
Adalet ve Kalkınma Partisi (AKP), Turkey 21,
    22–23, 40, 128–129; headscarf ban 40–42;
    Islamic women's groups 29, 31; women's
    political representation 27–28
Aherdane, Mahjoubi (Morocco) 137–138
Ahmadinejad, Mahmoud (Iran) 27, 39
Aït-Aoudia, Myriam 64, 66
AKP (AK Parti), Turkey *see* Adalet ve Kalkınma
    Partisi (AKP), Turkey
AL, Morocco *see* Armée de Liberation (Liberation
    Army, AL), Morocco
Alaouite monarchy, Morocco 136, 138, 140, 141,
    142, 143
Algeria 18–19, 77, 79
al-Quwwāt al-Lubnāniyya (Lebanese Forces, LF),
    Lebanon 46, 47, 49, 52, 55, 57, 58–59
Amal (Shia militia), Lebanon 14
Amnesty International 118
Anavatan Partisi (ANAP), Turkey 124
an-Nahda, Tunisia 23
'Aoun, Michel (Lebanon) 46, 49, 52, 58, 59
AP, Turkey *see* Adalet Partisi (AP), Turkey
Arab-Israeli conflict 148–149, 155
Arab Socialist Union (ASU): Egypt 15, 16, 79, 83;
    Libya 78
Arab Spring (2011) 61, 64
Arab states 2, 3, 10–11
Arab Uprisings 4, 11, 22–23, **24**, 25, 61
Arafat, Yasir (Palestine) 112, 146, 149, 151, 152,
    154, 155, 158
Arat, Zehra F. Kabasakal 6, 33
Armée de Liberation (Liberation Army, AL),
    Morocco 137, 139, 143
Asad, Bashar al- (Syria) 22, 78, 80, 82
Association for the Support and Training of
    Female Candidates, Turkey *see* KA-DER
    (Association for the Support and Training of
    Female Candidates), Turkey
ASU *see* Arab Socialist Union (ASU)
authoritarian regimes 79, 85, 88–89, 133

Balafrej, Ahmed (Morocco) 141, 142
Ba'th party 12, 14; Iraq 12, 13, 15, 19, 22, 25, 79,
    80, 81, 83, 84, 89, 106; Syria 12, 15, 19, 22, 25,
    79, 80, 81, 82, 84, 85, 89
BBP, Turkey *see* Büyük Birlik Partisi (BBP), Turkey
Behrouzi, Maryam 34, 37–38, 39
Belhadj, Souhaïl 83
Ben 'Ali, Zine al-'Abidine (Tunisia) 80, 86
ben Barka, Mehdi (Morocco) 141, 142
Berger, Peter L. 47
Bill, James A. 9
Bookchin, Murray 4
Bostan, Fatma (Turkey) 35, 41–42
Bourdieu, Pierre 7, 132, 133–134, 135
Büyük Birlik Partisi (BBP), Turkey 128

CAG, Iran *see* Communist Alliance Group
    (CAG), Iran
capital, forms of 134, 135, 136, 140, 142, 143
Çarkoğlu, Ali 120
Cavatorta, Francesco 1
centralization 3–4, 79, 84, 89
CGP, Turkey *see* Cumhuriyetçi Güven Partisi
    (CGP), Turkey
charisma 50–51, 56–57, 58
CHF, Turkey *see* Cumhuriyet Halk Fırkası
    (CHF), Turkey
CHP, Turkey *see* Cumhuriyet Halk Partisi
    (CHP), Turkey
CKMP, Turkey *see* Cumhuriyetçi Köylü Millet
    Partisi (CKMP), Turkey
collaboration movements 15
Communist Alliance Group (CAG), Iran 93–94,
    95, 96, 97, 101, 104, 106–107, 109–111,
    112–114, 115, 116
Communist parties 12; Egypt 12; Iran 12, 93–94,
    95, 96, 97, 101, 104, 106–107, 109–111,
    112–114, 115, 116; Iraq 13; Lebanon 14, 49;
    Morocco 137; Palestine 147, 148, 154, 155;
    Syria 12
Communist Unity, Iran *see* Organization of
    Communist Unity (OCU), Iran
Confederation of Iranian Students 108, 110, 115

Constitutional Democratic Rally, Tunisia *see* Rassemblement Constitutionnel Démocratique (RCD), Tunisia
Constitutional Socialist Party, Tunisia *see* Parti Socialiste Destourien (PSD), Tunisia
court parties 11
Cumhuriyetçi Güven Partisi (CGP), Turkey 124
Cumhuriyetçi Köylü Millet Partisi (CKMP), Turkey 124
Cumhuriyet Halk Fırkası (CHF), Turkey 121, 122, 124
Cumhuriyet Halk Partisi (CHP), Turkey 120, 121, 122, 123, 124, 125

Dahbi, Khalil 7
Dashnak party, Lebanon 14
DEHAP, Turkey *see* Demokratik Halk Partisi (DEHAP), Turkey
democracy 2, 9, 22, 46, 47–48
Democratic Front for the Liberation of Palestine (DFLP), Palestine 147, 148, 153–154, 155, 158
Democratic Union Party (PYD), Syria 4
democratization 10–11, 20, 22, 25
Democrat Left Party, Turkey 21
Democrat Party, Iran 12, 13
Demokratik Halk Partisi (DEHAP), Turkey 127
Demokratik Sol Parti (DSP), Turkey 129
Demokrat Parti (DP), Turkey 20, 21, 121, 129
Demokrat Türkiye Partisi (DTP), Turkey 127, 129
Destour Socialist Party, Tunisia 15
Dézé, Alexandre 64
DFLP, Palestine *see* Democratic Front for the Liberation of Palestine (DFLP), Palestine
Doğru Yol Partisi (DYP), Turkey 127, 128
dominant-party systems 16, 17, 22, 25
DP, Turkey *see* Demokrat Parti (DP), Turkey
DSP, Turkey *see* Demokratik Sol Parti (DSP), Turkey
DTP, Turkey *see* Demokrat Türkiye Partisi (DTP), Turkey
DYP, Turkey *see* Doğru Yol Partisi (DYP), Turkey

education, women's 123–124, 128
Egypt 1, 11, 16–18, 22, 23, 25, 61–63, 65, 77, 79, 80, 81, 83, 86–88; Arab Socialist Union (ASU) 15, 16, 79, 83; Communist parties 12; Freedom and Justice Party (FJP) 6, 62, 63, 65, 66–67, 69, 70, 71–76; *Gama'a* 62–63, 65, 66, 67–71, 72–73, 74, 75; Muslim Brotherhood (MB) 6, 12, 17, 18, 23, 62, 63, 65, 66, 69–71, 72, 74–75, 86; National Democratic Party (NDP) 16–17, 23, 79, 81, 82, 83–84, 85; National Progressive Unionist Party (NPUP) 17, 23; National Union 79; New Wafd Party 16, 17; Socialist Party 12, 83; *tanzim* 67–68, 73, 74, 75; Wafd party 10, 12, 16, 23; women's political representation 27
equality, women's 126, 127, 129, 130
Erdogan, Recep Tayyip (Turkey) 22–23, 35, 36

Fada'i Guerrillas, Iran *see* Organization of the Iranian People's Fada'i Guerrillas (OIPFG), Iran
Fassi, Allal al 19, 141, 142
Fatah, Palestine 3, 7, 102–103, 146, 147, 148, 151, 152, 153, 154, 155, 156, 157, 158, 159
Fazilet Partisi (FP), Turkey 124, 128
fields 134–135, 143
field theory 7, 65, 132–133, 135, 144
First Intifada, Palestine 146, 155
FIS, Algeria *see* Front Islamique du Salut (FIS), Algeria
FLN, Algeria *see* Fronte Liberation Nationale (FLN), Algeria
Freedom and Justice Party (FJP), Egypt 6, 62, 63, 65, 66–67, 69, 70, 71–76
freedoms, women's 126–127
Free Patriotic Movement (FPM, Lebanon) *see* Tayyār al-Wataniyy al-Ḥurr (Free Patriotic Movement, FPM), Lebanon
Fronte Liberation Nationale (FLN), Algeria 15–16, 18, 66, 79, 89
Front Islamique du Salut (FIS), Algeria 18–19, 66

Gama'a (Organization of the Muslim Brothers), Egypt 62–63, 65, 66, 67–71, 72–73, 74, 75
Gandhi, Jennifer 88–89
Geagea, Samir (Lebanon) 54, 55, 58, 59
Gemayel, Amin (Lebanon) 52, 55
Gemayel, Bashir (Lebanon) 52–53, 55, 56, 58, 59
Gemayel, Pierre (Lebanon) 52, 53–54, 57, 58
Genç Parti (GP), Turkey 127
gender discrimination 26–27, 33–34, 42, 43
gender equality 5, 6, 30, 31, 123, 126, 127, 128–129, 130
gender ideology 26–27, 32
GiE, Palestine *see* Government in Exile (GiE), Palestine
Gorji, Monireh (Iran) 34
governance 6, 78, 85–88, 89
Government in Exile (GiE), Palestine 149–150
GP, Turkey *see* Genç Parti (GP), Turkey
Green Movement, Iran 4

Ḥizb al-Katā'ib al-Lubnāniyya (Phalanges), Lebanon 13–14, 46, 47, 52, 54, 55, 57, 58–59
Habash, George (Palestine) 150, 151, 152, 153
habitus 134, 139, 140, 143
Halkçi Parti (HP), Turkey 125
Halk Fırkası (HF), Turkey 119, 122
Hamas (Islamic Resistance Movement), Palestine 155, 156, 157, 158, 159
Harik, Iliya 15
headscarf ban, Turkey 40–42
Herut (Likud), Israel 21
Hezbollah (Shia militia), Lebanon 14, 46, 49
HF, Turkey *see* Halk Fırkası (HF), Turkey
Hibou, Béatrice 80–81, 83
Hinnebusch, Raymond A. 5, 83
Hizb Misr al-Ishtiraki, Egypt *see* Socialist Party, Egypt

Hobeika, Elie 55–56
HP, Turkey *see* Halkçi Parti (HP), Turkey
human rights 117, 118, 149
Huntington, Samuel P. 14

IDP, Turkey *see* Islâm Demokrat Partisi
    (IDP), Turkey
independence movements 12
internal criticism 5, 30, 31, 39, 43
International Labour Organization (ILO) 126
Intifada, Palestine 146, 148–149, 150, 151,
    152–153, 154, 155, 156, 158
Iran 3, 5, 6, 11, 13, 18, 19, 30–31, 33, 90–91, 92,
    93, 103, 114–116; Communist Alliance Group
    (CAG) 93–94, 95, 96, 97, 101, 104, 106–107,
    109–111, 112–114, 115, 116; Confederation
    of Iranian Students 108, 110, 115; Democrat
    Party 12, 13; Iranian Revolution 3, 33, 34, 92;
    Iran Party 13, 96, 100; Islamic Republican
    Party 3, 18; National Front of Iran (NFI) 12,
    13, 92, 94, 95–96, 98–100, 104, 106, 108,
    110, 111, 114; Organization of Communist
    Unity (OCU) 6, 90, 91, 92–94, 95, 96, 97, 101,
    104, 106–107, 109–110, 112, 114, 115, 116;
    Organization of the Iranian People's Fada'i
    Guerrillas (OIPFG) 94, 95, 103, 105, 107,
    108, 110, 111–112, 116; Pahlavi regime 90,
    92, 95, 97, 102, 103, 104, 105, 106, 114; Star
    Group 103–104, 105, 106, 107, 110, 111, 112;
    Tudah Party 13, 94–95, 97, 99; United Front
    of Conservative Women 29, 38–39; women's
    political participation 34, 42; women's
    political representation 27, 28, 29, 30–31, 33,
    34, 35, 36–40, 43; Zeinab Society 29, 34, 37, 38
Iranian People's Party, Iran 97
Iranian Revolution (1979) 3, 33, 34, 92
Iran Party, Iran 13, 96, 100
Iraq 13, 19, 22, 25, 77, 79–80, 86; Ba'th party 12,
    13, 15, 19, 22, 25, 79, 80, 81, 83, 84, 89, 106;
    Communist parties 13; Istiqlal party 12, 13;
    Kurdish Democratic Party 13; National
    Democratic Party 12, 13
Islah party, Yemen 18
Islâm Demokrat Partisi (IDP), Turkey 121–122
Islamic Jihad Movement (Islamic Jihad),
    Palestine 155
Islamic National Salvation party, Turkey 21
Islamic party women 29–31, 32, 34, 43
Islamic political movements 5, 10, 12, 42;
    women's political participation 32–33, 34–35,
    43; women's political representation 28–29,
    30–31, 33–34
Islamic political parties 6, 16, 23, 27–29,
    31–33, 65
Islamic Republic of Iran *see* Iran
Islamic Republican Party, Iran 3, 18
Islamic Resistance Movement, Palestine *see*
    Hamas (Islamic Resistance Movement),
    Palestine
Islamic Salvation Front, Algeria 66

Islamic women 29–31, 32
Israel 3, 20, 21–22, 25, 102, 148, 149, 150, 151,
    152, 155, 156
Istiqlal party: Iraq 12, 13; Morocco 12, 19, 136,
    137, 138–139, 140–142, 143

Jordan 11, 19, 20, 25, 27, 150
Justice and Development Party (AKP), Turkey *see*
    Adalet ve Kalkınma Partisi (AKP), Turkey
Justice and Development Party, Egypt 23
Justice Party (JP), Turkey 21

KA-DER (Association for the Support and
    Training of Female Candidates), Turkey
    35–36, 42
Kar, Mehrangiz 36
Karamé, Elie 54
Katā'ib, Lebanon *see* Ḥizb al-Katā'ib
    al-Lubnāniyya (Phalanges), Lebanon
Katatni, Sa'ad al- (Egypt) 73
Khalaf, Samir 45, 46
Khatib, Abdelkrim (Morocco) 137–138
Khomeini, Ayatollah (Iran) 34, 37
Khumayni, Ayatullah Ruhollah (Iran) 103
Koselleck, Reinhard 49
Kurdish Democratic Party, Iraq 13
Kutla (National Bloc), Syria 12
Kuwait 19, 20

Laclau, Ernesto 2
Lahire, Bernard 65
leaders 52–54, 55
leadership 85, 86, 89
Lebanon 5, 11, 13–14, 25, 44–46, 47,
    48–50, 51–52, 56–58, 59–60; al-Quwwāt
    al-Lubnāniyya 46, 47, 49, 52, 55, 57, 58–59;
    Communist parties 14, 49; Ḥizb al-Katā'ib
    al-Lubnāniyya 13–14, 46, 47, 52, 54, 55,
    57, 58–59; Shia militias 14, 46, 49; Tayyār
    al-Wataniyy al-Ḥurr 46, 47, 49, 52, 55, 57,
    58–59
Leopardi, Francesco Saverio 7
LF (Lebanese Forces), Lebanon *see* al-Quwwāt
    al-Lubnāniyya (Lebanese Forces, LF),
    Lebanon
Liberal (Ahrar) Party, Egypt 17
liberalism 47–48
liberal oligarchies 10, 11–14, **24**
Liberation Army (AL), Morocco *see* Armée de
    Liberation (Liberation Army, AL), Morocco
Libya 15, 22, 78, 88

Mapai (Labour), Israel 21
mass competitive party systems 20–22, 25
mass-mobilizing parties 78–79
MÇP, Turkey *see* Milliyetçi Çalışma Partisi
    (MÇP), Turkey
MDP, Turkey *see* Milliyetçi Demokrasi Partisi
    (MDP), Turkey
Mexico 89

MHP, Turkey *see* Milliyetçi Hareket Partisi (MHP), Turkey
Middle East and North Africa (MENA) 1, 2–4, 9, 10
Millet Partisi (MP), Turkey 124
Milli Nizam Partisi (MNP), Turkey 123–124, 126
Milliyetçi Çalışma Partisi (MÇP), Turkey 122, 128
Milliyetçi Demokrasi Partisi (MDP), Turkey 124–125
Milliyetçi Hareket Partisi (MHP), Turkey 122, 128
Misr al-Fatat (Young Egypt), Egypt 12
MNP, Turkey *see* Milli Nizam Partisi (MNP), Turkey
monarchies 11, 19, 20, 25; Iran 90, 92, 95, 97, 102, 103, 104, 105, 106, 114; Morocco 136, 138, 140, 141, 142, 143
Morocco 1, 7, 19–20, 22, 25, 27, 133, 135, 136–137, 139–140, 143–144; Alaouite monarchy 136, 138, 140, 141, 142, 143; Armée de Liberation (AL) 137, 139, 143; Communist parties 137; Mouvement Populaire (MP) 137, 138; National Union of Popular Forces (NUPF) 19; Parti Communiste Marocain (PCM) 137; Parti de l'Istiqlal (PI) 12, 19, 136, 137, 138–139, 140–142, 143; Parti Democratique de l'Independance (PDI) 137; Union Marocaine du Travail (UMT) 140, 141, 142; Union Nationale des Forces Populaires (UNFP) 142, 143
Morsi, Muhammed (Egypt) 23, 62, 73, 75
Motherland party, Turkey 21
Mouffe, Chantal 2
Mouvement Populaire (MP), Morocco 137, 138
movement, women's 129–130
MP, Turkey *see* Millet Partisi (MP), Turkey
Mubarak, Hosni (Egypt) 23, 61, 63, 85
multi-party systems 6, 16, 18, 19, 44, 77, 80, 119
Musaddiq, Muhammad (Iran) 90, 92, 94, 96, 98, 99, 100, 114
Muslim Brotherhood (MB) 3, 65; Egypt 6, 12, 17, 18, 23, 62, 63, 65, 66, 69–71, 72, 74–75, 86; Palestine 155

Nasser, Gamal 'Abd al- (Egypt) 15, 16, 17, 62, 63, 67, 86–87
National Action party, Turkey 21
National Bloc, Syria *see* Kutla (National Bloc), Syria
National Democratic Party (NDP), Egypt 16–17, 23, 79, 81, 82, 83–84, 85
National Democratic Party, Iraq 12, 13
National Front of Iran (NFI) 12, 13, 92, 94, 95–96, 98–100, 104, 106, 108, 110, 111, 114
National Front of Iran Abroad 95, 96, 98–99, 114, 115
National Front of Iran in Exile 102
nationalist parties 12
National Liberals, Lebanon 14
National Progressive Unionist Party (NPUP), Egypt 17, 23
National Socialists, Jordan 12
National Union, Egypt 79

National Union of Popular Forces (NUPF), Morocco 19
Neo-Destour Party, Tunisia *see* Parti Socialiste Destourien (PSD), Tunisia
New Wafd Party, Egypt 16, 17
Nidaa Tounes, Tunisia 23
notable parties 11, 12, 25
Nour party, Egypt 23

Öcalan, Abdullah 4
Occupied Palestinian Territories (OPT) 146, 147–149, 151, 152–156, 157–159
ÖDP, Turkey *see* Özgürlük ve Dayanışma Partisi (ÖDP), Turkey
Organization of Communist Unity (OCU), Iran 6, 90, 91, 92–94, 95, 96, 97, 101, 104, 106–107, 109–110, 112, 114, 115, 116
Organization of the Iranian People's Fada'i Guerrillas (OIPFG), Iran 94, 95, 103, 105, 107, 108, 110, 111–112, 116
Organization of the Muslim Brothers, Egypt *see* Gama'a (Organization of the Muslim Brothers), Egypt
Organizations of the National Front of Iran Abroad 6, 97, 98, 108–109, 110–111
Organizations of the National Front of Iran Abroad, Middle East Branch (ONFME) 90, 91, 92–93, 94, 98, 103, 104–109, 110, 112–114, 115
Organizations of the National Front of Iran in America 100–102, 103, 108
Organizations of the National Front of Iran in Europe 99, 100–101, 102
Orthodox Christian (SSNP), Lebanon 14
Ottoman empire 11
Owen, Roger 14, 88
Özgürlük ve Dayanışma Partisi (ÖDP), Turkey 123, 126, 127, 129

Pahlavi regime, Iran 90, 92, 95, 97, 102, 103, 104, 105, 106, 114
palace-dominated multi-party system 16, 19
Palestine 3, 7, 27, 102–103, 145–146, 149; Communist parties 147, 148, 154, 155; Democratic Front for the Liberation of Palestine (DFLP) 147, 148, 153–154, 155, 158; Fatah 3, 7, 102–103, 146, 147, 148, 151, 152, 153, 154, 155, 156, 157, 158, 159; Government in Exile (GiE) 149–150; Hamas 155, 156, 157, 158, 159; Intifada 146, 148–149, 150, 151, 152–153, 154, 155, 156, 158; Islamic Jihad Movement 155; Palestine Liberation Organization (PLO) 146, 147, 148, 149, 150–151, 152, 153, 154, 156–157, 158, 159; political Islam 155–156, 157, 158; Popular Front for the Liberation of Palestine (PFLP) 7, 145–146, 147, 148, 149–150, 151–152, 153, 154, 155, 156–157, 158, 159; Unified National Leadership of the Uprising (UNLU) 146, 148, 149, 152, 153, 156

Palestine Liberation Organization (PLO)
146, 147, 148, 149, 150–151, 152, 153,
154, 156–157, 158, 159
Palestinian Communist Party (PCP) 147, 148,
154, 155
Palestinian National Authority (PNA) 159
PA regimes *see* populist authoritarian (PA)
regimes
Parti Communiste Marocain (PCM),
Morocco 137
Parti de l'Istiqlal (PI), Morocco 12, 19, 136, 137,
138–139, 140–142, 143
Parti Democratique de l'Independance (PDI),
Morocco 137
Parti Socialiste Destourien (PSD), Tunisia
12, 79, 85
party creation 64–67, 75–76
party development 11–17, 18–22, 24–25
party ideology 10, 120
Party of the Iranian Nation, Third Force 97
party organization 5, 10
party systems 10–11, 16–23, 25, 64, 79
Payam-e Hajar (Hajar's Message, women's
magazine), Iran 36
PCM, Morocco *see* Parti Communiste Marocain
(PCM), Morocco
PCP, Palestine *see* Palestinian Communist
Party (PCP)
People's General Congress, Yemen 18
PFLP, Palestine *see* Popular Front for the
Liberation of Palestine (PFLP)
Phalanges, Lebanon *see* Ḥizb al-Katā'ib
al-Lubnāniyya (Phalanges), Lebanon
PI, Morocco *see* Parti de l'Istiqlal (PI), Morocco
PLO, Palestine *see* Palestine Liberation
Organization (PLO)
PNA, Palestine *see* Palestinian National
Authority (PNA)
political activism 2–3, 6
political culture 9, 10, 24
political field 132–133, 135, 141, 142, 143
political Islam 3; Palestine 155–156, 157, 158
political martyr 59
political parties 1–2, 4, 9, 10, 24–25, 64, 78–79,
117, 118, 135
political party field 7, 135, 140, 142, 143
political systems 3, 5, 9, 133, 143–144
politicization 5, 10, 11, 24
Popular Front for the Liberation of Palestine
(PFLP) 7, 145–146, 147, 148, 149–150,
151–152, 153, 154, 155, 156–157, 158, 159
populist authoritarian (PA) regimes 10, 14, 25
populist revolution 11, **24**, 25
post-populist authoritarianism 11, 16–20
post-populist regimes **24**, 25
presidency 79–80
Progressive Socialists, Lebanon 14
PSD, Tunisia *see* Parti Socialiste Destourien
(PSD), Tunisia

PYD, Syria *see* Democratic Union Party
(PYD), Syria

Qaddafi, Mu'ammar al- (Libya) 15, 22, 78, 88

Rassemblement Constitutionnel Démocratique
(RCD), Tunisia 79, 80, 81, 82, 83, 84
Refah Partisi (RP), Turkey 33, 34–35, 40, 124
regimes 5, 10–11, 16, **24**, 25
Republican People's Party (RPP), Turkey
20, 21
revolutionary Marxism 6, 91
revolutionary regimes 14–16
ruling parties 79, 80–85, 88–89

Saadet Partisi (SP), Turkey 126, 128
Sadeghi-Boroujerdi, Eskandar 6
Sassoon, Joseph 6
Second National Front, Iran 94, 95, 96–97,
98–99, 100, 114
sectarianism 59–60
secular nationalist parties 12
self-criticism 80
Shia militias, Lebanon 14, 46, 49
single-party systems 6, 10, 14–16, 19, 22, 25, 77,
89, 119
Six-Day War (1967) 3, 88, 102
Social Democratic Populist Party, Turkey 21
Socialist Labour Party (SLP), Egypt 17
Socialist League of Iran 97, 100
Socialist Party, Egypt 12, 83
Socialist Union, Egypt 79
Social Nationalist Party (SSNP), Syria 12
Sosyal Demokrasi Partisi (SODEP), Turkey
123, 125
Sosyal Demokrat Halkçi Parti (SHP), Turkey 125
SP, Turkey *see* Saadet Partisi (SP), Turkey
Springborg, Robert 9, 81, 85
Star Group, Iran 103–104, 105, 106, 107, 110,
111, 112
Storm, Lise 1
Syria 4, 11, 19, 22, 25, 77, 78, 79–80, 82, 83;
Ba'th party 12, 15, 19, 22, 25, 79, 80, 81,
82, 84, 85, 89; Communist parties 12;
Democratic Union Party (PYD) 4; Kutla
(National Bloc) 12; Social Nationalist Party
(SSNP) 12

Tahrir Square protests 4
Tajali, Mona 5
Taleghani, Azam (Iran) 34, 36
tanzim, Egypt 67–68, 73, 74, 75
Tayyār al-Wataniyy al-Ḥurr (Free Patriotic
Movement, FPM), Lebanon 46, 47, 49, 52, 55,
57, 58–59
Third National Front, Iran 94, 98, 100
Thuselt, Christian 5
tri-continental solidarity 91–92
True Path party, Turkey 21

Tudah Party, Iran 13, 94–95, 97, 99
Tunisia 19, 22, 23, 25, 27, 77, 79, 80–81,
    85–86; an-Nahda 23; Destour Socialist
    Party 15; Nidaa Tounes 23; Parti Socialiste
    Destourien (PSD) 12, 79, 85; Rassemblement
    Constitutionnel Démocratique (RCD) 79, 80,
    81, 82, 83, 84
Turkey 5, 6, 10, 20–21, 22–23, 25, 30–31, 33, 42,
    117, 119, **131**; Adalet Partisi (AP) 121, 124;
    Adalet ve Kalkınma Partisi (AKP) 21, 22–23,
    27–28, 29, 31, 40–42, 128–129; Anavatan
    Partisi (ANAP) 124; Büyük Birlik Partisi
    (BBP) 128; Cumhuriyetçi Güven Partisi (CGP)
    123–124; Cumhuriyetçi Köylü Millet Partisi
    (CKMP) 124; Cumhuriyet Halk Fırkası (CHF)
    121, 122, 124; Cumhuriyet Halk Partisi (CHP)
    120, 121, 122, 123, 124, 125; Demokrat Parti
    (DP) 20, 21, 121, 129; Demokrat Türkiye
    Partisi (DTP) 127, 129; headscarf ban 40–42;
    Islamic women 29, 31; Milli Nizam Partisi
    (MNP) 123–124, 126; Milliyetçi Çalışma Partisi
    (MÇP) 122, 128; Milliyetçi Demokrasi Partisi
    (MDP) 124–125; Milliyetçi Hareket Partisi
    (MHP) 122, 128; Özgürlük ve Dayanışma
    Partisi (ÖDP) 123, 126, 127, 129; Republican
    People's Party (RPP) 20, 21; Saadet Partisi (SP)
    126, 128; Sosyal Demokrasi Partisi (SODEP)
    123, 129; women's education 123–124, 128;
    women's political participation 34–35, 40–42,
    127–129; women's political representation
    27–28, 29, 30–31, 33–34, 35–37, 43, 129;
    women's rights 6, 35, 117, 121–123, 125, 128,
    129–130
Turkish Women's Union 129–130
Türkiye Birlik Partisi (TBP), Turkey 125
Türkiye İşçi Partisi (TIP), Turkey 125, 126
Türkiye Köylü Partisi (TKP), Turkey 123
Türkiye Sosyalist İşçi Partisi (TSIP),
    Turkey 126

UN (United Nations) 148–149, 155
Unified National Leadership of the Uprising
    (UNLU), Palestine 146, 148, 149, 152, 153, 156
Union Marocaine du Travail (UMT), Morocco
    140, 141, 142
Union Nationale des Forces Populaires (UNFP),
    Morocco 142, 143
United Front of Conservative Women, Iran
    29, 38–39
US (United States) 151

Vahid-Dastejerdi, Marzieh (Iran) 39
Vannetzel, Marie 6

Wacquant, Loïc J.D. 134
Wafd party, Egypt 10, 12, 16, 23
Wasat (the Centre), Egypt 68
Welfare (Refah) party, Turkey *see* Refah Partisi
    (RP), Turkey
White, Jenny B. 33
women 5, 124–125; education 123–124, 128;
    equality 126, 127, 129, 130; freedoms
    126–127; movement 129–130; political
    participation 27, 28–29, 31–33, 34–43, 82,
    127–129
women's rights 26–27, 31, 35, 42, 118; Turkey 6,
    35, 117, 121–123, 125, 128, 129–130

Yemen 15, 18, 25, 27
Yemen Socialist Party 15, 18
Yeni Türkiye Partisi (YTP), Turkey 129
Young Egypt *see* Misr al-Fatat (Young
    Egypt), Egypt
youth groups 11–12, 82

Zanan (Women, women's magazine), Iran 36
Zartman, William 20, 143
Zeinab Society, Iran 29, 34, 37, 38
zuama blocs, Lebanon 14